The Tyndale New Testament Commentaries

General Editor: Professor R. V. G. Tasker, M.A., D.D.

THE GOSPEL ACCORDING TO ST. MARK

THE GOSPEL ACCORDING TO

ST. MARK

AN INTRODUCTION AND COMMENTARY

by

R. A. COLE, Ph.D., M.Th.

Wm. B. Eerdmans Publishing Company
Grand Rapids, Michigan

Library of Congress catalog card number, 61-18908

ISBN 0-8028-1401-8

PHOTOLITHOPRINTED BY EERDMANS PRINTING COMPANY
GRAND RAPIDS, MICHIGAN, UNITED STATES OF AMERICA

GENERAL PREFACE

ALL who are interested in the teaching and study of the New Testament today cannot fail to be concerned with the lack of commentaries which avoid the extremes of being unduly technical or unhelpfully brief. It is the hope of the editor and publishers that this present series will do something towards the supply of this deficiency. Their aim is to place in the hands of students and serious readers of the New Testament, at a moderate cost, commentaries by a number of scholars who, while they are free to make their own individual contributions, are united in a common desire to promote a truly biblical theology.

The commentaries are primarily exegetical and only secondarily homiletic, though it is hoped that both student and preacher will find them informative and suggestive. Critical questions are fully considered in introductory sections, and also, at the author's discretion, in additional notes.

The commentaries are based on the Authorized (King James) Version, partly because this is the version which most Bible readers possess, and partly because it is easier for commentators, working on this foundation, to show why, on textual and linguistic grounds, the later versions are so often to be preferred. No one translation is regarded as infallible, and no single Greek manuscript or group of manuscripts is regarded as always right! Greek words are transliterated to help those unfamiliar with the language, and to save those who do know Greek the trouble of discovering what word is being discussed.

There are many signs today of a renewed interest in what the Bible has to say and of a more general desire to understand its meaning as fully and clearly as possible. It is the hope of all those concerned with this series that God will graciously use what they have written to further this end.

R. V. G. TASKER.

CHIEF ABBREVIATIONS

AV	English Authorized Version (King James).
RV	English Revised Version, 1881.
RSV	American Revised Standard Version, 1946.
NEB	New English Bible: New Testament, 1961.
Arndt and Gingrich	*A Greek-English Lexicon of the New Testament* edited by William F. Arndt and F. Wilbur Gingrich, 1957.
Cranfield	*The Gospel according to St. Mark* (Cambridge Greek Testament, new series) by C. E. B. Cranfield, 1959.
Eusebius	*History of the Church* edited by Burton, 1856.
Grollenberg	*Atlas of the Bible* by L. H. Grollenberg, 1956.
Huck	*Synopsis of the First Three Gospels* by Albert Huck, 1949.
Lightfoot	*The Apostolic Fathers* edited by J. B. Lightfoot, 1889–90.
Moule	*An Idiom-book of New Testament Greek* by C. F. D. Moule, 1953.
Moulton	*A Grammar of New Testament Greek*, Vol. I, by J. H. Moulton, 1930.
Singer	*Authorized Daily Prayer Book of the United Hebrew Congregations of the British Empire* with translation by Singer, 1949.
Strack-Billerbeck	*Kommentar zum Neuen Testament aus Talmud und Midrasch* by Strack-Billerbeck, 1922–28.
Taylor	*The Gospel according to St. Mark* by Vincent Taylor, 1952.
Wikgren	*Hellenistic Greek Texts* edited by Wikgren, Colwell and Marcus, 1947.

CONTENTS

AUTHOR'S PREFACE

THIS little book cannot pretend to be scholarly, but it does at least attempt to be theological. There are many excellent commentaries on Mark already in existence, but perhaps this slender volume may yet find a place on the shelves of those who are too busy to read the larger volumes, or who feel themselves to be too ill equipped to enjoy the scholastic riches available elsewhere in such embarrassing abundance. It is an attempt at a practical work-a-day commentary for the use of those engaged in the humbler levels of Christian service, and it has at least the merit of being produced by such a one himself. The absence of reference to many works of proven value does not correspond to scorn for their contents, but simply to the limitations of library necessary to one whose calling has been to work with his fellow Christians in the Church of South East Asia. For inadvertent lack of acknowledgment, if such there be in places, the author apologizes humbly. It, too, is not intentional, but the result of assimilation so complete that the material has become part of the author: and, rightly seen, there could be no truer compliment to the now forgotten original authors. This book now goes forth with the prayer that it may lead the readers into as much blessing as it led the writer, through the same means of the careful study of the actual text of Scripture. If it had a dedication it would be to his brethren in the Church of South East Asia, to whom the author has given so little, but from whom he has learnt so much.

R. A. C.

INTRODUCTION

I. THE GOSPEL AND THE CHURCH

W HEN we open our English Bible, we are confronted by four books that bear the title of 'Gospel': and this commentary deals specifically with one of them, the Gospel according to St. Mark, or Mark's Gospel for short. We may then well ask ourselves: what is the gospel?

Etymology, while philologically interesting, is no safe guide to the modern meaning of a word; to this, accepted contemporary usage is the only guide. Nevertheless, etymology is not without its value, for it often shows us what was the primary meaning of a particular word in the minds of our ancestors. If a new word was coined, it was because the very idea to be expressed was new: and this in itself adds to the value of such a study, for we can see how this strange new thing, the Christian gospel, appeared to our pagan forefathers. Nor is this purely a study in the archaeology of religion, for we may be able to realize something of the original richness of the term, lost to our jaded ears through its very familiarity, by recapturing vicariously its richness to our forbears.

We do not know when the term 'Godspell' was first coined by the Anglo-Saxons; but in this term we have the first reaction of Saxon folk to the strange new faith from the Mediterranean. Nor indeed is the exact meaning of the word plain: is it 'good tidings' or 'tidings about God'? If we press etymology to its roots in a dim Indo-European past, there may well be little ultimate difference: but both the traditional interpretation, and the original meaning of the Greek, of which the Roman church at least may have been still aware in this missionary preaching, support the meaning 'good tidings'. Moreover, the Anglo-Saxon suggests that this 'good news' comes as a spoken 'story' or message, as naturally it must, to a people largely illiterate before the coming of Christianity, though no doubt possessing a not inconsiderable epic literature at least, judging from abundant pre-Christian references in *Beowulf* and other fragments.

Thus to early speakers of English the gospel meant good news, passed on by word of mouth: and, since no further definition is thought necessary, we may assume that the gospel was seen as *the* good news *par excellence*.

But what relation, if any, does this spoken message, whether preached by first-century disciples or by St. Augustine's men at Canterbury, bear to this pale, silent book encased in dark covers, as it lies before us? This is a weighty theological question that has vexed the mind of the Church over centuries, and never more than during the last hundred years. Some relation there must needs be: but how close is it? Is it complete identification, or is the bond something vague and tenuous? Is there indeed a 'quest of the historical Jesus'? or is He already there, patently before us? Is there need to 'demythologize'[1] or not? If the written Gospel is a witness to Christ, how faithful a witness is it?

Not every culture and nation either received or regarded the Gospel primarily as a spoken word; for some, it came primarily as a written word, and therefore, to them, the problem is more immediate and urgent, although a little reflection will show that ultimately all except the first generation of disciples must face the same issue. To the Chinese, it is the *Fu-Yin-Shu*, the 'Happy Sound Book': to the Malay, or to any whose cultural life has been moulded by Arabic, it is the *Kitab-Injil*, the 'Writing of the Evangel'. Indeed, the concept of a holy book, borrowed no doubt from the Judeo-Christian world, has shaped the whole thought-life of Islam: although to them, by its very name, the *Qur'an* is a book to be heard by reading aloud, as was the universal custom in ancient days, rather than a static revelation to be scanned on paper. Here is the bridge between *spoken word* and *book*: it is the *read word*. But

[1] The attempt made by certain modern scholars of the critical school to penetrate what they regard as the mythological trappings of the Gospel and to discover the assumed underlying historical basis.

with fully literate groups came the Scriptures: long before, in
AD 635, the very year that Aidan of Iona reached Northum-
bria, a Persian bishop named Alopen completed a daring ride
across the steppes of central Asia to the court of China in the
north: and before the present writer hangs a paper-rubbing of
the 'Nestorian Stone', erected some hundred and fifty years
later by the Chinese church in memory of that Christian
caravan (AD 781). True, he brought images in his saddlebags
(column 10, top), that doughty but unreformed bishop: but
he also brought 'the true Scriptures', as the tablet makes clear
(column 9, top). Moreover, to judge not only from the express
statement of the tablet (column 9, middle) but also the manuscript discoveries by Sir Aurel Stein at the Tun Hwang Caves,
this bishop or his successors took steps to translate these same
Scriptures into Chinese, so important a witness to the Gospel
did they at least deem them. It is possible, to judge from the
jumbled manuscript remains, that they initially translated the
Gospel, not from four independent Gospels, but from Tatian's
Diatessaron, or 'Four-in-Hand'—a sort of running Harmony of
the Gospels which we know to have been a favourite of the
middle-eastern Christian churches of the day. The four
Gospels as such, nevertheless, either he or his successors certainly knew; for there is a clear reference to the 'twenty-seven
books' of the New Testament (column 6, top) while 'the Old
Law of the Twenty-Four Sages' Discourses' (column 4,
bottom) is, equally clearly, the Old Testament. This interpretation is reinforced by numerous other similar Patristic
correspondences in the phraseology of the tablet, superficially
concealed by the allusiveness characteristic of classical style
in Orient as well as West, showing that this remote Chinese
church was in the full tradition of eastern Patristic thought and
exegesis.[1]

---

[1] Those who are interested may care to consult a readable little book *The
Church of the T'ang Dynasty*, by John Foster (S.P.C.K., 1939), or the relevant
chapters in the same author's *World Church* (S.C.M., 1945), or the same
author's *Beginning from Jerusalem* ('World Christian Books' series, Lutterworth Press, 1956). Other books of a more scholarly nature are not easily
accessible to the western reader: but Saeki, the Japanese scholar, has done
some interesting research, as has Mingana.

Yet the point is, after all, a fine one; for whether this church used one Gospel-book or four, a Gospel-book they used, and were sufficiently convinced of its value as a written witness to Christ to translate it laboriously from (presumably) Syriac into Chinese. Of all the Gospels, the Gospel-outline that may be recovered from these Tun Hwang fragments bears the closest resemblance to Matthew, but this may not be significant. It is also true that Tatian's *Diatessaron* is considered as having heretical tendencies, but even this does not affect the main issue of the felt value of a written Gospel to a primitive church, like that of the T'ang Dynasty in China.

If, then, so many of the early churches considered the written Gospel as so important, were they justified in their view? To put it bluntly: how trustworthy a record of the sayings and doings of the Christ have we here? For it seems that we are peculiarly dependent on these four books, plus a few isolated references in the Epistles, if we wish to form any idea of the Person or claims of Christ. We have no 'oral tradition' running parallel to the written word as Judaism has, handed down from countless generations, professing both to give a scheme of interpretation, additional information, and independent corroboration of the stories in these books. Even the Church of Rome, with all its stress on tradition, knows nothing of valid extra-canonical (that is, non-biblical) sayings or stories of Jesus. To Rome, tradition is confined to the origins and interpretation of the existing canonical Scriptures. Thus the Church bears no independent witness to the nature of the Christ, although it can and does bear continual glad witness to His reality in the living experience of the Christian body. The Bible indeed *is* the witness of the Church to Christ: it was the Church herself, acting under that unerring spiritual instinct that is the proof at once of the Spirit's indwelling and of the possession of the mind of Christ, that ruled 'out of court' the vast heterogeneous mass of non-canonical tradition, both oral and written.[1] So the Christ of experience is the Christ of the written Gospel: for when men's professed experi-

[1] This may conveniently be studied by English-speaking readers in such work as M. R. James, *The Apocryphal New Testament*.

ence of God ran counter to the data of the Gospels, the Church was quick to accuse them of heresy—that is, of choosing their own path, rather than that beaten hard by the feet of countless Christian pilgrims. The Christ of the Church *is* the Christ of the Gospels: the very existence of creed and formulary shows that. Different communions may, and do, disagree as to the theological interpretation of the data, but none deny that the data themselves are the sole ultimate criterion, and thus normative. So, try as we may, we know no Christ but the Christ of the Gospels; we cannot go behind the Gospels, unless we walk alone—as Marcion did, as the Gnostics did, and as many have done since: and such, by its very definition, is heresy.

Yet this very truth introduces what may be to some a grave problem: what if the Church fashioned the Gospel? It is apparent to any thoughtful reader that the Christ of the New Testament is not the same as the Christ of the apocryphal Gospels: and most scholars would agree that the picture of Christ in the New Testament is a unity, a consistent portrait, while the Christs of the Apocrypha are many and varied, according to the theological predilections of the author. 'Gods many and lords many' is true of the writers of the apocryphal Gospels: and in few cases do the portraits of Christ even overlap, let alone coincide. But might it not be that the unity of the Christ of the New Testament was a unity imposed firmly from the outside, a pattern stamped by the Church? Might not this also be the reason for the difference between the canonical and apocryphal pictures? Finally, might not this explain the firm rejection by the Church of all except the 'official' picture, all except the 'party line', so to speak?

If this were true, our position would indeed be hopeless. We have no absolute and independent criteria outside of the Bible by which to reconstruct an 'Original Jesus' or 'Jesus of History', whatever phrase we care to use. The Christian, should he abandon the doctrine of the trustworthiness of the written Gospel, would be at the mercy of countless interpreters who reconstruct and adapt at will the biblical material, as the data does or does not commend itself to their intellect, and does or does not conform to their preconceived notion of the Christ. This experience, in fact, has been ours over the last two or three generations: and at the last, all we have is yet another subjective creation. He who will not follow the light must follow will o' the wisps: and he who will not accept the traditional picture of Christ will ultimately have to accept one of the many individual (and therefore 'heretical') interpretations, by an equally great act of faith.

Fortunately, we are not left to this courage of despair, the stoical belief that, even if the Church's picture be wrong, we can form no other, and therefore, *faute de mieux*, may still cling to the old. First be it noted that the first-century Christian Church stood two millennia closer to the Christian event than any modern independently-minded scholar, and the same Church doubtless had many additional sources of information denied to us today. In addition, we say that, if the Christ of the Gospels is the Christ of the Church, it is because the Church as a whole, despite all heresies, clung fast to the Christ of the Gospels. Further, while the Church may well have written the Gospels, it did not create the gospel: rather, it was the gospel that created and moulded the Church. Thus it was that the Church became the custodian of the gospel: so it was that only four written Gospels out of many[1] commended themselves to the mind of the Church as being not only consistent with each other, but also consistent with the true historical Jesus. They were seen as the written equivalent of the spoken word that was the creation-word at the dawn of the Church's first day (see Gn. i. 1 and cf. Jn. i. 1).

For it must not be forgotten that, whatever date we assign to the written Gospels in their present form, the preached gospel antedates them all. It undoubtedly goes back to the circle of disciples who knew the Lord when He was on earth, and were eyewitnesses of the very events: so much is clear from Luke's prologue and various incidental apostolic references (e.g. Acts i. 21, 22). Our Gospels owe their existence to the fact that, in an age when such eyewitnesses were fast falling

---

[1] See the statement in Luke i. 1, confirmed and illustrated by the voluminous remains in M. R. James, *op. cit.*

asleep (1 Cor. xv. 6), these books were believed to enshrine the heart of this eyewitness, though naturally not the whole (Lk. i. 1, 2 and Jn. xxi. 25) and to contain nothing inconsistent with it. Our primitive spoken 'Godspell' has, in fact, become of necessity a written *Cristes bōc*, 'Christ's Book', with the passage of time: but there is no breach to the minds of the early Christians. The exact principle of the definition of the books of the New Testament Canon has never been satisfactorily settled, but it seems highly likely that a book was retained only if it was believed to emanate directly or indirectly from the circle of those who had known Christ when He was incarnate. It was accepted on apostolic authority, if an apostle was believed to be either author or guarantor. Thus we have pushed the problem back to the first Christian generation, immediately following the resurrection and ascension, to the days before such collections as 'Sayings of Jesus' or 'Doings of Jesus' or 'Old Testament Proof-Texts' were in circulation. Did the apostles, or did they not, bear faithful witness to the Christ whom they had known so intimately? If they did, we may accept the New Testament as a reliable witness: if not, we are lost, for we have no hope of an independent reconstruction.

Seen in this light, the problem is no new one: we stand today and every day exactly where the wondering crowds stood in the book of Acts as they listened to the first Christian preaching by the apostles. 'We all are witnesses', says Peter stubbornly (Acts ii. 32, etc.). It is by our acceptance or rejection of the apostolic testimony to Christ that we are justified or condemned, to use biblical language: for ultimately the faith that justifies is a casting of ourselves upon the mercy of a God who has revealed Himself in many ways and manners in the Old Testament, but supremely in the Christ of the New Testament, to whom this first Christian generation bears witness.

Further, Peter is quite clear that he is adopting no arbitrary position. Those who are apostles have been deliberately appointed to this position by God, in order that they may bear precisely this witness to Christ, *imprimis* to His resurrection

(Acts i. 22, ii. 32, etc.) but also to all the details of His earthly life, to which the apostles so confidently appeal (Acts ii. 22, 23, etc.). The believing Christian will also note, and take seriously, both the Lord's promise of the Spirit as aid to the sluggish memory (Jn. xiv. 26) and the express testimony of Scripture as to the Lord's continual presence with His disciples for the six weeks between His resurrection and ascension, 'speaking of the affairs of God's rule' (see Acts i. 3).

These are points that will commend themselves only to the convinced Christian, although any man must take account of them, as further data in the situation, however he may interpret them. More cogent in an absolute sense is the confident way in which Peter can appeal to his non-Christian audience for confirmation of the historical facts of the life and death of Christ (Acts ii. 22). About His resurrection there were naturally other stories, as Matthew xxviii. 11–15 makes clear: but it also makes clear the very good reasons for their fabrication. Further, the crowd were at least suspicious of these alternative explanations of the resurrection. This may be seen from the fact that whenever Peter or the others spoke of the resurrection, they never rejected his evidence out of hand (Acts ii and iii). They were, presumably, largely influenced by the Pharisees, for whose piety and patriotism they had a high regard, rather than by the wealthy Sadducean priestly aristocracy (Acts iv. 1, 2). For the Pharisees, of course, resurrection in itself was no stumbling-block, as Paul's successful court counter-attack in Acts xxiii. 6 shows. They might dispute that this Jesus of Nazareth had in fact been raised, but not the general concept of resurrection—contrast the Greeks, for whom the very concept was pure tomfoolery (Acts xvii. 32). It was the inclusion of the Gentiles in God's plan, not the resurrection of Christ, which Jews found intolerable (Acts xxii. 22). So then, Peter can confidently appeal to his unbelieving, and therefore 'unbiased', Jewish hearers to confirm the historicity of his account of the life and doings of Christ. Nor is this confined to Peter: half a generation later, Rabbi Saul the tentmaker, who had given opinions 'in the name of Rabbi Gamaliel', as the saying was, when on trial before King

Agrippa, can still confidently appeal to the common know-ledge as to the historicity of the account of the life and death of Jesus the Carpenter, the unlettered Rabbi of Nazareth, who dared to give decisions in His own name (cf. Acts xxvi. 26 with Mk. i. 22).

Now we are at the crux of the whole matter, and the heart of the Christian faith: as to the historicity of their *facts*, Peter or Paul could convince their Jewish or Gentile hearers (if not our modern minds), but not as to their *interpretation*. This latter can be accepted only by faith; and, by definition, faith was just what these unbelieving hearers had not. Here, then, is the last ditch of Liberalism, either old or new: the facts of the life of Christ they will accept (often with certain reservations about the miraculous), but not the biblical interpretation. They will admit that the interpretation goes back far behind Paul to the early sermon outlines in Acts i–xii.[1] Here, they will say, is where the misunderstanding started: the apostolic interpretation of the simple facts is itself misleading, and from thence as fountainhead there wells and flows the whole New Testament—a glorious misconception, they say, and a unity at that, because it all springs from this one *fons erroris*.

Were this so, it would indeed be most serious, but to talk in this way is to ignore two basic principles: the first is concerned with the very nature of revelation, while the second deals with the reason for the preservation of some of the sayings and doings of Christ, doubtless only a tiny fragment of the whole available material. It would be useless, to take the first point, to argue with such a man that, if the six weeks' communion of the Lord with His disciples between His resurrection and ascension means anything by 'speaking of the matters dealing with God's rule' (see Acts i. 3), it must refer to the interpre-tation of the well-known events in our Lord's life, and not to the events themselves. It would be useless, because he would regard this as but another 'covering clause', to justify the apostolic position. But what such a one often fails to realize is

---

[1] See F. F. Bruce, *Acts of the Apostles* (Tyndale Press, 2nd ed., 1952), Leon Morris, *The Apostolic Preaching of the Cross* (Tyndale Press, 2nd ed., 1960), amid a host of other works, old and new.

that the whole concept of revelation is at stake here. We are apt today to be so blinded by the true concept of the 'God who acts' that we forget the equally true correlative that He is also the 'God who speaks'. Unexplained activity is not revelation: it may be only darkness. It is the capricious godlings of heathendom who act suddenly and devastatingly, and leave men to guess their whim or desire. The God of revelation is One whose every act is consistent with His already revealed nature and whose action, when its significance is explained and appreciated, is further and independent confirmation of that known nature. Put briefly and schematically it might be phrased thus: act plus interpretation equals revelation. What is true of Jesus Christ in the New Testament is true of the entire sweep of God's revelation, that is the whole Bible. Act without interpretation is meaningless mystery: interpretation without act is unreal, for it would then be imaginary. In the first case, we would indeed be worshipping an unknown God: in the second, we would be worshipping an unreal God, for He would not, after all, have done those things in which we claim He showed His nature. Paul's blunt words on the impossibility of the whole theological position of Christianity, if even the resurrection be a pious fabrication, are a useful corrective here (1 Cor. xv. 15).

And yet there are two schools of theological thought today which deny one or other of these two factors. One school will hold fast to the acts of God, and admit their substantial historicity, but deny the primitive biblical interpretation. The other school will accept the interpretation, but not the historicity of the facts upon which alone the interpretation is based. We have seen that, as regards the basic facts at least, the apostles can appeal to the public of their day for confirmation. The interpretation, by the very nature of the case, can neither be proved nor disproved; it can only be accepted or rejected; and it is this whole-hearted acceptance of both fact and interpretation which is one of the biblical meanings of the word 'faith'. For fact may be accepted by intellectual assent: but to accept the interpretation is to undergo a spiritual experience as well: and it is the conjunction of these two that is saving faith, in the biblical sense.

To fail to accept the interpretation, then, is not only to refuse to accept the apostolic testimony, proven to be veracious over the only area where it can be checked, i.e. that of historical accuracy: it also involves a refusal to accept the biblical concept of revelation. More, it is to refuse to face a profound psychological principle—the principle of the selection of significant fact, as a necessary ingredient of authorship of any kind. Every history, except mere chronicle, is written under the influence of a process of selection: this in turn is influenced by one's system of interpretation, for such interpretation alone determines what facts are seen as relevant and important, and what as trivial. The history of the Christ is no exception: and that the Gospel is no mere all-embracing chronicle is shown by the well-known difficulty of constructing any satisfactory chronological scheme at all, let alone harmonizing the four accounts into one. Therefore the stories and sayings that we have are those selected and preserved by the Christian community because they seemed to them to be peculiarly relevant. If we accept even the most general doctrine of inspiration by the over-ruling of God's Spirit, we must say at the least that the disciples were not wrong in making such a choice, and that these sayings and incidents do indeed give us a clear picture of who Jesus Christ claimed to be. But even without this admission, we must still admit our utter inability to go behind the Gospels: for, so far from being able to separate fact from interpretation, the very fact is only recorded because of the associated interpretation. There is no such thing as an 'unbiased' picture of Christ: every Gospel must be written either by a believer or an unbeliever. Sometimes this interpretation comes directly from the lips of our Lord Himself (Jn. xiii. 10); sometimes it comes in an explanatory note from the Evangelist (Jn. xiii. 11); sometimes it is verbally unexpressed; but underlying all is the same psychological principle. Thus, once again, we are thrust back to an acceptance or rejection of the message as it stands: for if this particular incident has been preserved by the primitive Church only for the sake of its interpretation, what value has the account if divorced from this interpretation? Assuredly, to the early Christian community, it would have had none.

There is another danger in some streams of modern scholarship which assume that, if the Church has preserved a particular story because it illustrated a particular truth, the Church has therefore created or altered the story, purely as a vehicle for teaching that truth. But a moment's thought will show that this is a gratuitous assumption. For how would the Church have seen or even thought of those truths in isolation, without first seeing them embodied in word or action? Truth as an abstract principle is an ideal of Greek philosophers; it is not germane to the genius of Hebrew religious thought, let alone a group of peasants and fishermen; and all the Lord's apostles were Jews. Had there been some long 'tunnel period' before the emergence of the written Gospels, such a view, however objectionable, might perhaps be tenable. Now that the continual discovery of still earlier papyri has pushed the probable date of the first drafts of the written Gospels to a generation after the crucifixion, the suggestion is ludicrous. The real 'tunnel period' is now seen to be after, and not before, the written Gospels—if, indeed, there be any such period. There would not be time for such a set of ideals to be formed *in vacuo*; nor could numerous such imaginary incidents be safely created and fobbed off on a theological 'lay figure', as long as the first generation of witnesses were still alive to deny them. Not until lapse of time, and the Roman devastation of Israel in AD 70, had well-nigh wiped out the generation who remembered Christ's earthly ministry, would such wholesale fabrication have been safe. But by then, at least the sayings of Jesus would have been widely known, and so there would have been a critical 'yardstick' by which to test the genuineness of other utterances.

Besides, there is a further cogent point to consider, which may best be seen in parable. In the Talmudic treatise *Pirqe Aboth*, amid a list of objects originally created by God we find one strange item—'The Tongs made with Tongs' (chapter 5). The reason for its presence in this heterogeneous list was so that a well-known Jewish philosophical difficulty might be solved: to make any pair of tongs, hammered and fashioned in the fire, another pair of tongs is necessary. Who, then, made the first pair? 'God', said the Hebrew briefly, after his fashion, to end the argument. Theologically speaking, he was undoubtedly correct, however we may regard the value of this particular piece of *Midrash*. Translated into terms of our present problem, the parable becomes: if the Church created the Gospels, who then created the Church? Of course, the ultimate answer is indeed 'God': but the Church is itself clear that it was the 'word of the gospel' that formed it (1 Thes. i. 5–10, etc.). And indeed, the existential fact of the Church demands such an explanation. We today have forgotten what a strange phenomenon came into being almost overnight— how men's characters were changed, and the whole bent of their lives altered. The pagan and Jewish worlds disliked the Church (Acts xvii. 6): they persecuted it (Acts viii. 1–3), but they dared not deny its existence and nature. The Church was thus, in selecting incidents for preservation, seeking to conserve and not to create; and her principle of selection was the principle of her own being, the constituent 'word of the gospel'.

II. SOURCE CRITICISM AND FORM CRITICISM

This leads to a consideration of what lies under and beneath our Gospels. We must not imagine some sort of primitive Diocesan Church House, with an editorial board carefully examining all extant accounts of, let us say, the miracles of our Lord, to decide which were most suitable for preservation, with files marked 'Q', 'L', and so forth. Such notions are utterly foreign to the times. What we have is the natural and spontaneous persistence of a vigorous living tradition, which, by healthy Christian instinct and not by deliberate choice, retains those things which are of proven value. It is only when the living oral tradition begins to fade away, with the death of the first Christian generation, that there comes the crystallization of oral tradition in written form. Writing ever comes when art is dying; and, with the passing away of the apostolic witnesses, the problem of recording teaching or evangelistic material had become acute. But the Gospels, as we have them, were of course not the first or the only formulations: and modern attempts at uncovering some of these early strata go under the headings of *Source Criticism* and *Form Criticism*. These two must be considered briefly: although, of these, the first has already passed out of favour nowadays, and the second is now, in its turn, itself in danger of being swamped by 'demythologizing', to use the modern jargon for an old approach.

It is apparent to any man, comparing the four Gospels, that there are many similarities between Matthew, Mark, and Luke, however they be explained: while John is in many respects *sui generis*. There have been many unsuccessful attempts to elucidate the exact relations between the first three Gospels or Synoptics.[1] As a matter of sheer description, it is true to say that there is a vast body of common material, the bulk of Mark, to which Matthew and Luke each make various additions peculiar to themselves. This solution of the 'Synoptic Problem' is usually expressed quasi-algebraically by the use of 'Q' (for German *Quelle* or 'Source') to denote the non-Marcan material common to Matthew and Luke, with 'L' for the material, often of medical or Gentile interest, peculiar to Luke, and 'M' for the material, often of Jewish interest, peculiar to Matthew. Of course, such algebraic or similar symbols may be multiplied *ad infinitum*, and we may have L^1 and L^2, etc. Yet it is well to remember that, having said all this, we have still only been attempting to describe the present position of each Gospel *vis à vis* the others: we have not explained how the Gospels came into being; still less have we proved that these algebraic symbols ever actually represented early written documents, or even complexes of oral tradition, that had any independent existence. Sometimes the Christian Church, in its zeal for analysis, has forgotten this: and has assumed not only specific documents, but also specific literary dependence.

Inevitably, scholars have then pushed farther along the

[1] So called because, taken together, they give a 'synoptic' or stereoscopic view of Christ, dealing with roughly the same selection of incidents.

road, to try to decide the relative dates of the composition of the Gospels. Here we do have some scanty extra-biblical tradition, of doubtful value, which will be considered specifically in its relation to Mark. Enough to say here that it is adherence to this extra-biblical tradition which has led the Roman Church and some Protestant scholars to hold fast to the 'primacy of Matthew'—i.e. the view that Matthew's Gospel was the first to be written, and is fundamental to the others as a source. That would make Matthew's Gospel very early in date, and allow it to be directly from the stylus of the apostle of that name. Most Protestant scholars, on the other hand, hold to the primacy of Mark, or an early version of Mark, pointing out that it is the shortest and baldest of all the Gospels. They consider it thus to have been a source for both Matthew and Luke, although not by any means the only source.

However, these questions are really only of academic interest nowadays, for, as in modern Old Testament scholarship, the neat 'Documentary Hypothesis' has now largely broken down under its own weight. With the bewildering multiplication of symbols in recent years, the various hypotheses ceased to be of any descriptive, let alone explanatory, value, and the net result was complete fragmentation. Most scholars today, if they thought in these terms at all, would think in terms of multiple early written sources, which later coalesced into several great blocks. This, besides seeming reasonable, agrees with certain hints in the New Testament (cf. Lk. i. 1 and Jn. xxi. 25). It also agrees with what we know from archaeology to have been the probable position with regard to manuscripts of the New Testament in the days before the great textual 'schools' of later days arose, and variant manuscripts were gradually assimilated to one or other of these schools. In this respect, at least, modern Textual Criticism is beginning to understand the early days of biblical manuscripts. Yet the chief reason why Source Criticism has now ceased to hold an important place in the field is that it has been largely ousted by Form Criticism.

In origins, it is probably true to say that Form Criticism

was a revolt, an escape from what had become the tyranny of Source Criticism, just as the Scandinavian Oral Tradition School in Old Testament studies was a revolt against the Documentary Hypothesis as a means of explaining the origins and present form of the Pentateuch or Hexateuch. True, Form Criticism in itself became, in its turn, just such a tyranny again; but in origin, it was an attempt at a fresh approach to the Gospel material. Again, like Source Criticism, Form Criticism began by being purely descriptive, and therein lay its best work. When it attempted to be explicative, then it, too, began to crumble. Form Criticism, instead of classifying material by source, does it by the nature of the material: these are Birth-Sayings, these Pronouncement-Stories,[1] and so forth. This is legitimate description; and, in so far as this remains a new system of grouping, we are able to see the old material in a new light and profit accordingly. It is even a legitimate deduction to say, 'This type of story was probably preserved by the Church because it presented such and such a Christian truth', although logically we can establish only two points: (a) that it *has* been preserved, and (b) that it *does* teach this truth. The further link is always possible, and may even be highly probable, but we cannot establish it by logic. But when Form Criticism says 'This has been created for the sake of that', or even 'This is more trustworthy than that', then it is passing out of its own sphere into another, where it has no right to be heard. The first statement is, by its very nature, incapable of proof, and thus remains a hypothesis to the last; while the second is a value-judgment and, as such, it is a theological question, and not germane to a descriptive science.

But even orthodox Form Criticism is now passing out of favour for other and newer forms of approach, of which Rudolph Bultmann's 'demythologizing' will serve as an example. 'Out of favour' is deliberately used here, and not

---

[1] The name commonly used by this school to describe some story that owes (according to them) either its origin, or at least its form and preservation, to a desire to provide a suitable 'backcloth' for some remembered sayings of Jesus.

'superseded': for such is the wind of theological fashion. The battlefront moves on to new positions, and the old are abandoned. It is not that old questions have been solved, but rather that both contestants have grown weary of a battle that has ceased to have any real theological meaning or relevance for them. The fashion has altered, and soon the whole field is in full hue and cry in another direction. To remember this will help to give us a sense of theological perspective as well as saving us from overmuch study of what is often now mere 'spiritual archaeology'. It will also warn us not to be swept off our feet by any new views, under the impression that new theories will necessarily endure.

Rudolph Bultmann's views are best studied in his own works: sufficient to say here that, like Dibelius, his concern is to penetrate what he too regards as the artificial 'crust' of the written Gospel to its real core. In other words, it represents but another modern reluctance to accept fact and interpretation alike as the warp and woof of revelation. Time will test such views: meanwhile, it is important to see if we can gain any fresh insights of spiritual value from a new line of study, no matter how much we may disagree with it.

But, laying aside these rather forbidding approaches, what lay behind all our written Gospels, by whatever process and in whatever order they reached their present form? In the present state of flux, a reverent 'provisional agnosticism' on these points seems the wisest attitude for a New Testament scholar to adopt. We may assume an initial period of direct oral tradition, manifold and thus diverse, as different tellers recalled different incidents, but tending to become stereotyped with repetition, especially when used for catechetical purposes within the Church. Then came written collections of the *Logia*, or *Sayings of Jesus*. Whether we are justified in making a separate division for the *Doings of Jesus* is uncertain: many of the doings seem to be preserved for the sake of the accompanying interpretative sayings, so perhaps we should see these as also coming under *Logia* rather than *Erga*. On the other hand, the constant twofold New Testament stress on 'all that Jesus did and taught' (see Acts i. 1, etc.), combined with the continual reference to His 'mighty works' as testifying God's hand upon Him (Acts ii. 22, etc.) may suggest two types of literature. The third step is quite distinct; there were apparently in circulation *Testimony Books*, drawn from the prophecies of the Old Testament, designed to prove to Jew primarily, and to all men secondarily, that Christ was no after-thought, but the fulfilment of God's mind and purpose from the dawn of revelation; in biblical language, that Jesus was the Christ (see Acts xvii. 2, 3 for this type of activity).

III. THE PAPIAS FRAGMENT

Now have we any evidence for this or is this just as hypothetical as any of the other lines of study outlined above? Evidence we have, and that of two kinds: traditional and archaeological. Traditional evidence is in itself of little value; for immediately after the brilliantly lit period of the New Testament, the Church plunges into the first of its so-called 'tunnel' periods, where the gloom is only partly illumined by the flickering lights of the apostolic Fathers. It is not until Justin Martyr in the second century, and then increasingly until Eusebius the historian in the fourth century, that we emerge into daylight again: and these men are themselves remote from the early traditions which they quote, sometimes with caustic comments as to their value. Nevertheless, let us look at these early traditions that at least survived the so-called 'tunnel' period: for if they contain any suggestions which are supported by archaeology, they are deserving of high respect.

Papias of Hierapolis was a contemporary of Justin Martyr, about the middle of the second century. We owe the preservation of his fragments to Eusebius of Caesarea, the Church historian, writing in the fourth century—as far from Christ as we are from the Reformation, and as far from Papias as we are from the revolt of the Americas. That in itself warns us against overcredence; and Eusebius himself passes an uncomplimentary remark about the intelligence of Papias in connection with his millennial views. Now, Eusebius had the books of Papias before him as he wrote, and we have not. And for faithful testimony of this sort, great brainpower is not essential: in fact, it might be a hindrance. An unintelligent man may not understand the meaning of a tradition, but he is more likely to pass it on faithfully than an intelligent man who may question it or emend it. It is the old story of the unintelligent scribe—he may make a mistake, but he will not introduce emendations into the text; and to this extent, he is the more trustworthy. Further, Papias claims to be a disciple of John in Asia: and this would bring him into direct contact with the closing years of that vital first Christian generation, while he himself could of course lay no claim to belong to it. Therefore his evidence may well be much more valuable than appears at first sight. His evidence on Mark will be considered in more detail later: at this point all we shall stress is his emphasis on the existence of *Logia* of the Lord, of which he wrote an 'Explanation'.

'Mark', says Papias, 'wrote the things *said* or things *done* by the Lord'—where the old twofold division re-appears—though not apparently in order: 'for he was not', says Papias, 'just making a harmony of the Lord's *Logia*' (2. 15. 6)—which certainly seems to imply that such collections or groupings existed. 'Similarly, Matthew', says Papias (2. 16), 'arranged the *Logia* in Hebrew'—by which he probably means Aramaic, as the New Testament does (Acts xxii. 2). Others then worked out varying translations from this common source. Of course, it has been pressed that Papias does not use the word *euangelion*, 'gospel', at all, while Eusebius does, in the same context: and therefore it has been argued that *Logia* is merely the old term for what later was known as *euangelion*. The analogous use of *logia* in the New Testament as referring to the Old Testament scriptures has been quoted (Rom. iii. 2). But this is not strictly fair. In the first place, even the Epistles knew and used the term *euangelion* for the gospel-message itself, though naturally not for the as yet non-existent four Gospels (Gal. ii. 2, etc.). This would seem an easy extension of meaning. In the second place, all four Gospels were certainly in existence long before Papias, and Mark at least bluntly begins by introducing his book as a *euangelion* (i. 1). It may well be that it is from this initial usage—which Mark may have meant to refer not so much to his whole book as to a particular aspect of its contents—that the title was applied, first to Mark's complete work and then, by analogy, to the other three. That still does not alter the position that the title was well established long before the days of Papias. Thirdly, and most important of all, even if Papias does not use the title *euangelion* for the finished work, his whole point is that there is a very real distinction between the initial *Logia* and the final product of the Evangelist; the two are not one. But this whole question is much debated, and those who wish to pursue it further may easily do so by consulting any of the standard New Testament Introductions.

Archaeologically, this theory can be tested by the known fact that 'Sayings of Jesus' (presumably *Logia* of this very type) existed in papyrus form, certainly in Egypt, and therefore probably in other areas, well before the time of Papias. How much closer to the days of the earthly ministry of Christ we can place them, remains a moot point. An interesting phenomenon is that such fragmentary pieces as have survived seem to be mostly either heretical or extra-canonical sayings: but this may well be by pure accident. We know from Luke's prologue that our present Gospels were but four among many earlier Gospels, which they superseded; and we have no reason to suppose that all the others were of the heretical type that has survived in the so-called apocryphal Gospels. Luke may well be making a sidelong reference to Mark, for instance. Many of these may have contained parallel accounts of the same incidents as those recorded in our canonical Gospels, but in the present imperfect state of our knowledge, it would be dangerous to make general pronouncements. Meanwhile, a work like Skeat and Ball, *Fragments of an Unknown Gospel*, is a wise reminder of how little we know of this formative period, and therefore how unwise it is to dogmatize over what must or must not have taken place.

Secondly, the existence of *Testimony Books*, collections of Old Testament proof-texts, applicable to the Messiahship of Jesus, and useful in controversy, while not specifically mentioned in very early Christian tradition, had been rendered exceedingly probable by the repeated occurrence of the same or similar Old Testament texts in similar controversial contexts in the New Testament. It would be difficult to go into this question in detail without considering the whole question of 'Catechetical Forms' in the New Testament Church—the stereotyped outlines, as it were, of various aspects of Christian doctrine and behaviour, used for the methodical instruction of the thousands of adult converts absorbed into the Christian Church in the first few decades of its life. But such a subject is too wide to be discussed here: the reader is referred initially to E. G. Selwyn's *Commentary on the First Epistle of Peter*, and secondarily to Archbishop Carrington's work on the subject. The present writer's own small monograph *The New Temple* (Tyndale Press, 1950) is also relevant to the subject. Sufficient to say that, without the aid of archaeology, all we could prove is that certain groups of prophetic scriptures had, as it were, become 'stereotyped'—presumably by constant repetition in teaching —as the 'classic passages' referring to the Messiahship of Jesus of Nazareth, and were constantly so used in what the Bible calls 'testifying' to the Jews (which seems to be a technical term in Acts xviii. 5 and elsewhere). But we now know, not only that oral repetition had stereotyped such collections, but also that they existed in papyrus form, thanks to a find in the sands of Egypt.

We have now seen that before any Gospel, and thus before Mark's Gospel as it confronts us, there were in existence at least collections of the sayings of the Lord, probably also collections of His doings, and certainly Testimony Books drawn from the Old Testament. What, we now ask, has tradition to say of the way in which this heterogeneous mass was transformed into homogeneous Gospels? Much every way: and the reader who has neither time nor opportunity to refer to the original texts *in extenso* will find a good summary of early Patristic evidence in Albert Huck's *Synopsis* (pp. vii ff.), where most of the relevant sections are quoted briefly in the original. Greekless readers will find many of the relevant passages reproduced and translated in H. M. Gwatkin's *Early Christian Writers*.

Papias (*Frag.* 2. 15) gives the tradition he has received about Mark, as follows: 'The Presbyter (i.e. the presbyter John) was in the habit of saying this too: Mark, seeing that he was Peter's interpreter (or "explainer") wrote down carefully all that he remembered, but not, however, an orderly chronicle, of the sayings or doings of the Lord. For he had neither heard the Lord nor been His disciple, but afterwards, as I said, he had been Peter's disciple. Now he (Peter) used to teach according to the needs (*sc.* of his hearers), but not as if constructing an orderly summary of the Lord's sayings. So Mark was not wrong (or "was not mistaken") in thus writing down some things (i.e. not a complete account?) as he (? Peter) recalled them. For his (? Mark's) one care was this—not to leave out anything that he had heard, and not to falsify anything in them.' The exact identity of this presbyter is a fascinating question—is it John bar-Zabdai, or a shadowy Ephesian John the Elder? And what is his relation to the Gospel of John and the Apocalypse? These questions we must leave unsolved here, and simply note that the elder, whoever he be, is taken to be a fount of apostolic tradition, and is so quoted here.

This fragment of Papias is notoriously difficult, and scholars will note that in the above loose translation by the present writer, the Gordian knot has been cut in places by interpretative additions in brackets. Yet this is not so unfair as it seems, for some such interpretative additions there must be: and if these suggested be wrong, others must be found and inserted in their place. Frustrating though the fragment is because of its brevity, there is always a peculiar satisfaction in handling acknowledged first-hand evidence, even if there be endless dispute about its interpretation. Here, maybe, we find the answer to the riddle of Mark's Gospel. Certainly to Papias it was the answer and, moreover, an answer received at the hands of tradition: for Papias' claim to fame, both in his own and posterity's eyes, is that he is one of the great repositories of Johannine tradition (Eusebius, *Hist.* 3. 39). There is always the possibility, as some scholars have said in polite academic terms, that Papias was a garrulous old liar, trading on his connections with John: but at least some connections with John he must have had, or the very stories would have had no meaning. Further, we may of course, after sifting and evaluation, reject these traditions: but if so, we are more in darkness than if we followed them, for we have no others of such early date, and later tradition is at least in agreement in broad outline with Papias. It may be that this is by assimilation to the tradition of Papias, whether known directly (for his books were still evidently circulating in Palestine in the days of Eusebius, in the fourth century) or through the work of the great historian who quoted and thus preserved him. We would then be dealing with only one line of evidence and not two: but that would not weaken this one line, though it would leave it unsupported. In addition, it would mean that not only was the Papian testimony widely accepted as true, or at least likely, in early days—which is good presumptive evidence in itself—but also that no alternative explanation was known, which is stronger evidence still. Further, there is the psychological point that the early Church obviously felt that no further explanation was necessary, and was thus quite content with the Papian tradition, and does not seem to have questioned its veracity till much later. All this is cumulative evidence of no small value, especially as the scornful words with which Eusebius dismisses Papias' millennial views shows that this tradition was accepted because it commended itself to the mind of the Church as true, and not merely because it was hoary with antiquity, and associated with venerated names (again, see Eusebius, *Hist.* 3. 39). John's name might be venerated by the Church at large, but the name of Papias was not.

What, then, is the problem of Mark, to which the early Church, like ourselves, was trying to find a solution? First, it is the very shortness of Mark, and his blunt, clipped style: why should Matthew and Luke contain so much more? (John we may leave altogether out of account in any such comparison, because he is so different in plan, content, and execution from the three Synoptists.) Why, moreover, should Mark's account seem at times to vary from that of the others, even when describing what is presumed to be the same incident? Further, Mark seems, on the face of it, to be an attempt at an ordered chronological sequence of our Lord's life: but is it? The reader is referred to the other standard Commentaries or Introductions for discussions on the historicity of Mark, and the notorious difficulties of bringing the chronological scheme of his Gospel into line with that of the others. So the problem resolves itself into two heads—the principle of selection used by Mark, and the chronology of Mark. It will be appreciated that at this stage we may use 'Mark' as a convenient algebraic symbol for 'the Second Gospel in its present form', without necessarily inferring anything as to the identity of the author or authors.

It is obvious from the tradition quoted by Papias on the authority of John ('Rab' Papias said on the authority of Rab' Yohanan'—we are still close to Jewish-Christian days) that these very problems vexed the early Church, a point which satisfies us that such problems are not the product of some capricious modern criticism, but apparent to any thoughtful reader of the Gospels in whatever century he may live. The problems were seen. Does the solution proposed by the early Church satisfy us? From the wording of the fragment above, irrespective of the details of translation, it is clear that the reliability of Mark was impugned on the following grounds: some blamed him for omissions, some for carelessness, some for failure to preserve chronological sequence, some for falsification and some for an unusual principle of selection. How does Papias—or John—deal with these? He obviously has a high regard for the reliability of Mark, and rebuts all these criticisms very simply, by saying that Mark's Gospel is not a primary source of knowledge of Christ, but a secondary: the primary source was the preaching of Peter. Thus the omissions were due to the fact that Mark's Gospel was necessarily limited to the recollections of the aged Peter: and such recollections are notoriously illogical, as anyone can test from the spasmodic memories of childhood, where certain times are full of vivid recollections, while long periods are a complete blank. Mark, says the tradition, was very careful to omit nothing of what he had heard from Peter: but he also seems to have restricted himself to this one source. The same answer deals with the charge of carelessness: the very curtness of Mark, says the tradition, is a proof of his exactness, not of his carelessness: for he was careful to reproduce his Petrine material as it was, without addition or subtraction. The charge of falsification is rebutted at the same time: Mark is a faithful witness to Peter—if there is any question, it must be pushed back to the first generation, to the witness of Peter.

The charges of a lack of chronological sense and a peculiar selection of material are not really charges against Mark, but against his source, if Mark is really a one-source Gospel, as the tradition affirms. Mark could not construct an exact chronological sequence of the Lord's earthly life for the simple reason that he was not an eyewitness of the events, nor had he any personal knowledge of them. Peter, on the other hand, had not constructed a chronological sequence simply because it was not his purpose to do so: he was not, after all, constructing a 'Gospel', but various *Didascaliai* or 'Catechetical Forms', for use in his preaching and teaching work at Rome or elsewhere. We now have one of the clearest explanations of both the lack of chronological sequence, and the superficially odd principle of selection, as well as a primitive justification for some kind of Form Criticism at least. Peter's choice of material varied from time to time no doubt: but, says the fragment, it was always dictated by the simple basic principle of the needs of the hearers. So the preaching of Peter took shape gradually, guided in its choice of material by the needs of the infant Christian Church, whether at Rome or elsewhere: and no doubt from the mass of Petrine reminiscence of Christ, certain points hardened and crystallized through their constant repetition in teaching; around them clung other points, while many incidents or sayings were tacitly dropped or forgotten. What had no doubt at first been spontaneous and varied utterance was through sheer repetition gaining a fixed and quasi-liturgical form—a common psychological phenomenon, especially among those of advancing years.

There remains only one question more, in connection with

this fragment: what does it mean when it says that Mark was the *hermeneutēs*, 'interpreter' (or 'expositor') of Peter? No scholar can seriously suggest that Peter was ignorant of Greek, though no doubt the Galilaean dialect of Aramaic, with its guttural peculiarities (Mk. xiv. 70), was his mother tongue. The Petrine Epistles pose many problems in themselves, but, quite apart from them, the fact that Peter was seen as the first preacher to the Gentiles both by others and by himself (Acts x. 34 ff., xv. 7) would make nonsense were he not conversant at least with colloquial Greek. Thus he needed no 'interpreter', in the narrow sense of the word, in Rome or elsewhere. The Roman Church used Greek at least for the first century of its life, as early liturgical fragments show: and Paul never seems to contemplate the Roman Church finding any difficulty with his Epistle to them, though written in Greek. No: the key must be sought in the fact stated below, that, just as Peter had been the Lord's disciple, so Mark had been Peter's. We are, then, back in early Jewish-Christian days again; as Peter had recorded and expounded the words of his Rabbi, so Mark in his turn did the same for the treasured words of his venerated Rabbi, Peter. As Papias was preserving the sayings of John, and expounding their meaning and relevance, so Mark was preserving and expounding the preaching of Peter.

It is *a priori* unlikely that Mark would have written this down until the primary source, in the spoken word of Peter, was either passing away, or had already gone; and it is probable that it was not written down until the secondary witness felt that his time was drawing near—as is true, no doubt, of the Papian recording in writing of the Johannine tradition. It is not exclusively in modern times that few men write their reminiscences or compose autobiographies until they are aged: this is not only due to the natural desire to live on in men's memories; it is also for the very practical reason that, in earlier days, such reminiscences are of less value in that they are not unique—many others may share them. It is only when a man is the last of his generation that his reminiscences become really valuable, as the sole remaining link with a lost age. Some kind of chronological scheme or at least orderly presentation Mark, then, undoubtedly attempted: but if so, it was either a scheme of Peter's (which is unlikely) or his own reconstruction, made nearly two generations after the events. We say it is unlikely to have been Peter's scheme because, by the very nature of the preaching of Peter, any such chronological scheme (except the crudest one, dealing with birth, baptism, death, and resurrection) was ruled out. Peter's material was neither selected nor organized as such a scheme: it was grouped by subject, not by chronology. Further, Mark's sole available material was prescribed for him in advance by Peter's choice, which had been in itself dictated by the needs of the Christian community, a fact which incidentally may account for the proven value of Mark's Gospel as a teaching medium on the mission field today. The sole task that lay before Mark, then, was to seek to arrange in some meaningful chronological or other sequence the various *Didascaliai* or 'Teaching Outlines' which he had received on the authority of Peter. Whether he succeeded or not is quite a separate question: but at least he could not, any more than we cannot, go behind his single source.

IV. OTHER EARLY EVIDENCE ABOUT THE GOSPEL OF MARK

Even if we cannot accept Johannine authority for this tradition of Papias, or at best see this John as the shadowy Asiatic elder, and not John the apostle, yet here at least is good early-second-century belief on the matter, claiming to go back still further to a first-century figure. What of other early Patristic evidence—does it confirm or deny the Papian account? The anti-Marcionite Marcan prologue sheds little, though welcome, light on the question. The questions connected with these prologues are interesting but too complex to be considered here. Enough that here we have testimony of approximately the same date as that of Papias: but is it independent evidence, and is it of any value? That the author of these prologues is acquainted with Papias is shown by his prologue to the Fourth Gospel; but nevertheless, it may well be independent testimony, first, because it is too close in time to

Papias to have been assimilated to his tradition, and secondly, because, while it agrees in the main with him, it fills in various gaps. It tells us what we suspected—that Mark only reduced the preaching of Peter to writing after the death of his source; it says that the written Gospel was produced in Italy—where it is almost certain that Peter was preaching before his death; and it also adds the information that Mark was known as *kolobodaktulos* or 'stumpy-fingered'. This it explains by saying that his fingers were disproportionately short in comparison with his tall stature.

Now this type of nickname, derived apparently from physical peculiarity, was common enough in the ancient world, and not unknown even in the apostolic circle. James of Jerusalem was called 'Camel-knees', though this was presumably more from his habits of earnest prayer than from the physical deformity to which it was alleged to lead. As mentioned below in the commentary, many of the apostles had such nicknames: but they were usually given for mental attitudes rather than physical characteristics. This trait persisted in the pagan world: old *Chalkenteros*, 'Copper-guts', was so named for his ability to study, not from the result of some internal surgery! Likewise, no-one would dream of referring 'golden-mouthed', the nickname of John Chrysostom, to dentistry rather than eloquence. This in itself should warn us that the adjective as applied to Mark may contain a deeper meaning than the worthy anti-Marcionite editor realized. Further, this is a nickname which would arise only in a Greek-speaking community; and if Mark grew up in Jerusalem, it is highly unlikely that he moved in such a society. But the Christian Church that read and used Mark's Gospel, whether in Italy or elsewhere, was Greek-speaking; and it was this Church that was so conscious (as we have seen above) of Mark's omissions and inadequate chronology that also called him 'stumpy-fingered', for whatever reason. Taking all the above together, it may be that the quick Greek wit which coined the term *Christiani* (with its probable pun on *Chrēstos*, 'good' or 'useful'—a common slave name) for the followers of the new god, now coined, within the Church, another uncomplimentary adjective for what may well, in spite of Patristic tradition and Roman Catholic scholarship, have been the first written Gospel of all. In any case the point is not important, for Mark obviously suffered, in the eyes of the early Church, by comparison with other Gospels: so, let us say, the priority of Matthew would only strengthen the case here. As to the exact meaning of the nickname, we cannot be sure; it might just mean 'ham-handed', or it might refer to the clipped style of Mark, often with the various grammatical members of the sentence reduced to the bare minimum. If so, we have yet another testimony to the fact that Mark, just as we know it, 'warts and all' (to use Cromwell's phrase) was known to the early Church, and that thus our problems were their problems. It is even possible that the early Church was as puzzled as we are by Mark's abrupt ending.

Irenaeus (*Against Heresies* 3. 1. 1) confirms this general tradition, but in words that suggest that he is not independent of the Papian source. Of course, if the Papian tradition is indeed Johannine, this is not surprising, as Irenaeus has links with Asia Minor, the home church of John in later years, as well as with south Gaul. He reiterates that Mark was disciple and 'interpreter' of Peter (the continual recurrence of this unusual word certainly suggests a common original tradition); that he wrote after the death of Peter, the primary witness as far as he was concerned; and that he conceived his work as a handing-down of tradition, now reduced to writing. The contents of that tradition, Irenaeus bluntly says to have been Peter's *kērussomena*—the habitual sermon-material of his spoken addresses. It is true that in the same context he holds to the primacy of Matthew, but that is irrelevant to our purpose here, as it does not affect the main issue.

The late-second-century *Muratorian Canon* is textually corrupt at this point, and all we can learn of Mark's Gospel is in the cryptic half sentence '*quibus tamen interfuit et ita posuit*'. At least it seems clear that it was arguing along the now familiar line, that Mark was not himself an eyewitness of most of the events which he records, though possibly of some: secondly, it is the familiar defence of his accuracy—he set things down just as he heard them—*ergo*, the author of this second-century book-list was at least aware of the criticisms against Mark, and was adducing this as defence.

Clement of Alexandria, as quoted in Eusebius (*Hist.* 6. 14. 5), makes the observation that the 'earliest of the Gospels are those concerned with the genealogies'. This would account for Matthew and Luke, at least in part: as Mark is thus left out on a limb, as it were, he hastens to explain its origin in the traditional way, as a record by a faithful disciple of the spoken and preached word of a beloved master (and Origen, again as quoted in Eusebius, *Hist.* 6. 25. 3, points out, from the wording of the Petrine Epistle in I Peter v. 14, that apparently this bond of affection was mutual). Clement lays stress on the fact that Mark was an old disciple of Peter's (unless *porrōthen* refers to distance in space and not duration of time, in which case it will refer to John Mark's long journey from Jerusalem to Rome for the sake of, and presumably in company with, his revered master) and thus well qualified to record his traditions. He also lays stress on the fact that this is no 'Gospel of Peter', who neither encouraged nor condemned the idea (which he hardly could do if, as is highly likely, the book was not produced until after his death!), but that it was produced in response to a demand from the people, who had so often heard Peter preach to them, but to whom he would now preach no more. This in itself seems highly likely, and indeed a very natural process, whether in Rome or elsewhere. It would be most unsafe to reckon on finding any reliable independent tradition as late as this. Origen but repeats the general view briefly, already busily fighting for four Gospels, and four only, as Gospels of the Church Universal. Eusebius, who records all these opinions, is really in much the same position as we are, although, aggravatingly enough, he had access to far more evidence than we, for much has now been irrevocably lost. He does, however, pass the interesting observation that it is only possible to call them 'synoptic' Gospels within certain limits (*Hist.* 3. 24. 5).

Jerome (*Introduction to Commentary on St. Matthew*, para. 6), too, is but gathering up old traditions when he tells us that

Mark was an *interpres* of Peter; that he never saw the Lord in the flesh; that he was exact in recording the incidents which he had heard at Peter's lips—was more concerned, in fact, with exactness than with historical sequence. But when he tells us that Mark was first bishop of Alexandria, he must be recording some fresh local tradition of his residence there. It is strange that neither Clement nor Origen, in their surviving fragments, refer to this, for, right or wrong, it was obviously living tradition in Alexandria at least. Moreover, the fact that Jerome could, without fear of contradiction, quote this tradition side by side with the other, shows either that substantially the Papian tradition as to the origin of Mark was held in the Alexandrian church (as it must have been in the Roman church, or the frequent references to Rome in all the traditions lose their point), or that, at the least, no violently opposing tradition as to the origin of the Gospel was known there, for all the Alexandrian claim to be associated with Mark. In such early traditions, the psychological assumptions that can be made from the very existence of a certain tradition may be almost as important as the truth or falsity of the tradition itself, and this is one particular instance of that general rule.

V. THE VALUE OF THE PATRISTIC TRADITION

What, then, have we as sum and substance of these views? We find a strong and continuous Patristic tradition which, when translated into modern terms, is that the second Gospel is not the first formulation of the sayings or doings of Jesus; nor indeed is it perhaps the first full 'Gospel', though it is not formally dependent on any other full written Gospel, be it Matthew, Proto-Matthew or any other. It is basically a one-source Gospel, and that source is the apostolic preaching of Peter—an oral, not a written, source, though doubtless obtaining in later days something of the fixity of a written tradition. The nature of the source determined the nature of the Gospel; and the admitted limitations of the Gospel are thus due to the exigencies that, by selection, moulded the source. The Gospel, like the source, was called into being by the needs of the infant Christian community, and not until the age of oral tradition was well-nigh over, with the passing of the apostolic age, was it written.

So far, the tradition is clear, universal, and reasonable; it conforms remarkably well with what little we know of conditions in this misty period, and with what literary criticism of the Gospel has shown as inherently probable. So far, therefore, it may be cautiously accepted. As to place of composition and identity of the author, we may prefer to keep an open mind; the Gospel itself gives no clear internal evidence, intentional or unintentional, but at least such hints as we can gather are not opposed to the traditional view. These 'hints' will be discussed below as they occur in the text: here it will be sufficient to point to the young man in the linen garment of Mark xiv. 51, which has often been taken to be a sidelong reference to the author (cf. possibly Jn. xix. 35). Of course, this may simply be one of those irrelevant but vivid memories that cling around deeply emotive moments: the present writer has etched on his memory to this day the sight of a robin, perched on a spade-top, the first object that met his eyes as he wandered outside after hearing over the wireless the news of the outbreak of the Second World War in 1939. But at least we have here Jerusalem eyewitness evidence; and there are numerous other passages hard to explain without such evidence. Now while this would fit John Mark of Jerusalem (see Acts xii. 12, 25), known to have been a junior member of the apostolic circle in lands far beyond Judaea (Acts xiii. 5, xv. 39) and later traditionally associated with Paul (2 Tim. iv. 11), and with Peter (1 Pet. v. 13) at 'Babylon', which we know to have been a sort of code word for Rome in the early Church (Rev. xiv. 8), yet it could all be traceable to Mark's use of a Petrine source of information, for Peter the apostle was nothing if not a Galilaean and Jerusalem eyewitness (Mk. xiv. 70).

Here it should be noted that the argument is strengthened and not weakened by any highly critical attitudes to the Pastorals or the Petrine Epistles, although the present writer finds no difficulty in seeing in them an apostolic source.[1] For even supposing that such Epistles had been written later, in the name of these apostles, by a group of zealous disciples seeking to preserve and expound their respective apostolic traditions, it is even more clear evidence that, as early as then, Mark was believed to have been at Rome with Peter, acting as his amanuensis; and it seems fairly certain that the early Church took this Mark to be John Mark of Jerusalem, the nephew of Barnabas. There is a lot to be said for this simple identification. After all, the Church—and above all, the apostolic circle—was not yet so large as to have numerous homonymous Christians; and such a Gospel was more likely to be written by one at the centre of things, as John Mark incontrovertibly was. How then can we explain the Papian tradition that Mark had no personal knowledge of the events described, if in apostolic days he was so closely associated with the Church, even by blood? The answer may simply be that his youth was spent in Jerusalem, where the Lord spent little time except at festivals, when there were doubtless many other preoccupations for a lad. In that case, there is nothing inconsistent in combining the traditions that Mark did not know the Lord personally with the suggestion that the author of the Gospel—perhaps in an earlier 'edition'—was the young man of Mark xiv. 51, where the very wording suggests a youngster, aroused from sleep, desiring to see the excitement, rather than a devout follower of the Lord.

Petrine source there certainly is, whoever the actual author of the Gospel be: there are too many minute psychological touches to jettison this tradition lightly. And it has often, and wisely, been remarked that this Gospel is set in a Gentile milieu. *A priori*, Mark is not an unlikely amanuensis: there are not many 'central' characters in the period which bridges the apostolic and sub-apostolic ages, and Timothy and Mark are two of them. If Paul called for Mark to come to Rome (2 Tim. iv. 11), or was even believed to call for him (which, as above,

---

[1] See D. Guthrie, *The Pastoral Epistles* and A. M. Stibbs and A. F. Walls, *I Peter* (*Tyndale New Testament Commentaries*, 1957 and 1959), for recent approaches along these lines.

would be even stronger evidence, for it would prove that the Church knew that Mark was, in fact, at Rome in this formative period, and closely associated with the apostolic circle there), there is no *a priori* reason why he should not also have assisted Peter in his preaching, as tradition states, if Peter was in Rome also, as all early tradition agrees. However much we may dislike some of the claims of the modern Roman pontiff, there can now be little doubt that in fact Peter spent his latter years at Rome, and was martyred there, possibly at the same time as Paul, or possibly even later. The early tradition of Peter's Roman episcopate—which, in this context, makes no mention of Paul—is thus easily explicable: Paul was in prison, and Peter was not. If Paul died a martyr, he was executed as a Roman citizen; but Peter was presumably lynched as a wandering Judeo-Christian, in some judicial pogrom after Nero's fire (AD 64) or later. He would have been free in the interval to wander about Rome and Ostia and 'Three Taverns', shepherding the flock of God, while fiery Paul chafed in prison, or poured out his heart in the captivity Epistles.

This, too, would serve to explain John Mark's close connection with Peter: he may have been summoned to Rome to aid Paul, but Mark was not a prisoner, as Paul was. Therefore, what more natural than that he should be a disciple and assistant of Peter and hear him preaching to Roman Christians for years? And who ultimately more fitted than he to record such preaching? If Paul had two Roman imprisonments and not one, with an interval of further missionary travel in between, then the case is further strengthened; for Paul's links were always closer with Timothy, and we have no hint that Mark ever accompanied him on further missionary journeys: he may therefore have stayed at Rome with Peter. Mark's links with Peter would thus have become closer, now that only one of the two apostles was left at Rome. Should Paul have died before Peter, this would have been even more so: but tradition is strong in favour of a simultaneous death for both apostles in one and the same persecution.

The association of Mark with Alexandria, which must have

been a strong Alexandrian local tradition, is harder to explain: such traditions are not gratuitously invented, and it must contain at least some kernel of truth. Either there was another homonymous Mark in early days who was presbyter of the Alexandrian church, or else John Mark visited Alexandria late in life, possibly after the death of his master at Rome, and quite likely as a fugitive from one of the anti-Semitic edicts published so frequently by the Julio-Claudian emperors. Such edicts could send Jewish Christians far afield, as we see from Acts xviii. 2: a Jew of Pontus, late resident of Rome, is settled now in Corinth, and later found in Ephesus (Acts xviii. 26). Thus there is nothing inherently impossible in a Jerusalem Jew, after sojourn in Rome and expulsion or flight from there, finding refuge in Alexandria—always a great Jewish centre, and doubly so after the sack of Jerusalem in AD 70. In that case, the Gospel may have been produced at Alexandria just as easily as at Rome; but tradition and probability favour a western production. In any case, it would be the western preaching of Peter that was the source, so the point is not important.

Seen from this angle, the question of the 'primacy of Mark' or 'primacy of Matthew' is not important either—*pace* our Roman scholar-friends. Later mutual assimilation of text is much more likely than any early conscious and deliberate documentary dependence, although naturally all alike drew on a common storehouse of apostolic traditions, rounded and smoothed, like water-worn stones, by constant repetition. Even initially, we have no reason to suppose that the preaching of Peter (Acts ii, etc.) differed greatly from the preaching of Stephen (Acts vii) and indeed, the preaching of James and the preaching of Paul are expressly said to be identical in theological content (Gal. ii. 9) although naturally the choice of incident would vary with the individual's own recollections or source.

For what it is worth, early Christian tradition is broadly in favour of the primacy of Matthew, as we have seen. A full discussion of this question belongs more properly to a commentary on the Gospel of Matthew: here it will suffice to say that this neither necessitates a St. Matthew's Gospel in the present form in which we have it, nor yet, more important, any use of such by Mark as a secondary source. But we have seen that the obvious criticisms of Mark in the early Church would be easily explained by assuming that at least *some* other 'proto-Gospel' existed, as a sort of spiritual yardstick against which Mark's 'defects' could be measured. All that Papias says (*Frag.* 2. 16) is that Matthew made a collection of the *Logia* or 'Sayings' of Jesus, in Aramaic (which, as has been noted,[1] is almost certainly what he means by 'the Hebrew tongue'—petty distinctions of kindred barbarian dialects were not for the Greek) and that others thereafter 'interpreted' them (or 'expounded' them—the same Greek word as is used of Mark's activity in connection with the preaching of Peter) as they were able. It would seem that he is only postulating a collection of colloquial Aramaic *Logia*, which were believed to rest on the apostolic witness of Matthew, plus numerous collections of variant Greek *Logia*. The variations between these Papias puts down to the problems of translation and the varying ability of the translators. Here he may be right or wrong: we pass no judgment, but merely record his opinion and the possible reasons for it. So far as we know, Papias does not even press for the primacy of this 'Proto-Matthew': he simply records its existence.

Unfortunately, the anti-Marcionite prologue to Matthew is lost, so we do not have its evidence which would have clarified the Papian position: but the prologue to Luke mentions it as the traditional belief that Matthew and Mark were in existence before Luke wrote, Matthew's Gospel being produced in Judaea and Mark's in Italy. Here the polemic author may simply be relying on the statement of Luke i. 1, that many Gospels were already in existence: but as he also in the context gives us some extra-canonical traditions about Luke, it is likely that he had an external independent source, which may well have been some other lost fragment of Papias. Apart, however, from the order in which they are mentioned, there is no hint in the context of the primacy of Matthew: rather

[1] See p. 29.

Matthew and Mark are classed as 'early', as opposed even to Luke, and certainly to John.

From Irenaeus (*Against Heresies* 3. 1. 1) onwards, the tradition is either first recorded or first created, that Matthew was earliest of all. Matthew's writing-date is placed as *during* the ministry of Peter and Paul at Rome, while Mark's is put after their death. The *Muratorian Fragment* has a lacuna here: Origen, Eusebius and Jerome repeat what now looks suspiciously like a 'party-line', but they are too late to be good primary evidence. Clement of Alexandria is more original and interesting, as well as being at least one generation nearer the living tradition even than Origen. It is *a priori* to be expected that the third-century persecutions caused a great snapping of lines of tradition, as no doubt earlier persecutions had done in lesser degree. Clement is quoted in Eusebius (*Hist.* 6. 14. 5). His view, as has already been noted,[1] was that the earliest Gospels were those containing the genealogies, i.e. evidently Matthew and Luke, for he discusses Mark at length below. But this may be only a retrospective and reflective argument, of which Clement was well capable: and in any case the translation of the fragment in question may perhaps be 'the earliest parts of the Gospels are those that surround the genealogies', which may well be true, but takes us back from the study of the Gospels to a study of their Judaean sources, not to Matthew's Gospel but to Proto-Matthew's *Logia*—a very different thing.

We thus find no *early* tradition of the primacy of Matthew, still less of Mark's dependence on it, but only a strong tradition of the existence in Palestine of at least one collection of Aramaic *Logia* (and possibly some genealogies and birth-stories) plus numerous variant similar collections in Greek, at a date anterior to the date of Mark's Gospel. This we have already seen to be inherently probable for many other reasons, and so we may provisionally accept it. Mark—possibly in an earlier 'edition'—would thus become the first written Gospel, and a possible source, with the *Logia* of Proto-Matthew, of Matthew's Gospel as we have it: while it seems that at least

[1] See p. 40.

the existence of Mark was known to Luke. Once again, let it be emphasized that we do not call for any direct literary dependence, but simply use of the same, or similar, tradition blocks. Any who come from a Celtic or Scandinavian background, where oral tradition is still a living force (as the *seanachaidhe*—Anglicized 'Shanaghy'—in the Gaelic west of Ireland) will not despise the tenacity and formalism of a living oral tradition.

It is interesting to speculate whether the traditional order of the writing of the Gospels is not an inference from the order in which they usually appear in biblical MSS: it would be a simple step to seek an explanation, and even simpler to give this answer. But behind this easy answer lurks the nagging question —why were they assembled in this order? Is it not at least equally probable that they were arranged in this order because it corresponded to the traditional views of their respective dates of writing, be such views right or wrong? But we know too little of the principle that guided even the arrangement and order of the Pauline corpus to dogmatize here; and in any case, this could only show the views of the Church at a comparatively late date, when the four Gospels had begun to be produced together. The publication of the four Gospels probably did not occur till after the uproar over the *Diatessaron*, and possibly not till the days of Origen, for it is then that the cry first appears of 'Four Gospels and only four', as has already been noted.[1] In any case, the existence of such a belief would prove nothing as to the correctness of the belief: it is evidence, but not proof.

So much, then, for the background, date, and probable authorship of the second Gospel. But there remains the old question of the reliability of Mark, which is but one aspect of the whole question of the reliability of the Scriptures as we have them. We have seen that the early Church was somewhat troubled by what appeared to be discrepancies between the Marcan account and that of the other Synoptists, both in chronology and in fact. The first was, to judge by modern

[1] See p. 40.

mission-field psychology, less of a problem to the early Church than the second: but we have seen how the Church saved Mark's reputation, and solved the problem to its own satisfaction at least, by transferring responsibility for these points from Mark to Peter, the *fons et origo*. Presumably the Church felt itself able to accept these apparent discrepancies on direct apostolic authority, though not on secondary Marcan authority. But can we, with our analytical western minds, do the same? or has the early Church found only a false solution, in projecting the problem to a deeper level, where we can scarcely follow? We have seen that, like the first Christians, we must in any case accept the apostolic witness to Christ if we desire to find the Christ of salvation: for there is no other— we know no Christ but the Christ of the Gospels. But can we extend such credence to details, and how can we give any such credence to two accounts that seem to conflict in detail? Must we descend to a pettifogging harmonizing that attempts to explain away, often by unworthy means, such apparent inconsistencies? Such an over-scrupulosity seems to betray a small mind: far wiser and far bigger is the attitude of Jerome. His task, he says, is not to dispute about words and names, but to expound the gospel. There is a robustness, almost a gustiness, of faith here which would find echo in Paul's impatient dismissal of what he regarded as trivialities (see Rom. xiv. 17; 1 Cor. xi. 16). John Calvin says roundly that, if there *are* any apparent discrepancies, it is because it is God's will that they should be there and that in such superficial variants there is no real contradiction.

It is our basic attitude of reverent and assenting faith, displayed towards the Bible, which is the key. Such an attitude is buoyant enough to allow some unresolved superficial problems of this sort to go unchecked, whether or no it chooses to express itself in terms of the famous much-maligned 'lost Princeton Bible'[1] of inerrant fame. But this latter is more than

---

[1] This term was coined by liberal scholars in derisive allusion to the attitude of a group of conservative scholars of Princeton, N.J., of whom B. B. Warfield is best known. They held strongly to the doctrine of the infallibility of the Bible as originally given by God, while prepared to admit errors in the biblical manuscripts now before us.

a theological 'swear-word': it is, at its best, a reverent expression of the belief that, did we have all the facts at our disposal, and clear eyewitness account of every incident, then no problems would remain. This is surely a self-evident truth to any thoughtful man: and the second 'form' embodied in the concept of the so-called 'Princeton Bible' is the ready acknowledgment that we do not now have such full knowledge, and that therefore certain problems will ever remain unsolved. This also can scarcely offend: it merely expresses a reverent 'provisional agnosticism' on certain peripheral points, which is in no sense a barrier to further research or continual attempts at solution, as more and more evidence, from linguistic, textual, or archaeological quarters, gradually appears. *Adhuc sub judice lis est*: but just because the Christian is so sure of the final verdict, so he welcomes, more than others, every fresh shred of genuine evidence. Only he is cautious: there is too much at stake for him to allow himself to be chivvied about from position to position, at every fresh whim of biblical interpretation: *securus orbis terrarum judicat*.

That is why, in a commentary of this kind, due care has been taken of the *consensus fidelium*, the agreement of the minds of thoughtful, humble commentators of past or present, of whatever communion they profess themselves; for to us, in biblical commentary, all men are of the Communion of Christ. Any new or startling interpretation of God's Word is *ipso facto* unlikely to be right: sheer humility teaches us that, and all wise men strive to heed it.

ANALYSIS

I. PREPARE YE THE WAY: THE PRAEPARATIO EVANGELICA (i. 1–13).

    a. The title of the book (i. 1).
    b. The forerunner (i. 2–8).
    c. Christ's baptism (i. 9–11).
    d. The temptation (i. 12, 13).

II. HIS OWN RECEIVED HIM NOT: THE EARLY GALILAEAN MINISTRY (i. 14–iii. 6).

    a. The kingdom of God in Galilee (i. 14–45).
       i. First Galilaean preaching (i. 14, 15).
      ii. The call of disciples (i. 16–20).
     iii. Christ at Capernaum (i. 21–28).
     iv. Peter's mother-in-law (i. 29–31).
      v. The evening healings (i. 32–34).
     vi. From Capernaum to Galilee (i. 35–39).
    vii. The cleansing of the leper (i. 40–45).

    b. The beginning of conflict (ii. 1–iii. 6).
       i. The healing of the palsied man (ii. 1–12).
      ii. The ministry of the Christ (ii. 13).
     iii. The call of Levi (ii. 14–17).
     iv. Controversy about fasting (ii. 18–22).
      v. Controversy about the sabbath (ii. 23–28).
     vi. The man with the withered hand (iii. 1–6).

III. AS MANY AS RECEIVED HIM: THE CALL AND TRAINING OF THE DISCIPLES (iii. 7–viii. 26).

    a. The conflict increases (iii. 7–35).
       i. Breach with the religious leaders (iii. 7–12).
      ii. The call of the Twelve (iii. 13–19).
     iii. Mounting opposition and the Beelzebub controversy (iii. 20–30).
     iv. Christ's true brethren (iii. 31–35).

b. Parables of the kingdom (iv. 1–34).
   i. The parable of the sower and the reason for the use of parables (iv. 1–25).
   ii. Two more parables of growth (iv. 26–32).
   iii. Summing up of the parabolic section (iv. 33, 34).

c. Ministry round the Lake of Galilee (iv. 35–vii. 23).
   i. Christ calms the storm (iv. 35–41).
   ii. The Gadarene demoniac (v. 1–20).
   iii. Two more healing miracles (v. 21–43).
   iv. Christ's own city rejects Him (vi. 1–6).
   v. The sending out of the Twelve (vi. 7–13).
   vi. Herod's estimate of Christ (vi. 14–16).
   vii. Martyrdom of John the Baptist (vi. 17–29).
   viii. The feeding of the five thousand (vi. 30–44).
   ix. The walking on the water (vi. 45–52).
   x. Healings at Gennesaret (vi. 53–56).
   xi. Further clash with Judaism (vii. 1–23).

d. Ministry in Northern Palestine and back to Galilee (vii. 24–viii. 26).
   i. The Syrophoenician woman (vii. 24–30).
   ii. The deaf and dumb man (vii. 31–37).
   iii. The feeding of the four thousand (viii. 1–9).
   iv. The Pharisees seek a sign (viii. 10–13).
   v. Beware of leaven (viii. 14–21).
   vi. The blind man of Bethsaida (viii. 22–26).

IV. HE STEDFASTLY SET HIS FACE: THE ROAD TO JERUSALEM (viii. 27–x. 52).

a. Confession and transfiguration (viii. 27–ix. 10).
   i. Peter's confesssion of Christ (viii. 27–33).
   ii. The cost of discipleship (viii. 34–38).
   iii. The transfiguration (ix. 1–10).

b. The passion foretold (ix. 11–50).
   i. 'Elijah redivivus' (ix. 11–13).
   ii. The epileptic boy (ix. 14–29).
   iii. Second passion-prediction (ix. 30–32).
   iv. Who is greatest in the kingdom? (ix. 33–37).
   v. The man casting out devils (ix. 38–40).
   vi. On stumbling-blocks (ix. 41–48).
   vii. The salt of the earth (ix. 49, 50).

c. Departure from Galilee (x. 1–34).
   i. Local setting (x. 1).

ii. Christ's teaching on marriage (x. 2–12).
iii. 'Suffer little children' (x. 13–16).
iv. The rich young ruler (x. 17–31).
v. Third passion-prediction (x. 32–34).

d. The sons of Zebedee (x. 35–45).

e. Blind Bartimaeus (x. 46–52).

V. THE ZEAL OF THINE HOUSE: THE JERUSALEM MINISTRY (xi. 1–xiii. 37).

a. Entry into Jerusalem (xi. 1–14).
   i. The entry (xi. 1–10).
   ii. The return to Bethany (xi. 11).
   iii. Cursing the fig tree (xi. 12–14).

b. The cleansing of the Temple (xi. 15–19).

c. Exhortation and debate (xi. 20–xii. 44).
   i. Meaning of the withered fig tree (xi. 20–26).
   ii. By what authority? (xi. 27–33).
   iii. The wicked husbandmen (xii. 1–12).
   iv. Tribute to Caesar (xii. 13–17).
   v. The Sadducean question (xii. 18–27).
   vi. The greatest commandment (xii. 28–34).
   vii. Who is the Son of David? (xii. 35–37).
   viii. Woe to the scribes! (xii. 38–40).
   ix. The widow's mite (xii. 41–44).

d. The Olivet discourse (xiii. 1–37).
   i. Doom on the Temple (xiii. 1–4).
   ii. Signs of the end (xiii. 5–8).
   iii. The beginning of the troubles (xiii. 9–13).
   iv. The abomination of desolation (xiii. 14–20).
   v. False Christs and false prophets (xiii. 21–23).
   vi. The coming of the Son of man (xiii. 24–27).
   vii. The parable of the fig tree (xiii. 28, 29).
   viii. The date of the coming (xiii. 30–32).
   ix. The end of the discourse (xiii. 33–37).

VI. BEHOLD THE LAMB OF GOD: THE PASSION NARRATIVE (xiv. 1–xv. 47).

a. The Last Supper (xiv. 1–25).
   i. Christ's death is decided (xiv. 1, 2).
   ii. The anointing at Bethany (xiv. 3–9).

COMMENTARY

I. PREPARE YE THE WAY: THE PRAEPARATIO EVANGELICA (i. 1-13)

a. The title of the book (i. 1)

The first clause, as well as being the title of the book (which, be it noted, is *the gospel of Jesus Christ*, not the Gospel of Mark) is also a summary of its contents. The Gospel is the 'news' or the 'tidings'. How far the first-century reader was conscious of the meaning 'good news', as inherent in the Greek word *euangelion*, is uncertain. There is Old Testament evidence to suggest that the word ought usually to be translated 'reward for bringing good tidings' at this late date. But, in any case, from the very nature of its content, the gospel soon took on this meaning of good news for the Church—a good example of how the early Church moulded its own vocabulary to express itself.

The subject of this news is one named *Jesus*, a common enough biblical name both in its Hebrew form of *Joshua*, in Old Testament days, and in this Hellenized form, derived from the Aramaic form *Jeshua*, in the New Testament world. Both by common etymology and by historic example, the name meant 'Jehovah is salvation', the name given to the divinely-appointed leader, sent to God's people in their hour of need. So, when the angel announced to Joseph the coming birth, it was both appropriate and natural to the ears of a pious Jew that he should say 'You shall call his name Jesus, for he will save his people' (Mt. i. 21, RSV). The subsequent phrase 'from their sins' is, when understood at the deepest level, the distinctively New Testament concept; this salvation is not now to be merely physical, but also moral.

Not alone, however, is He to be Saviour; He is also to be

God's appointed agent upon earth. This singling out for a particular task is described in terms of being 'anointed' for that task, as any king or priest of Old Testament days would have been anointed. Both the concept and the word are very common in the New Testament, occasionally in the Semitic form of *Messiah*, but more commonly as *Christ*, or 'the Christ', using the Greek root *chriō* that has the same meaning as the Hebrew root *mšh*, i.e. 'to anoint'.

Whether or not in this verse the clause *the Son of God* should be included is doubtful; the manuscript evidence is inconclusive.[1] But in any case, it is a title of Christ that has abundant testimony elsewhere in the New Testament (e.g. Rom. viii. 3), and was indeed the very claim for which Christ was condemned to die by the Sanhedrin (Mt. xxvi. 65). This Sonship, to the early Christians, was no spiritualized metaphor, nor did it simply mean the adoption of a mortal man into the Godhead. For its full understanding and interpretation, it demands the developed doctrine of the virgin birth, though this is not specifically mentioned by Mark (nor indeed by Paul); Matthew i and Luke i are the primary sources of authority. It seems as if this was a doctrine taken for granted by the Church rather than one explicitly propounded and discussed; the doctrine of the Trinity is another similar example.

b. The forerunner (i. 2–8)

2, 3. Further, this good news stands in direct relation to God's whole revelation to His people in the past. The New Testament is thus not a breach with the Old, but a fulfilment of it (Mt.

---

[1] Since both RSV and *The New English Bible* have adopted 'Son of God' here, to weigh the evidence may be of interest. Against its inclusion are Sinaiticus (i.e. its original, not corrected, reading) and Koridethi, of the great uncials; 28, and a few other minuscules; some Oriental Versions, and the bulk of early Patristic evidence. Supporting the clause (either with or without the definite article) are the uncials Alexandrinus, Vaticanus, Beza, and Freer; and several important families of minuscules. This makes a strange problem, in view of the Patristic silence; but it is easier to see why such a clausule should be added later (from other New Testament contexts), than to see why it should be omitted by the Fathers. It may therefore be considered an early addition.

v. 17). Yet, strangely enough, the scriptural prophecy quoted here[1] to provide the necessary 'link' has primary reference not to Christ, but to John the Baptist. It is as if Mark would have us know that the gospel era was ushered in by John. This same point is made abundantly clear by the elaborate dating by which Luke introduces his account of the birth of John the Baptist in chapter iii of his Gospel, and by the early stage (also in his first chapter) at which John the Evangelist introduces the Baptist. The Baptist is God's messenger and Christ's forerunner; his status, unrecognized by Jewish officialdom, is unequivocally stated here. His task is to make a road for God, and his method is by preaching; the content of his preaching is a stern uncompromising call to men to prepare themselves for the divine coming.

4. John's baptism was not Christian baptism, nor was it associated with the gift of the Holy Spirit (see Acts xix. 2, where disciples of John are re-baptized by Paul, as being ignorant of the very existence of the Spirit, and as not having been baptized in the name of Jesus). But note also that there is no evidence for the re-baptism of those disciples of the Lord who had previously been John's disciples, and who may thus be presumed to have received his baptism already. John's baptism was therefore one of the initiatory and purificatory rites of later Judaism, and was an outward sign and symbol of the message that John preached. He called men to a change of heart and purpose, which would result in a forgiveness of their sins by God; and it is clear from the common Gospel tradition that John demanded a changed life as proof of this truly changed heart.

5–8. The initial response to John's message showed him to be in the true Old Testament prophetic succession; men recognized him at once as bringing a word from the Lord. Dress and food and dwelling-place alike marked him out as being in the rugged tradition of Elijah and the other desert

---

[1] The prophecy, loosely quoted here with a reference to Isaiah, is in fact a combination of Malachi iii. 1 and Isaiah xl. 3, perhaps coming from some early Jewish collection of texts relating to the Messiah.

prophets (cf. 2 Ki. i. 8, RV mg.), as did his eschatological and 'forward-looking' preaching. But in John's case there was an urgency and imminence about the messianic preaching, that had been lacking of old; God's intervention, that was to result in the establishment of His rule upon earth, was at the very doors. All this was accompanied in John by an overwhelming consciousness of the relative unimportance of his own work and ministry, compared with that of the 'Coming One'.

c. Christ's baptism (i. 9–11)

9. To receive John's baptism came Jesus; not, of course, through any consciousness of sin (a difficulty felt by the heretical 'Gospel of the Hebrews'), but through a desire to 'fulfil all righteousness' (Mt. iii. 15), i.e. to fulfil every ordinance of God for His people. That John himself protested against any idea that Jesus had need of such baptism of repentance is clear from the previous verse in Matthew.

10, 11. This is one of the great 'trinitarian' passages of the New Testament. Here the Spirit and the Father both bear witness to the Son. As in the book of Genesis God created by His word and through the Spirit, so it was fitting that, at the very commencement of God's new work of re-creation in the hearts of men, there should be the same operation of the whole Godhead. Here, on Jordan's banks, God speaks His word again, and again the Spirit is brooding over the waters.

The *voice from heaven* (11) is a combination of the messianic Psalm ii. 7 and Isaiah xlii. 1, which deals with the suffering Servant. This creative fusion is a perfect expression of the double nature of the work of Christ. The Greek word *agapētos*, translated *beloved*, has also the nuance of 'only' Son, and was thus doubly appropriate.

d. The temptation (i. 12, 13)

12. The Spirit (RV) is seen here in two lights. He is the gentle 'dove' (10) hovering over the waters, as Noah's dove hovered over the ark of salvation and the waters of judgment (Gn. viii.

8ff.); but He is also the mighty Spirit of creation, hovering over the baptismal waters, out of which God will call His new creation, in terms of new-made men and women (2 Cor. v. 17). It is this mighty Spirit of power who irresistibly impels Christ *into the wilderness*, the place where so many of the Old Testament prophets received their commission and revelation.

13. In the loneliness of the desert, Christ remained for *forty days*, probably corresponding to the forty years of testing that Israel, God's child, endured in the wilderness (Ps. xcv. 10). The desert was, to the Hebrew, a gloomy place of terror, the abode of devils and unclean beasts. To be *with the wild beasts* had no such romantic associations for them as it has for a world of jaded city dwellers today. There may be the further thought of divine protection; as God shut the lion's mouth to save His servant Daniel (Dn. vi. 22), so He preserved His servant Jesus from the wild beasts. Again, like Israel in the desert (especially to the eyes of later Jewish orthodoxy), He enjoyed angelic ministry. From the fuller account in the other Gospels (see Mt. iv and Lk. iv), it is clear that the purpose of this wilderness period was that Christ might face and conquer the peculiar temptations involved in His calling as Messiah, and thereafter commence His mission.

II. HIS OWN RECEIVED HIM NOT: THE EARLY GALILAEAN MINISTRY (i. 14–iii. 6)

a. The kingdom of God in Galilee (i. 14–45)

i. First Galilaean preaching (i. 14, 15). At this point, Mark merely refers in passing to the whole story of John's denunciation of Herod for immorality, and his consequent imprisonment and death. The incident serves only as a date-line, for from that moment began the preaching of the good news by Jesus. That the initial point of preaching was hard-pressed, stubbornly nationalistic *Galilee*, always first target for any invader from the north, is seen by Matthew to be no accident (Mt. iv. 12–16). As in the words of the prophet, so in Christ's earthly ministry, Galilee symbolizes God's people in bondage, to whom the light of salvation would come (Is. ix. 1, 2).

15. The news which Christ thus heralded in Galilee was that God's hour had struck, the time to which all the Old Testament had looked forward. God's reign upon earth—a concept familiar to the prophets—was about to begin. Men were called to a change of heart and an acceptance of this news for which John had prepared the way. What men had yet to learn, and what proved to be the hardest lesson of all for the Lord's disciples to learn, was that the reign of God was not to be a cataclysmic external triumph by an earthly Messiah, but a quiet rule over the hearts of men; the rule of God, said Christ, was 'within' His disciples (Lk. xvii. 21).

ii. The call of disciples (i. 16–20). The Lord called Simon and Andrew to be *fishers of men* (17), and while the use of the metaphor in their case may have been suggested by their occupation at the moment of their calling, yet this is a calling to every disciple of the Lord.[1] Fisherman, farmer, builder, reaper, shepherd, steward, servant—the Gospels abound in such homely metaphors, each describing a different aspect of our common obligations to our Lord and our fellow-men.

Both pairs of brothers found obedience to the call of Christ costly; it meant abandonment of all that they held dear, and all earthly security, in simple committal to Christ. Nor can we say that those who left father and hired servants left more than those who left their nets alone, inasmuch as each left all that he had; that is always the minimum requirement for the Christian (Lk. xiv. 33).

It has been well pointed out by Köhler that to the Eastern mind, unaccustomed to walking abreast and side by side as Westerners would naturally do, to *come . . . after*, or to 'follow', means to 'walk with', in our idiom. To walk with God as Enoch had walked (Gn. v. 22), these men gave up all earthly

---

[1] It has been noted (e.g. Cranfield, *Cambridge Greek Testament*) that, while this is a common Old Testament metaphor, it is used there in a bad sense only: but in Jeremiah xvi. 16 the fishers are at least sent forth by God, and thus find a place in this purpose for Israel.

prospects. Nevertheless it is true that, by New Testament times, the phrase 'to follow' had added to itself an ethical aspect, for it is always the superior who walks ahead, and the inferior who follows: therefore, at the least, a rabbi-disciple relationship was implied.

iii. Christ at Capernaum (i. 21–28). It was the consistent practice of Christ to attend the Temple and synagogue. Like any other adult Jewish male, He could exercise a teaching ministry in the synagogue; but, unlike any other teacher whom they had heard hitherto, He neither quoted nor leaned on any other rabbinic names as precedent. Men were amazed, not only at the content of His teaching, but also at the quiet assumption of personal authority displayed in the manner of its presentation. This was in direct contrast to the caution and pettifogging of the scribes, to whom the Lord's handling of law and tradition must have seemed cavalier, to say the least.

23–26. The immediate result of Christ's preaching was not harmony, but division and strife, exactly as He later warned men (Mt. x. 34). This strife might lie concealed in the minds of the congregation, but was made plain in the outcry of the demoniac. He, at least, bears unwilling witness to the Person and work of Christ, though he recoils instinctively from His purity, realizing that here is a preacher with whom he has nothing in common (*What have we to do with thee . . .?*). Capernaum, the scene of the miracle, was the proud city of unbelief, compared with which Tyre and Sidon would fare well in the day of judgment (Mt. xi. 23, 24). It is a strange commentary on the spiritual situation in Capernaum that a demoniac could worship in their synagogue with no sense of incongruity, until confronted by Jesus, and apparently with no desire to be delivered from his affliction. The Lord's instant response was to muzzle this involuntary demon-testimony and free the man of the incubus. (The Greek word *phimōthēti*, *Hold thy peace* (25), is better translated 'Be muzzled'.)

27, 28. This exhibition of power only confirmed the impression left in men's minds by hearing His teaching, that here was one invested with authority. But, though it led men to wonder, the miracle did not lead men to belief. This seems to be the reason why the Lord performed miracles so sparingly and selectively, and only for those in whom faith already existed, in no matter how small a degree (Lk. xvii. 6).

iv. Peter's mother-in-law (i. 29–31). This 'domestic miracle' gives us one of the rare glimpses into the home lives of the apostles. Simon's wife may even have accompanied her volatile husband on his missionary travels later, as she is mentioned specifically by Paul in 1 Corinthians ix. 5.[1]

As so often in the Gospel narrative, the touch of Christ brought instant healing (31); and the consciousness of healing brought grateful devotion to Him, expressed in glad service— in this case, within the four walls of a home.

v. The evening healings (i. 32–34). The miracle in the synagogue and the miracle in the home are the natural preludes to the general healing described in these verses. These two isolated miracles had taken place on the sabbath; but now, after sunset, with the sabbath over and past, crowds assembled to seek healing. The Evangelist may have felt that it was appropriate for such general healing and blessing to be on the Lord's Day of the Church. The question of healing on the sabbath does not seem to have yet arisen as a controversial question; presumably this was because the healing of the demoniac was well-nigh involuntary, and the healing of Peter's mother-in-law was inside a private house, and thus roused no stir of scandal among the orthodox.

34. Once again, the Lord refuses to accept demoniac testimony to His Godhead. All such testimony is non-voluntary, an unwilling recognition of an empirical fact, and thus corresponds to no moral or spiritual transforming discovery. Christ is prepared to await the revelation to be made by God to men that alone will enable them to say with Peter, 'You are

---

[1] Although the Greek verb *periagein*, 'to lead about', may be weaker in meaning, and simply refer to Peter's married state, not to his wife's movements.

Messiah' (see Mk. viii. 29). James ii. 19 shows that such grudging acceptance of God as an unwelcome reality is poles apart from true Christian faith: demons may well believe, but they do not trust.

vi. From Capernaum to Galilee (i. 35–39). All the varied healings mentioned here must have taken a considerable time. We know that on some occasions at least, the miracle was accompanied by a conscious flow of healing power from the Lord to the patient (Mk. v. 30) and may thus have been exhausting to the Lord.

It was after a busy sabbath of worship and ministry in the synagogue, at a time when others might seek rest and relaxation, that Christ sought God in private prayer. In this way the Lord was accustomed to spend His 'preacher's Monday morning'. The earliness of the hour and the pains thus constantly taken to secure a quiet place for uninterrupted prayer left an abiding impression on the disciples. Simon at least thoroughly disapproved of the Lord's 'unrealistic' strategy in withdrawing from the bustle and opportunity of Capernaum to the silence of the lonely spot. He must have been still more puzzled when Christ saw, in this heightened local interest roused by His healing work, the signal to move on, and to preach in other villages. This, Christ explains, was in fulfilment of His divine mission, which thus became a general preaching and healing mission of a peripatetic nature, based on the synagogues of Galilee.

vii. The cleansing of the leper (i. 40–45). This account of the cleansing of the leper is a little vignette of a type of incident that must have been repeated many times in the unrecorded ministry of our Saviour, which (as John reminds us in xxi. 25) was much more extensive than our scanty records show. In this miracle, there are only two characters involved. The first is an untouchable, conscious of his own state, earnestly desiring to be cleansed, humble enough to ask for cleansing and believing that the Christ had power to heal him. The other figure is the compassionate Christ, who does not shrink from laying His hand even on the loathsomeness of leprosy. Wherever the compassionate Christ and the yearning sinner meet, there then comes instantaneous and complete cleansing. In the antiseptic cleanliness of modern hospitals we lose sight of the wonder of the pure Christ stooping to touch the *odiosus peccator*, the 'stinking sinner', to use the strong term beloved by our forefathers. To the pious Jew, so conscious of the ritual uncleanness of the leper (Lv. xiii. 3, etc.), the wonder became staggering.

43, 44. Once again, the commands of the Christ run counter to all natural human thought. To the cleansed leper, the most natural thing in the world, and the spontaneous expression of adoring love, would have been to tell others. This, in his case, was forbidden in the most explicit terms. This was surely because Christ never desired men to be drawn to follow Him simply in hopes of material and bodily benefits to be obtained from Him. Unwise witness to a physical healing would attract others from wrong motives. This is one of the paradoxes of the Christ. He sees the hungry multitude, has pity on them and feeds them; and yet He rebukes multitudes who come to Him for feeding (Jn. vi. 26). He has compassion on the sick, and does not turn them away when they come for healing; but He makes no attempt to seek out the sick and heal them. Rather, He withdraws Himself when the throng of those seeking healing becomes too great, for this makes His teaching ministry, that is alone able to interpret His healing ministry, impossible. He was primarily Teacher, not Healer.

For the man to show himself to the priest, on the other hand, and to make the necessary offerings, was both a fitting expression of gratitude to God for his healing, and also an obligation to the law that was at once the medical and hygienic, as well as the ceremonial, code of Israel (cf. Dt. xxiv. 8, reinforcing the injunctions of Lv. xiv).

45. Disobedience to the express command of Christ, even if undertaken from the best possible motives, can lead only to a hampering and hindering of Christ's work.

b. The beginning of conflict (ii. 1–iii. 6)

i. The healing of the palsied man (ii. 1–12). Whenever the Messiah entered a house, the simple verdict of the Gospels is that it could not be concealed (see Mk. vii. 24), so pervasive was His presence. Thus the crowds gathered again in Capernaum, which, after the move from Nazareth, now became His home town (Mt. ix. 1; for the move, see Lk. iv. 31). But this time they came, not primarily to be healed of bodily afflictions, but to hear the word of God. The temporary withdrawal of i. 38, and the Galilaean preaching tour of i. 39, had served their purpose; the wheat had been separated from the chaff.

Nevertheless, because the needs of those in Capernaum were many and varied, and because the Christ would meet all those needs, however diverse, there was still healing by Christ; and healing, after all, was another messianic sign (Lk. vii. 22; cf. Mt. viii. 17). The crowd that milled about the door of the house—either Mary's new home or the house of Simon's wife's kindred—were hungry to hear the word of God; and so the poor had the gospel preached to them.

3–5. The four, who came in such faith carrying their sick comrade, were anxious to obtain physical healing for their friend; it was granted. The paralysed man himself, to judge from the Lord's dealing with him, was not so much conscious of his physical need as of his spiritual burden; so the Lord gave forgiveness. Only the scribes, arrogantly self-satisfied, and conscious of no need, received nothing from Christ. Verse 17 is the Lord's quiet comment, not without wry humour on this seeming anomaly.

As usual, the Lord healed only in response to faith. Here Scripture does not make clear the attitude of the sick man himself. He, too, may well have had faith, but it may be that he was too conscious of his own sin to have any confidence in thus approaching the Christ. It is simplest to assume that the Lord worked the miracle in response to the robust and active faith of the four friends, who brought a helpless comrade and laid him at Jesus' feet. Their faith showed its reality by its very obstinacy and stubbornness in refusing to give up hope. This could be a veritable sermon on the text of James ii. 26, showing that faith, unless it manifests its reality by action, is unreal and self-deceptive.

6, 7. These scribes were men of theological acumen. They were not the local synagogue wiseacres of provincial Capernaum, but a fact-finding commission of the type that had minutely cross-questioned John the Baptist (Jn. i. 19; Lk. v. 17). They saw at once down to the theological roots of the matter. Of course, none but God could forgive sin; how dare a man like Jesus claim such authority? Again and again during the life of Christ the same dilemma was to re-appear. If He were not divine, then He was indeed a blasphemer (*aut Deus, aut homo non bonus*); there could be no third way out. If the scribes did not accept Him, then they must condemn Him outright. At least some of them had early seen the logic of this (see Mk. iii. 6) and so they began to plot His death in cold blood.

8, 9. Nevertheless, in the case of others of the scribes, the bewilderment may have been genuine enough, as it surely was in the case of the honest scribe of xii. 34. To help such men to make the staggering equation between the man Christ Jesus and Godhead, the Lord gave an unasked sign of divine power, in healing the paralytic before their eyes.

Of course, it is equally easy to *say* the two phrases in the text, and equally easy for divine power to vindicate the note of authority in either phrase. But there is no outward sign by which the reality of the forgiveness of sins can be tested, while it is patent to all whether a lame man actually walks or no. In other words, in this sphere it could most readily be seen whether the Lord's assumption of authority was justified or unjustified. So, as often, the Lord took His enemies on their own terms and refuted them; verse 8 shows that He acted thus in full knowledge of their thought processes. It was, in point of fact, a much lighter thing to heal the body than to restore the soul, for a prophet might heal, but no mere prophet could ever forgive sins; but the scribes, with their incessant demands for signs, were unlikely to see this (see viii. 11). In any case,

Christ both healed and forgave on this occasion, leaving them speechless. Had they eyes to see it, here was the very sign they sought; but none are so blind as those who will not see.

10, 11. There are two ways of understanding this passage; both lines of exegesis are fruitful, and, if pursued far enough, merge into one. The first interpretation is to paraphrase, 'You say that only God can forgive sins? but I will show you that here is a *man* who has the same power', thus leading the thoughtful scribe to the equation of the man Christ Jesus with God. This would involve understanding the *Son of man* as merely the common Semitic paraphrase for 'mortal man' (Ezk. ii. 1, etc.). The second interpretation would take *Son of man*, in this instance, as the Lord's own self-chosen title for Himself, as it must be in Luke xix. 10, etc.[1] If it be taken as the Lord's personal title, then we should paraphrase as 'to show you that I in person have this power to forgive sins . . .'. In either case, the miracle has evidential value.

12. Once again Christ's word proved to be effectual, a word of authority. As in Genesis God had created from nothingness by a word, so, at a word, God's Son could bring strength out of impotence. Thus that which was impossible by nature took place, and a paralysed man walked home, carrying his mattress. The natural reaction of the unbiased section of the crowd was to praise the God who had committed such power (i.e. authority) to men (see Mt. ix. 8), thus vindicating the Lord's reason for performing the miracle. The crowd at least realized that an entirely new factor had now entered the situation, the 'finger of God' (cf. Ex. viii. 19; Mt. xii. 28). But they were as yet content to wonder at the authority thus committed to mortal man, without asking the further question as

[1] *Son of man* as a title of the Christ is derived primarily from the use in Daniel vii. 13, with development during the intertestamental period. This title of the Messiah speaks of Him in His capacity as 'representative man', the human agent of God, especially as vindicated by God and returning in judgment. In Matthew xxvi. 64, the title is linked specifically with 'the Christ, the Son of God'. This identification of man's son with God's Son was the ultimate blasphemy for which Christ was condemned to die by the Sanhedrin (Mk. xiv. 61–64).

to who this Son of man was. The full answer to that question was not to come till Caesarea Philippi (viii. 27–30) and it was a question for which not even His disciples were ready as yet.

ii. The ministry of the Christ (ii. 13). The Lord frequently is described as engaged in open-air preaching, and especially beside the Sea of Galilee, where many villages were clustered round the shore of the lake. One reason for this choice may have been that the sloping shore provided a convenient amphitheatre for a large audience, especially if the Lord habitually preached from a boat moored in shallow water (as apparently in iv. 1). Perhaps the same practical reason, as well as the geography of the area, influenced the Lord's fondness for teaching on hillsides. He had grown up in hilly Nazareth (i. 9), where His (presumably already married) sisters apparently still continued to live (vi. 3) even after His own move down to the lake (Lk. iv. 31). (See the note on ii. 1 for Capernaum as His home in later years.) Matthew xi. 20, 21 mentions Bethsaida and Chorazin as scenes of some of His mightiest works. Several of His disciples are specifically mentioned as coming from the Bethsaida area in any case (Jn. i. 44). As far as the three active years of His ministry go, the area immediately around the Sea of Galilee was therefore His home base, rather than the hills of central Galilee, although the Sermon on the Mount may well represent a summary of His teaching in these highlands (Mt. v–vii). As Luke vi has a Sermon on the Plain instead, it is reasonable to suppose that this represents a summary of the corpus of teaching given on the level land by the lake. In that case, the teaching mentioned, but not particularized here by Mark, may have formed part of this Lucan corpus, for we may assume a generally similar pattern throughout the Lord's Galilaean ministry.

The ministry of the Christ is explained in different terms. He 'heralds' the news (i. 14); He teaches (i. 21); He speaks the word (ii. 2). Perhaps we may see here a rough division into evangelism, systematic instruction and informal teaching respectively; we have examples of all three types recorded in the Gospels.

iii. The call of Levi (ii. 14–17). *Levi,* usually equated with Matthew (Mt. ix. 9), was a tax-collector and, being in Galilee, doubtless an agent of the hated Edomite Herod (cf. Lk. xxiii. 6, 7). This made him as much an outcast from orthodox Jewish society as the leper of i. 40 had been. Such men were often, if not always, rapacious and immoral, apart altogether from the nationalistic prejudice against them, especially if they were working directly for the Romans. Yet, as the Lord had laid His hand on the leper and cleansed him, so He called Levi to be one of the Twelve, one of the foundation members of His new society (cf. Rev. xxi. 14 with Eph. ii. 20), one of the twelve *phylarchs,* the tribal heads of His new Israel (cf. Lk. xxii. 30). The treacherous Levi of Genesis xlix had already in this man become the faithful Levi of Deuteronomy xxxiii.

15. It seems from Luke v. 29 that this meal was in the nature of a reception given by Levi to his old business acquaintances, to enable them to meet his new-found Master. This verse, and indeed the biting criticism of the Pharisees in Matthew xi. 19, seem to prove that the Lord already numbered many such tax-collectors among His followers.[1]

16. Christ never excused or condoned sin; no scribe or Pharisee ever condemned it in stronger terms than He. This criticism of Christ by the Pharisees was ill based for several reasons. First, when a man or woman became a friend or a follower of Jesus, then they ceased to be *sinners.* Secondly, the reason that the Lord mixed so freely with this stratum of society was because their need was so great, because they, unlike the religious, were conscious of their need and thus responsive to His message, and because He desired to change them. It was indeed a common complaint that the Lord was not particular enough in choosing His friends. 'This man welcomes sinners and shares the meal-table with them', said they (see Lk. xv. 2) apparently with much justification. Simon

---

[1] Cranfield prefers to take the *many* as simply introducing an awkward reference to the numbers of the Lord's disciples in general, and not tax-collectors in particular; but syntactically the traditional interpretation seems preferable.

the Pharisee was charitably certain that, if the Lord had only been possessed of a true prophetic insight, and had thus been able to divine the true nature of the loose woman who approached Him, He would at once have shrunk from contact with her (Lk. vii. 39). But the other Pharisees here were at once less charitable than Simon and more correct in their forecast of the Lord's probable reaction. The Lord Himself knew that the common Pharisaic view of Him was as a greedy and hard-drinking fellow, a friend of tax-collectors and sinners (see Mt. xi. 19). Nevertheless, in spite of this holy horror, it was probable that the main objection of the Pharisees to such strata of society was not a truly moral scruple, but merely a fear lest they themselves should contract ceremonial defilement by contact with the ritually unclean (cf. Jn. xviii. 28). So the Lord would willingly touch the leper (i. 41), but the priest and Levite, by virtue of their office, dared not help even an injured man at the roadside (Lk. xi. 31, 32).

17. The Lord not only refused to deny the imputation; He claimed that to act in this fashion, by seeking out the sinful, was the whole purpose of His mission, and indeed an irrefutable proof of His Messiahship. As in the case of Zacchaeus, the Son of man came on purpose to seek and to save the lost ones (see Lk. xix. 10). His whole mission was directed towards the sinful, or the *sick*, to use the imagery of the present passage. He did not mean that any were in truth just or healthy and thus without need of His spiritual healing. The point made is that, without the one primary pre-requisite of a sense of need, there could be no healing for them, for they were unwilling to come to Him, the sole Source, to seek it (cf. Jn. v. 40).

iv. Controversy about fasting (ii. 18–22). John's disciples, and thus, we may infer, John himself, were all meticulous in keeping the ceremonial law. This the very Pharisees grudgingly admitted, even in their criticism of Jesus. John was thus no heresiarch, but a bastion of orthodox Judaism, although as caustic in his remarks on the priesthood as many a prophet before him had been. Since several at least of the Lord's dis-

ciples had been John's followers before the Baptist's testimony
sent them away to follow Jesus (Jn. i. 35-37), this strictly
orthodox background is important. Both to the Pharisees, and
to John himself at times, it must have looked suspiciously as
though these were disciples who had chosen an easier way.
Although regular weekly fasting was not part of the Law of
Moses, by this date such fasting had become an important
part of the practice of Judaism, whence it passed into early
Christianity, with a change in the actual day observed.[1] To
the Jew this one minor point of fasting thus raised the whole
question of the attitude of Christ to the ceremonial law. He
had already healed on the sabbath (i. 26), though this had not
yet become an issue, while His disciples ate food without prior
ceremonial hand-washing (vii. 2), and even husked corn on
the sabbath (ii. 23). Taken together, this was highly suspicious.

19-22. As often, the Lord answered the Pharisaic criticism
at two levels; first, He replied superficially, on the level at
which these carping questions were usually asked. Then,
having already demolished their objection on their own
premises, He proceeded to deal with it at a far deeper theological level. Here one might paraphrase, 'in a time of joyous
fellowship, who thinks of fasting?' Fasting is, in the Bible,
either a sign of disaster or of voluntary abasement of the
spirit. The sorrow which finds expression in fasting will come
soon enough of its own accord, when the fellowship is broken;[2]
they will have sorrow then, at the Lord's departure to the
Father (Jn. xvi. 20). To apply the analogy, which so obviously
fits human affairs, it might be said that the Lord's time with
His disciples on earth was in many ways an interim period
and not normative for the Church. No generalization should
therefore be drawn from the practice of His disciples then,

---

[1] See *Didache* viii. 1 for some curiously naïve reasoning here. Paul's
words in Romans xiv. 5 may refer to this custom, especially as the context
treats of fasting: but it may equally well refer to sabbath observance by
converted Jews.

[2] See Cranfield for the very plausible view that John's disciples were
probably even then fasting in mourning for the martyrdom of their rabbi:
this, taken with the *aparthē*, 'is (violently) *taken away*', gives the whole saying
a grim point, and makes it indeed a passion-prediction of the Lord.

without careful comparison with the subsequent practice of the New Testament Church, after Christ had ascended into heaven and the Holy Spirit had been outpoured.

But there was a far deeper question, which not even the disciples saw until their forcible expulsion from the pale of orthodox Judaism in the days of the Acts of the Apostles. Was the whole structure of Jewish ceremonial, fasting naturally being included, indeed consonant with the new spirit of the followers of the Messiah? A new spirit must find new forms of expression; that is the lesson of the parable, and the book of Acts shows with increasing clarity the utter impossibility of containing young Christianity as a mere 'Reformed Sect' within Judaism. It was no accident that not only the Judaizers but even the non-heretical Jewish-Christian churches known to Eusebius died out in later centuries. Whether recent modern attempts to revive them are wise or no, is a moot point.[1]

v. Controversy about the sabbath (ii. 23-28). To neither the 'accidental' nor the 'essential' reason did the Pharisees give any reply; indeed, it is hard to see what they could have said. None the less, the next two incidents with which this chapter closes, and the next chapter begins, show further clashes on two other points of ceremonial observance, so it is obvious that, on the wider issue, the orthodox Pharisees were still far from satisfied. Here it was the behaviour of the disciples with which they found fault. It is very noticeable that they were not able to bring anything against Jesus personally, not even the most trivial charge of breach of the ceremonial law. The sole proven case against Him was that of healing on the sabbath. That this charge would not stand in the religious court of the Sanhedrin as true sabbath-breaking is shown by their failure to bring it forward at the trial of Jesus, when they were catching at any straw of evidence against Him as a make-weight. Like Pilate, try as they might, they could find no fault in Him (Jn. xix. 4).

The disciples were charged with 'working' on the sabbath on two scores; as they walked through the grain they not only

---

[1] See, for instance, Lev Gillet, *Communion in the Messiah*, Lutterworth Press.

pulled the ripe ears, but also husked them between their palms (Lk. vi. 1). The actual eating was of course not culpable, even in Pharisaic eyes. The disciples acted thus quite unself-consciously, and thus not for the first time, we may be sure. But then, they had not been trained in the niceties of the rabbinic schools. We know how bitterly the Pharisees despised the *'am hā-āres*, the common people, ignorant of the law, and thus accursed (Jn. vii. 49). Even the Lord was regarded with great suspicion as an unlettered Rabbi (Jn. vii. 15), that is, one without formal training at the feet of some already recognized religious teacher. Such ignorance displayed by His disciples with regard to subtle points would but condemn their Master further in rabbinic eyes. It was, in the last resort, the professional jealousy of the Jewish theologians that hounded Christ to death. None were so blind as those who boasted themselves of their theological insight (Jn. ix. 41), a solemn warning to us today, if we pride ourselves on our 'enlightenment'.

Again, the Lord's answer was twofold. First, He showed that there was biblical evidence for the law of need taking precedence over the law of ceremonial,[1] and that in the case of no less a personage than David. Further, He showed that this was no mere question of husking corn, but the much more serious charge of eating the presented bread which, after its presentation to God, was hallowed from secular uses, and might be eaten only by the priests.

This action of David, though they must needs admit it as an historic fact (whether or not in the priesthood of Abiathar[2]) and also that it passed unreproved in Scripture, they might

[1] *Pace* many modern commentators, this seems the plain meaning of the text before us. David had been in need, and so were Christ's disciples. To argue that they were not dying of hunger is beside the point.

[2] There is a well-known crux here, in that Abiathar became priest (the title 'high priest' does not seem to have been used in his day) only after the slaughter by Saul of Abimelech his father because of this deed of David's. Many mss omit the clause in whole or part, almost certainly because of the difficulty. We may cut the Gordian knot with the stout-hearted Jerome, by arguing that our concern is not with names and such like (cf. i. 2, where the citation from 'Isaiah the prophet' (rv) actually covers Malachi as well), or else say that *epi* should be translated 'in the passage dealing with'; cf. *epi tou batou* (xii. 26): see rv.

nevertheless have deprecated, and regarded as at best a poor palliative of the offence of Christ's disciples.

27. So the Lord now makes a far deeper claim. He claims that the Pharisees, with all their hedging restrictions, originally designed to avoid any possibility of infringing the sabbath, had ended by making it an intolerable burden (cf. Mt. xxiii. 4). They had thus quite forgotten that in origin the sabbath was God's merciful provision for man. Man was certainly not created simply to exemplify and observe an immutable theological principle of sabbath keeping, as certain of the extremists were quite ready to uphold.

28. Even this principle, that the sabbath was made for man, the Pharisees might endure, but the Lord goes further. If the sabbath was made for man's spiritual and physical good, and not vice versa, then *the Son of man* is Master of the sabbath and can interpret its regulations with reference to need. This, in fact, was what the rabbis had been trying to do themselves, though in a wrong-headed way. Once again, if the Lord is using *Son of man* as a personal title for Himself at this point, and if His opponents understood His use of it so (neither point is certain), then the claim becomes even more pungent. It would mean that, instead of denying the charge, the Lord freely admits it. He claims to have the absolute right to overrule the sabbath if He will, because of His Person and work as God's representative man. Such a claim leads naturally enough to the major clash over sabbath healing at the beginning of chapter iii. It is at last dawning on them that His sabbath healings in i. 25 and i. 31 were no mere accidents, but undertaken because He regarded the sabbath as His by right. So they resolve to lay a trap for Him, to make a deliberate test case; but as so often in the New Testament, the issue, when forced, moves them from the judge's bench to the prisoner's dock.

vi. The man with the withered hand (iii. 1–6). There is no evidence as to which *synagogue* this was, except that it was in Galilee, and the likelihood is that it was in Capernaum, since the theological delegation from Jerusalem still apparently held its watching brief. This miracle concerned a man powerless to work until he received the healing touch of Christ. One interesting early tradition[1] says that he was a plasterer, to whom naturally the use of both hands was particularly important. Many of these extra-canonical details preserved in such sources may well be true; otherwise, it is hard to see why they were invented, since they prove no theological truth. Much oral tradition about Jesus must have lingered in Palestine, at least until the cataclysm of AD 70.

2. The condemnation of the Pharisees is that they failed to see in this man a case of need. All they saw was a possible ground of accusation against Jesus if He took advantage of this sabbath encounter to heal. By such moral blindness, they stood self-condemned.

3. If the man truly desired healing, he must be willing to confess his need and to show his faith in the power of Jesus to meet that need by standing up in the face of the whole congregation. To a sensitive person, such public display of a maimed limb would be a cup of shame, bitter to drink; but such the Lord often demanded (cf. the woman with the haemorrhage in v. 33).

4. The Lord's query, like the question about the source of John's baptism in xi. 30, was one which they could not answer without at once abandoning their own position. Matthew xii. 11, with the homely parable of the animal which falls into a pit and is at once retrieved by his owner, sabbath or no sabbath, makes the point even more obviously. The Galilaean farmers would have slapped their thighs and chuckled at that, as no doubt they made merry at the thought of these city rabbis, who advocated leaving horse or mule without food and water on the sabbath (Lk. xiii. 15), though there were stories in the Talmud about pious rabbinic mules who would refuse to eat untithed corn. Yet every man, by admitting the justice

---

[1] 'Gospel of the Hebrews', quoted in Jerome's commentary on Matthew xii. 13.

of the parable, admitted that it was therefore lawful to do good on the sabbath day; for to save the life of a helpless beast was unquestionably good. Further, to abandon the helpless beast would be to cause it to die; this would clearly be to do evil. So, whatever course of action he chose, the owner was forced to do something on the sabbath day; his only freedom of choice was as to whether he did good or ill. Deliberately to refrain from doing good is to do evil (Jas. iv. 17), and technically speaking, this evil deed would be just as great a profanation of the sabbath as the good deed that they were scrupulously refusing to do. Matthew xii. 12 quietly points out that, if this is true of saving a brute beast, it is *a priori* true of saving a man who was created in God's image.[1]

5. This is the first reference in Mark to that *hardness* of heart experienced by the Lord, not only among the Pharisees, as here, but also among the common people (Jn. xii. 37–40), and even among His own disciples (Mk. vi. 52). Such hardness of heart angered Him when found among His enemies; it grieved and amazed Him when among His own disciples. 'Hard-hearted' to us means callous or cruel, but to the Hebrew it meant a stubborn resistance to the purpose of God, the very opposite of that humility and gentle teachableness which God requires. It is a form of pride and, like unbelief, it is in part at least an attitude of the will. Thus, if wilfully sustained, it can end in the unforgivable sin against the Holy Spirit. It should be noted that this is a sin to which, to judge from Scripture, the theologian and the religiously-minded are more exposed than are the publican and sinner: and if any man fears this sin, it is proof that he has not committed it.

6. The result of the man's faith and obedience (if the two

---

[1] It is possible that the second clause, 'or to do evil', may merely be a Semitic pleonasm to balance the first clause. The meaning would then be the same as the simple 'to do good'. But the above exegesis seems more natural and satisfactory, since it gives an appropriateness to both halves of the clause. Alternatively, we may take 'to do good or ill' as the common Semitic idiom for 'to act' in general, or 'to do anything', since all possibilities are included here. But in either case the problem is more linguistic than theological.

concepts can be distinguished) was complete healing. Mark, alone of the Gospel writers, tells us that from this moment the Pharisees and Herodians[1] began to plot the death of Jesus.

The Pharisees were outraged at what they regarded as a clear and deliberate breach of the law. But it is hard to believe that in their plot to kill Jesus they had already secured the backing of the authorities at Jerusalem, to whom as yet Jesus cannot have appeared a very formidable antagonist. Why the Herodians were involved in the plot is not so clear; although that party numbered many scribes in its ranks, they were scarcely zealous for the law. Their anxiety may have been purely political, as was that of Caiaphas (Jn. xi. 50).

III. AS MANY AS RECEIVED HIM: THE CALL AND TRAINING OF THE DISCIPLES (iii. 7–viii. 26)

a. The conflict increases (iii. 7–35)

i. Breach with the religious leaders (iii. 7–12). These verses seem to mark the decisive breach between the Lord and organized Jewry. This breach thus took place near the start of the ministry of the Christ, and is quite as marked and decisive in the Synoptic Gospels as it is in John. The Lord moved away from those who had become His enemies, almost as a deliberate act of separation, and His disciples accepted the consequences of separation by following Him. Not only so, but big crowds poured down, not merely from Galilee now; from Edom in the south to Tyre in the north and Transjordan in the east they gathered, eager to be healed. It is as if the Lord's action in the

---

[1] This name loosely describes those Jews who saw in the house of Herod the hope of Israel; blood-stained tyrant though he was, he was at least a native ruler, and had saved half the land from coming under the direct rule of Rome, as Judaea was. They appear to have been largely members of the priestly aristocracy, wealthy and shrewd, numbering many Sadducees within their ranks. The Pharisees, previously bitter enemies of the house of Herod (see Josephus), had now reached an uneasy understanding: but while many a scribe could well be a Herodian, a Pharisee could scarcely be so termed.

synagogue was being vindicated by the common man, though official Jewry repudiated it. It is a marked biblical stress that in spiritual matters the plain judgment of the simple heart is a truer guide than the wrangling of the learned. What is hidden from the wise is revealed to babes (Mt. xi. 25, 26).

9, 10. There are several references to the Lord's practice of sitting in a ship moored off shore, and preaching to the crowds on the beach, when other means of reaching such large numbers failed. It was but one of the instances in which it was proved that the prior life and training of His fisherfolk disciples was by no means wasted, though they had forsaken it to follow Him. Frequently He used their skill and strength to cross the sea by boat, although they had to learn that, even in the sphere where they felt most at home, Christ was still Lord (cf. iv. 41). There is at least one Gospel reference to Peter fishing with rod and line at the Lord's command (Mt. xvii. 27), and one of the resurrection appearances finds the disciples fishing again, this time with their nets (Jn. xxi. 3). It is thus reasonable to suppose that the skill of the disciples may often have supplied the little band with a meal.

11, 12. Note the Lord's steady refusal to accept demoniac testimony to His Person or work, though such testimony would have been irrefutable. The Lord wanted men to find out who He was by listening to His words and by watching His deeds. This is made clear in His reply to the puzzled disciples of the imprisoned John, who sent them to ask bluntly whether Jesus was the Christ or not. 'Go . . . and tell John what things ye have seen and heard' (Lk. vii. 22), said the Lord. Here were messianic signs in plenty; but it needed the eye of faith to interpret them.

But the scribes and Pharisees, who, of all men, ought to have known from their close study of the Old Testament how to recognize the Christ when He came, not only watched His deeds unmoved; they actually attributed the expulsion of demons to demonic power (Mt. xii. 24). This was a deliberate distortion of the truth which called forth from Jesus the solemn warning as to the necessarily unforgivable nature of such sin against the Holy Spirit. When a man so steels his heart against God's love, there can be no hope for him; for only to a broken and repentant heart can forgiveness come, and this is the way that he himself has consistently refused to take.

ii. The call of the Twelve (iii. 13–19). Following this breach with the church of Jewry, the Lord began to constitute His own Church. He retired from the lakeside into the hill country of central Galilee (this is more probably the meaning of the Greek *oros*, rather than some one particular hill near Capernaum),[1] and spent a whole night in prayer (Lk. vi. 12) before selecting for special training twelve men from out of the general company of His followers.[2]

14, 15. The primary purpose of the appointment of the Twelve was that they should be continually in the company of their Rabbi, who was at once Teacher and Leader of the group. They would thus receive both formal and informal instruction, and treasure and lay to heart His casual sayings, in the manner familiar to us from the disciples of Socrates and Confucius as well as from the common rabbinic practice of the Lord's day and later. The secondary purpose was that He might send them out as His own personal representatives, on missions for Him. At this stage, their mission was defined as that of being heralds of the news of the establishment of God's rule. By virtue of this, they had an authority, delegated from Christ, to expel from men's lives the demon forces that had hitherto ruled them.

---

[1] To biblical writers 'the Highlands' mean either the hilly country of central Galilee, or else the mountain plateau of Judah, with 'Lowlands' elsewhere, especially along the seashore or lakeside.

[2] Just as the old Israel had twelve 'Founding Fathers', so had the new; and even some of the names of the phylarchs are the same. In both old and new, there is a Simeon and a Levi, as well as a Judah. Other correspondences unknown to us may well exist, for Andrew and Philip almost certainly had a Hebrew 'name in religion' as well as their Greek names (see Cranfield). As there had been of old a beloved tribe, Benjamin, so there was now a beloved disciple, John; but in the new Israel all are both priestly and royal (Rev. i. 6).

16–19. Mark's list of the apostles contains more of the loving personal nicknames, naturally Aramaic,[1] than do any of the lists in the other Gospels. If, as suggested in the Introduction, and as supported by tradition, Mark depends directly upon the Petrine tradition, this is very understandable. *Simon* (16) is to be *Peter*, or *Cephas* in Aramaic, 'the rock'. *James* and *John* (17) are a hot-tempered pair; they are *Boanerges*, i.e. *Donner und Blitzen, The sons of thunder. Thaddaeus* (18) is probably to be equated with Lebbaeus—an equation specifically made in some manuscripts—and equally probably to be translated 'Big-Hearted', though whether the reference is to bravery or affection is unsure. *Simon the Canaanite* (18) is better translated 'the Zealot' or 'the Extremist', following Luke vi. 15. This is more likely to be an affectionate nickname than to denote actual membership of the party later so called. If we translate it 'the Keen', we can recapture some of the original pun on the place-name, as well as the sense of the word. Perhaps *Canaanite* is not so much a mistranslation as a deliberate precaution against Roman suspicion of treason. Mark's Gospel was written early, and there was no certainty that it would not fall into the wrong hands. Other instances of caution in Mark's wording will be mentioned below.[2] Likewise *Iscariot* (19) is at least as likely to mean 'the dagger man' (the ancient equivalent of the modern 'gunman') from the mixed Graeco-Latin word *sikariōtēs*, as it is to mean 'the man from Qerīyōth' (either 'the villages' in general, or a specific place–name). If translated 'knife-man' it could be either a pure nickname, or a hint of political associations with the various extremist parties loosely grouped together under that name.

[1] There can be little serious doubt that the Lord and His disciples habitually used Aramaic both in conversation between themselves, and in teaching outsiders, although there is much dispute over the exact dialect and vocalization. Matthew Black is the safest modern guide here: few now would hold with Torrey's extreme views, upon which see Albright. Written Aramaic sources for the Gospels (see Introduction) become progressively less likely in view of the dearth of Aramaic literature in this period (apart from certain of the Dead Sea Scrolls), but that spoken Aramaic was very much alive is shown especially by Mark—naturally enough, if he has a Petrine source. See also v. 41 and vii. 34, for entire 'fossilized phrases'.

[2] See, e.g., commentary on xiii. 14.

If these last three instances are indeed to be understood as nicknames, it is true that there is no direct evidence that they were names conferred by Christ; but there can be no doubt that they were names used within the group, from their later use in the Church. The Talmud is full of similar nicknames, used to distinguish homonymous rabbis.

In the choice of the disciples, there is an example of what is a mystery to the modern man. Christ chose at His own sovereign will, and those whom He chose responded to His call (cf. Jn. vi. 37, although this is not, as so often said, purely a Johannine emphasis). But why choose this particular twelve? Or has this question any meaning when applied to God's sovereign grace? It is easy to say that He chose those who had already proved themselves most responsive to His teaching, since He was choosing the Twelve from among those who were already His followers, and had thus been to some extent sifted and tested already. It may even be said cautiously that the parable of the talents would tend to support this general line of argument. But this cannot plumb the mystery, for perfect divine foreknowledge (Jn. ii. 24, 25) chose Judas. Perhaps it was because He saw capacity for response to divine truth, even in Judas; or perhaps the choice was like the handing to Judas of the sop at the Last Supper—a supreme token of divine love, that would either win the man over for ever, or else condemn him irrevocably. It was after the rejection of that supreme act of love that Judas took the irrevocable step (Jn. xiii. 30); so it is that Paul fears most for those who reject the tokens of supreme love in the Lord's Supper (1 Cor. xi. 29).

iii. Mounting opposition and the Beelzebub controversy (iii. 20–30).

The consequence of Sonship of the heavenly Father was complete misunderstanding of the Christ by His nearest and dearest upon earth. His own brothers did not believe in Him during His ministry (Jn. vii. 5), although Acts i. 14 shows that afterwards some at least were numbered among the Church. Although Mary had believed the word of the angelic messenger (Lk. i. 45), although she wondered and pondered (Lk. ii. 18, 19), although she might lay all to heart

(Lk. ii. 51) and doubtless recounted it later to Luke or to his informant, yet at this stage she does not seem to have understood her Son. That the misunderstanding sprang directly from His consciousness of His vocation as Son of God is shown by the wondering words of the child Jesus in the Temple, 'Why was it that you looked for Me? Did you not know that I must be engaged in My Father's business?' (see Lk. ii. 49). To translate, as traditionally, 'in my Father's house', makes no difference to the general sense. Even at Cana of Galilee, though Mary had undoubted faith in her Son, she showed a failure to understand Him that brought a gentle rebuke from the Lord in the 'Woman, what have I to do with thee?' (Jn. ii. 4; lit. 'what have we in common?'). She must learn not to presume upon her position, highly favoured though she was (Lk. i. 28).[1]

In iii. 31, Mary again tried to presume upon a physical mother-and-son relationship, and again received a loving rebuke from the Lord. When the Lord said 'a man's enemies will be those in his own home' (see Mt. x. 36), He may well have been speaking from bitter experience. Why should His relatives say, doubtless with rough kindness in spite of their obvious irritation, that He was beside Himself (lit. 'out of His wits')?[2] What had made those who knew Him best so convinced that He was mad, that they were even prepared to detain Him by force, if necessary? It was not, apparently, because of the content of His preaching, but because of its unexpected results; such numbers came to hear or to be healed that set mealtimes were impossible. This, to them, was the last straw; like Peter when he heard of the cost to Christ

[1] The unreformed churches of the world, with their undue exaltation of Mary, have not always realized the consequence of this principle, that a temporary physical relationship to the incarnate Lord gives no special call on Him. See Luke xi. 27, 28, where the Lord deals with the question gently but firmly, by the application of the same principle as in the present passage. 2 Corinthians v. 16 is a wider extension still of this principle.

[2] It is, however, possible that *elegon* should be translated in the vague sense of 'people were saying', or 'it was rumoured'. The subject would thus be men in general, and not specifically the relatives of the Lord. Their action would then be taken in response to a widespread rumour which had reached them, and would not be the result of a considered judgment on their part.

of the road to Jerusalem (Mt. xvi. 22), they decided that they must save Jesus from the consequences of His own vocation. Like Peter, they thought that they acted as His friends: but such friends were more dangerous than enemies. Like the disciples at the well of Samaria, they had no concept of the true food that sustained the Lord—the moment-by-moment obedience to the Father's will (Jn. iv. 32–34).

There is a theological snare here, into which we may inadvertently fall. We may not identify ourselves with the misunderstood Christ, and thus make false martyrs of ourselves and become filled with self-pity at the greatness of our own sacrifice. That is a form of deceptive sentimentality that is never encouraged in the New Testament. We must see ourselves rather as those who consistently fail to understand the Christ, consistently are scandalized at His doings, consistently make impossible demands upon Him in spite of our outward relationship to Him. Scripture never allows us the attitude of the third-party bystander; we are always either the prisoner at the bar, or the witness in the box, never the judge on the bench. We are never encouraged to weigh and ponder in abstract nicety that which has no direct relevance to ourselves.

22. Relatives and close friends might misunderstand Him; even His followers might be puzzled by Him. But it was left to the theological commission of enquiry to misinterpret Him deliberately. There is a calculated bitterness in their terse judgment which is lacking in the rough words of His family, sore to the Lord though the family misunderstanding of Him must have been. The commission were less concerned with speaking the truth than with speaking cutting words. We may compare 'He is demon-possessed and mad; why listen to Him?' (see Jn. x. 20) and 'Are we not right in saying that you are a Samaritan and are demon-possessed?' (see Jn. viii. 48). The more subtle sting of 'We were not born out of wedlock' (see Jn. viii. 41) must surely have been part of the suffering that was to pierce through Mary's own soul like a sword (Lk. ii. 35), for if Joseph knew the truth, then others must have guessed (Mt. i. 18, 19). The Lord's own quotation of their description of Him as 'a greedy fellow, fond of the winecup, a friend of taxcollectors and sinners' (see Lk. vii. 34) shows how the sting of the taunt remained.

It is a strange paradox that in times of religious revival and manifest working of God's Spirit, it is often the religious leaders who oppose the work of God most strenuously, and seem to misunderstand it most wilfully. This is because every man's danger of being offended in the Christ comes through that which he takes to be his strong point, in which he prides himself. God, says Paul, traps the wise by their own wisdom (1 Cor. i. 19–21); by wealth the rich man falls (Jas. v. 1); by morality the man who prides himself on his impeccable life is himself condemned (Rom. ii. 21).

These Jewish ecclesiastics could not deny that Jesus had expelled demons from the lives of men. Yet, running counter to all common sense, as the Lord pointed out in His homely parable, they attributed this good work to an evil agency. This would assume a dichotomy of evil, a veritable civil war within the kingdom of evil itself, which would not only be a practical impossibility, but also a theological absurdity in which no Jew could believe. Prejudice, in its full sense of a prior conceived judgment, had blinded their eyes to what was at once obvious to simple souls. Yet we may not condemn them; we must each ask himself the question of John ix. 40, 'Are we blind also?'

23–26. Nevertheless, the Lord dealt graciously with them, in spite of their stubborn blindness. He first shows by parables the patent absurdity of their position in this assumption of a fatal division within the realm of evil which would be tantamount to the suicide of Satan. The other two Synoptists add that He also asked the relevant question as to what power was used by confessedly orthodox Jewish exorcists in performing a similar task with similar results; was that then demonic power also? (See Mt. xii. 27; Lk. xi. 19.) We may note, too, the casual references to the one casting out demons in the name of Jesus, who was no professed follower of His (Mk. ix. 38), and the unfortunate experience of the sons of Sceva, the exorcists of Acts xix. 14, as illustrations of the widespread nature of such exorcism in Jewry. Exorcism was thus not a new or isolated phenomenon, that the Pharisees should misunderstand it so. What may have been new was the universal success with which the Lord Himself employed it, in contrast to the occasional experience of His own disciples (see Mk. ix. 28).[1]

27. There was only one possible corollary; if the Lord thus expelled demons, it must be because He was in possession of a power and authority stronger than that of Satan. This, to any Jew, could only be the power of God (Lk. xi. 21). This in turn meant that Satan's reign of sin and death is over, and that God's reign has already begun, in the hearts and minds of men whom Christ has ransomed and redeemed from Satan's power. Nor is there to be any triumphal return for Satan; his very weapons, in which he had trusted for so long, have been taken from him (so Paul in Col. ii. 15, and, at length, 1 Cor. xv). Death was Satan's greatest weapon and, since the resurrection of Christ, the weapon has lost its keen edge.

28–30. This leads to one of the most solemn pronouncements and warnings in the whole of the New Testament, coupled, as often, with one of the great promises. There is forgiveness with God for every sin and blasphemy except one, which seems to be the deadly sin of which John speaks so cautiously in 1 John v. 16. This is the sin of the wilfully blind, who persistently refuse the illumination of the Spirit, oppose the Spirit's work, and justify themselves in doing so by

[1] A brief note on demon possession may not be without interest here. Those who live and work among the younger churches will recognize the reality of this phenomenon as an empirical fact in Christian experience and the life of the Church, while perhaps adopting a reverent agnosticism as to its explanation. Even in cynical Europe two World Wars have unleashed such demonic powers that Western man is now more inclined to accept demon possession as a fact, even if the outward forms be different. Psychological explanations are merely explanations of the mechanism, and are no doubt valid as far as they go; but they cannot exhaust the meaning, for they leave unsolved the nature of the driving force under and behind such cases. The Bible never encourages idle speculation on these matters; our thought and speculation is to be Christocentric, not demonocentric. Certainly it seems that in the days of Christ there was a great outburst of Satanic activity, just as there was an outpouring of the Holy Spirit's power, manifested in miracles of healing.

deliberately misrepresenting Him. For such, as stated above, there can be no forgiveness, for they have refused the only way of forgiveness that God has provided. Yet, as always in the Bible, we are not encouraged to survey with complacency the downfall of others, but rather to search our own hearts with fear lest we fall in like manner (cf. 1 Cor. x. 12).

iv. Christ's true brethren (iii. 31-35). Presumably this arrival of His mother and brothers is still to be seen in the context of verse 21, where they were ready to restrain Him by force, through a misunderstanding of the nature of His ministry. A similar total misunderstanding underlay the plan of the multitude to seize Him by force and make Him king, after the feeding of the five thousand (Jn. vi. 15).

There are still great crowds coming to Christ and still He is teaching them, in systematic fashion, to judge from the *sat* of verse 32, which to an Eastern mind would imply a pupil-teacher relationship. Mary, who 'sat at Jesus' feet' and heard His doctrine (Lk. x. 39), is an obvious instance.

Here Mary, the mother of the Lord, along with His brothers and sisters, tried to presume upon an earthly relationship with Jesus, as she had done first in the Temple at Jerusalem, and then at the wedding of Cana of Galilee. In this, Mary was but a type of the whole Jewish nation in the days of Christ. They came, claiming a prior right to the kingdom because of their physical descent from Abraham (Mt. iii. 9; Jn. viii. 39).

Those who brought the message through the crowd to Jesus obviously agreed that such an external relationship constituted a prior claim on Christ. There is even a note of mild rebuke in their words, a certainty that as soon as the Christ knows the true facts of the case, He will at once acknowledge the justice of their view. But of such a claim, based on such a relationship, the stranger Christ shows Himself utterly unaware. There had been a genuine surprise in the Lord's words at Cana (Jn. ii. 4). Even to Mary, this Christ was a stranger, until she learned the nature of the new relationship that must bind her to Him. For, having destroyed the vain fleshly confidence with which they came, the Lord shows that there is, in the realm of God, a new relationship just as intimate, which does indeed bring such a claim; but this relationship is spiritual and inward, not outward and automatic, as was assumed by Jewry and as is sometimes assumed in Church life even today.

35. There is but one condition for admission to this position of peculiar intimacy with the Christ; we must know and participate, as He did, in *the will of God*. It is a constant New Testament stress that mere knowledge of the doctrine, even with intellectual assent and appraisal of its truth, is inadequate. Such knowledge in fact only condemns us (Lk. xii. 48). Such intellectual assent ultimately leads to our self-deception and downfall, as the illustration of the two houses, one built upon the rock and one built upon the sand, makes clear (see Lk. vi. 47–49). Luke viii. 21 makes the two steps quite plain; it is those who listen to the word of God and carry it out who receive this blessing. This is the difference between intellectual assent and true faith: and the distinction is made by asking whether or not knowledge is accompanied by obedience (Jas. ii. 21–24). Knowledge of God is not abstract and intellectual; it is personal, moral and empirical. It is not static but dynamic, since He is the living God. It is thus not an intellectual discovery, as other knowledge is, but a transforming and life-giving spiritual experience, brought to us, as to Peter, by the illumination of the Spirit of God (Mt. xvi. 17).

b. Parables of the kingdom (iv. 1–34)

i. The parable of the sower and the reason for the use of parables (iv. 1–25). If we are to stress the Greek word *palin*, again, 'a second time', in this verse, it would mean, as in iii. 7, a determined turning of the back on those who so misunderstood the Christ, and thus a fresh acceptance of the divine vocation.[1] But while in iii. 7 those who had obstinately misunderstood Him were His enemies, here they were His relatives and friends. Christ's path was ever a lonely path (as

---

[1] It is only fair to say that most modern editors (e.g. Cranfield *ad loc.*) take the following block of material as composite. But this, even if true, does not weaken the force of the argument above: Christ turns from His fleshly kin to His spiritual kin.

Heb. xiii. 11–13 makes plain). He must suffer outside the camp (outside the pale, in modern idiom). But, as in Hebrews, so here; there were many others who were prepared to risk the wrath of official Jewry, and go out to Him outside the camp, bearing His reproach.

Indeed, so great was the response that the Lord was forced to resort to an unusual manner and mode of teaching. He taught, as we have seen, sitting in a boat, doubtless anchored in shallow water, while the listening crowds sat on the fore-shore all around; and He taught by parables, a system of instruction specifically designed to sift the wheat from the chaff among His hearers. Other teachers might rejoice when great crowds followed them, but not so the Lord; for He knew only too well the mixed motives of the human heart (Jn. vi. 26, ii. 24, 25). Here is a strange Teacher; His parables are designed to test, not the intelligence, but the spiritual responsiveness of His hearers. Further, there is a sort of arithmetical progression in things spiritual; to him that already has something, more will be given (Mt. xxv. 29), and insight into the meaning of one parable will lead to spiritual perception of the meaning of other such parables. Contrariwise, failure to apprehend will lead us further and further into the fog, until we are completely mystified, groping in darkness. In this, as in all other spiritual things, either we see or we do not see; and to see is the proof that we have received the illumination of that Holy Spirit who alone can open our spiritual eyes, blind by nature, to the truth of God.

2. The parable of the sower is not the first of the parables used by Christ as recounted in this Gospel: iii. 23, in the Beelzebub controversy, is specifically stated to be parabolic, and ii. 19–22 (the children of the bride-chamber, and the new wine in old bottles) is equally obviously so. But this is the first sustained parable of which we have a full explanation given by the Lord Himself, and it stands, in all three Synoptic Gospels, at the head of a series of parables, obviously corresponding to a definite scheme of teaching that the Lord used at this time. Further, in a sense this parable is the key to all the other parables, for it deals with our reception of all of Christ's teaching (iv. 13). There was of course nothing strange in this method of teaching to a Jew: the Old Testament contains abundant examples of parable used for instruction (cf. Jdg. ix. 8–15) and it seems to have been one of the favourite forms in which the rabbis couched their pithy maxims, to judge from the Palestinian Talmud.[1] A good general rule of interpretation is to remember that the parable is designed for us to test ourselves, not to judge others, and we should not try to find a spiritual meaning in every detail, recognizing that some details are but the 'back-cloth'.

3. It is very possible that the subject of this parable was suggested by the sight of an actual sower at work on the hills above the lake: but there is no hint in the context as to the season of the year (compare the obvious connection between 'lift up your eyes, and look on the fields' of John iv. 35 with what the Lord's open-air congregation could actually see at the moment). He taught, not in a cloistered rabbinic school, but in the old familiar surroundings: and for this teaching, He used homely illustrations drawn directly from that life, for teaching divorced from daily life has no support in the example or word of Jesus.

4–8. This parable deals with the problem that is greatest of all to the thoughtful mind: how is it that scribes and Pharisees can so misrepresent Him? And how is it that His kindred and disciples can totally fail to comprehend Him? Why does not the hearing of the doctrine produce the same result in every heart? The answer, as given by the Lord Himself, is that the operation of the divine word on the heart of men is not automatic, and that, while the doctrine is unvarying, the nature of the response is dictated by the nature of the heart that receives it.

[1] It has been well pointed out that *māšāl* to the Hebrew had a far greater range of meaning than the Greek *parabolē* (see Brown, Driver and Briggs, *Hebrew and English Lexicon of the Old Testament*, p. 605; and Köhler and Baumgartner, *Lexicon in Veteris Testamenti Libros*, p. 576). It has, however, been less commonly recognized that, in biblical Greek, *parabolē* gradually extended its sphere of meaning to cover the wider range of the word that it was translating.

It is sometimes the fashion today for exegetes to blame the sower for the poor nature of the harvest, and to point to the indiscriminate nature of his sowing; but to adopt this attitude is to misunderstand the whole purpose of the parable as well as to ignore a great theological truth. God sends rain on just and unjust alike (Mt. v. 45) and sends His word to men, whether they will hear or whether they will forbear (Ezk. ii. 5). Also, we are not called to praise or blame the sower for his choice of methods: it is the empiric fact of the seed falling on different sorts of ground with which the parable is concerned. The hard heart, the shallow heart, the overcrowded heart, and the good heart—all are in fact present, whenever the Word of God is preached: and this does not merely refer to the initial preaching of the gospel and the initial response of man that we call 'conversion'. The whole of the Christian life is one of continual and progressive response to fresh spiritual revelation. It will thus be seen how appropriate it is that this parable should stand as the introduction to a long teaching passage, itself largely parabolic in nature.

9. This cryptic phrase is a warning to His hearers that the parable will bear deep thinking, a warning lest we dismiss it lightly without searching our own hearts. The constant peril facing the believing Christian is the temptation to apply the Word of God to others, without applying it first of all to himself.

10. Simple the parable may be when the explanation is known, but it was puzzling enough to the disciples, so that they seized the first opportunity, when they were alone with Him, to ask its meaning. Matthew xiii. 10 adds that they enquired wonderingly as to why He used the parabolic method of teaching at all. It is plain that even the Lord's disciples found this method taxing: the relief of the 'Now speakest thou plainly, and speakest no parables' (see Jn. xvi. 29) is obvious. Yet only by the use of parables could there be that process of spiritual sifting that would be either eternally rewarding or eternally baffling, according to whether men had 'ears to hear' or not—that is to say, whether or not they earnestly desired to understand God's ways. If their will was right, then intellect would present no problem (Jn. vii. 17).

11. The answer is given in solemn words, designed to make them realize how privileged was their position as disciples of Christ, and introduces some of the deepest theological mysteries of the whole New Testament. God had been pleased to reveal to this little group the 'mystery of the kingdom': they could talk with Christ face to face, and ask for explanations of what puzzled them, whereas to those outside, the only explanation would be by another parable and thus another puzzle. Perhaps a partial explanation may be sought in the verse that Matthew adds at this point (Mt. xiii. 13)—the law of consecutive spiritual assimilation or progressive spiritual atrophy. The judgment is written plain for those who hear and fail to appropriate: their capacity for apprehension and appropriation of spiritual truth steadily dwindles until it disappears. Contrariwise, the more of God's revealed truth that we assimilate, the more our capacity for assimilating truth will grow, in a sort of spiritual geometric progression. But even here there is no room for pride: we, in the first place, have nothing but that which we have received (Jn. iii. 27; 1 Cor. iv. 7), and further, spiritual perception of God's truth is perilous: it condemns us unless we act upon it. Increased knowledge merely brings increased responsibility (Lk. xii. 48). God's awful choice of man is thus far from favouritism, as indeed the history of Israel in the Old Testament makes plain.

12. Because spiritual truth is not a set of isolated intellectual propositions to be mastered, but a whole to be comprehended by that sudden flash of insight that is the revelation of the Christ made to us by God (Mt. xvi. 17), so, to those outside, all must be in parable, because it would be useless to teach them deep spiritual truths until they had mastered the elementary level. But in any parable there was enough to lead the thoughtful, questing soul on: as the Lord says below, the good ground would receive the word, would understand it (Mt. xiii. 23) and transmute that truth into life with steady persistence (Lk. viii. 15).

There are several ways of explaining this verse: one is by saying that in the Greek New Testament the particle *hina*, which should mean 'in order that' and express purpose, sometimes means 'so that' and simply expresses consequence.[1] The second is to see the antithesis´ as a strong Hebraism, saying more than it really means: this would come to the same result as the grammatical solution suggested above. The third is to see these strong words in their Old Testament context— quoted fairly fully in Matthew's version (Mt. xiii. 14, 15)— where it is plain that it is Israel herself who has thus obstinately shut her eyes and ears against God's pleading. Their deaf and blind condition is thus culpable (Jn. ix. 41) and a judgment which they have brought upon themselves; and so it is inevitable that they be taught in parables, and inevitable that they fail to understand them. The fourth possible explanation, which is not really essentially different from the third, is to take a strong theological position, and to say that God has been pleased to reveal His Son to some and not to others, and that what is revelation to some is merely baffling to others. This is again the mystery of God's choice: and it is at this point that Matthew introduces the Lord's solemn words: 'Blessed are your eyes, because they see, and your ears, because they hear . . . for . . . many prophets and just men have desired to see those things which ye see, and have not seen them' (see Mt. xiii. 16). Such divine choice in Old and New Testaments both brings responsibility, and has a wide ultimate aim: it is thus far removed from partiality in the human sense.

13. The Lord gives gentle warning that this parable is, as it were, the 'Parable of the Parables', for it describes the reaction of His hearers to the whole system of parabolic teaching. It is not only the easiest of the parables, it is the key to them all.

14. The parable of the sower owes its peculiar appropriateness to the fact that at that very moment when He was telling the parable, Christ was sowing the seed of the word, and thus, by telling the parable, He was actually exemplifying it, quite

---

[1] See Arndt and Gingrich, p. 378.

irrespective of whether an earthly sower was at the moment visible to all on the hillside or no.

15–20. There is another question: how are men to blame for the state of their hearts? Have they themselves, by multiple prior choices, determined whether their hearts are hard, or shallow, or overcrowded with cares and pleasures, or, instead, 'good soil'? This problem Scripture does not answer here: the sole point made in the parable is that men's hearts do in fact so vary, and that this variation governs their response.

21–25. It is probable that in this particular instance, the primary moral of the parable is not that pointed elsewhere: 'Let your light so shine before men . . .' (Mt. v. 16). The Lord's disciples must have felt as puzzled as any modern reader does. They must have asked, 'Is not this teaching of parables a deliberate obscuration of the truth to those outside?' No, says the Lord, answering as usual on their level: would that make sense—to light a lamp and then to hide it deliberately? If truth is temporarily hidden in parable, it is only that it may be revealed: the ultimate purpose of the parable is thus not to conceal truth but to reveal it. It is because of this that we must give good heed to the parables ('take note of what you hear', verse 24, NEB), remembering the double law of 'spiritual atrophy' and 'spiritual growth' mentioned above. To those who learn, and then pass on to others what they have learned, more will be given. This parable is an argument of 'minor to major'—*qal w'chōmer*, as the rabbis said: if man would not act so foolishly with a kindled light, how much less so God? (Cf. Mt. vii. 11 for this type of argument.) The same paradox is seen in the Christ: God is both veiled in Him, and revealed in Him.[1]

ii. Two more parables of growth (iv. 26–32). This is both a further explanation of the parable of the sower and an amplification of the law of spiritual growth, and a parable in its own right. As such, it illustrates the nature of the reign of

---

[1] Cranfield (pp. 164f.) discusses this Gospel paradox at length, and suggests a reason for it.

God in the hearts of men: it suggests the Christian doctrine of 'growth in grace' (2 Pet. iii. 18); and it inculcates a quiet trust in God, that 'he which hath begun a good work in you will perform it' (Phil. i. 6). The sower's sleeping and rising day by day, and his ignorance as to how the seed grows, is but part of the human 'back-cloth' of the parable and need not be spiritualized. But we may well compare the Lord's words to Nicodemus, the teacher of Israel: 'Thou . . . canst not tell whence it cometh, and whither it goeth: so is every one that is born of the Spirit' (Jn. iii. 8). The process of spiritual growth is 'natural' within the kingdom of God, but it remains a mystery to natural man. For the parable of 'fruitbearing' compare John xv *passim*, Luke vi. 43-45 and Galatians v. 22, 23, where in every case the natural inevitability of the process, given the necessary convictions, is stressed. The last sentence (verse 29) seems to be a warning of the coming end of the age. When the time is ripe, God will intervene decisively in the affairs of men (Joel iii. 13) and establish His rule, so that all may see. The metaphor of reaping, with its separation of wheat from weeds (Mt. xiii. 30), or wheat from husks (Mt. iii. 12), is a common picture in the Bible from Old Testament days of the end of the age.

30-32. The concept of the reign of God was still not clear to the Lord's disciples, who seem to have consistently looked for a cataclysmic establishment of the messianic kingdom in their lifetime; witness the selfish request of James and John (Mk. x. 35), and the eager question even after the resurrection, 'Lord, wilt thou at this time restore again the kingdom to Israel?' (Acts i. 6). This had been one of the temptations which the Lord had put from Him decisively in the desert (Mt. iv). The small beginnings and slow pervasive growth of the kingdom were past either the patience or the understanding of the disciples, but both were well exemplified in the life-history of the tiny mustard seed known to them all. It is quite beside the point to quibble, and to say that ultimately the mustard seed produces a bush and not a tree: the point is that, from a tiny seed, it far outstrips all other similar plants. Holy

Scripture must be read sensibly, and such pettifogging would be laughed out of court in the case of any other book.

The exact point of the reference to *the fowls of the air* (32) is not clear: it may be just indicative of size, for small birds could indeed perch in such a bush:[1] but this need not exhaust the meaning. Some commentators have seen in it a reference to the mixed nature of the Church, for, in the Bible, the phrase 'birds of the air' has usually a sinister sound. It is probably best to seek the explanation in the Old Testament context from which this is a quotation (Dn. iv. 14), where the birds in the branches, like the beasts that shelter below the boughs, are but part of the 'back-cloth' of the vision seen by the prophet. Those who prefer to see an unsavoury connotation in the word 'birds' will lean on passages like Genesis xl. 19, Joseph's interpretation of the dream of the royal baker.

iii. Summing up of the parabolic section (iv. 33, 34).
Mark has given the above specimens of the parabolic teaching of the Christ (to which Matthew adds a few others) and he here suggests both a reason for the employment of parables, and also for the careful gradation in their use, in the words *as they were able to hear it,* lit. 'to understand'. In the school of Christ, none may move to advanced lessons till he has mastered the elementary studies. Always to the outsider there was the stumbling-block of the form of the parable to be penetrated: only for His own disciples were there private explanations.

c. Ministry round the Lake of Galilee (iv. 35-vii. 23)
i. Christ calms the storm (iv. 35-41). With the parables closed, we enter a new section: here Christ is shown as Lord of nature. This is a new revelation (see Jn. ii. 1-11, where the Creator turns water to wine) yet a necessary one, if Christ is God: for, from the Law through the Prophets, God is seen as Lord and Controller of the natural world and natural phenomena. The God who blew with an east wind and dried up the waters of the Red Sea before Israel is now seen as making

[1] See Arndt and Gingrich (p. 419) on *kataskēnoō*: especially in view of Daniel iv. 21, their translation of 'nest' seems preferable to the usual 'perch'.

a path over the waves of Gennesaret for His disciples, the new 'people of God'. Already, Mark has shown Him as One who sees heaven opened, upon whom the Spirit rests, responsive to the Spirit's guidance, enjoying angelic ministry, and receiving the testimony of God to His Sonship, though refusing the testimony of demons to His deity. Christ preaches and teaches with a new ring of authority: He heals the sick, expels demons, and forgives sins. And now, only He who had created the wind and sea in the first place would dare to address them so: and their instant obedience shows His full deity as Creator as well as Redeemer. The wondering question of His disciples in verse 41 shows that they realized in part at least the implications of His activities here.

36. Mark is the only Gospel that tells us of the *other little ships* with the Lord here: it thus becomes a miracle of mercy on a wider scale than the mere salvation of the Lord's own boatload of frightened disciples. We might perhaps compare the closing words of Jonah, 'and also much cattle' (iv. 11), with its undertone of the infinite mercy of God.

37–39. This journey was undertaken at the Lord's suggestion, in unquestioning faith and obedience. This, for the disciples, made the storm harder to understand, and the Lord's attitude quite inexplicable. There is more than a note of reproach in their words, *Master, carest thou not that we perish?* (38)—compare Martha's and Mary's words to the Lord (Jn. xi. 21, 32).

40, 41. The Lord's sleep was not only the sleep of weariness: it was also the rest of faith, for there is a rest of faith as well as a watch of faith (Is. xxx. 15). Faith and fear are mutual exclusives in the Bible: it was the disciples' idea that they were perishing, not the Lord's. No command is more often reiterated in the Bible than the simple 'Fear not' (see Ex. xiv. 13, xx. 20, etc.), just because such fear is not compatible with this faith in God. But the disciples, inconsequential men, still feared;[1] a

---

[1] It is possible, however, that this is the indefinite use of the third person plural, corresponding to *on* in French: see Moule, p. 180. The reference would then be general, not specifically of the disciples.

friendly, human Jesus they would have, but a supernatural Son of God? No! Compare Peter's 'depart from me' (Lk. v. 8). The Church often agrees with the disciples, preferring the humanistic Christ to the divine: we would sooner have the suffering Jesus of a Pietà than the awfulness of the risen Christ (Rev. i. 17).

ii. The Gadarene demoniac (v. 1–20). After the section of teaching in parable, there follow these miracles of healing, of which the first is the healing of the demon-possessed man in the territory of Gerasa (a name with numerous orthographical variants). The Lord had healed demons before: there had been a first specific instance already mentioned (i. 26) followed by a general campaign (i. 32), and exorcism of demons was a general power entrusted to the disciples (iii. 15), as surely as was the task of heralding the news. But this particular demon-expulsion has several peculiar features, which merit its inclusion here. For this was a man long 'under treatment' (as was the woman suffering from a haemorrhage, mentioned later in the chapter): it was in the despair and failure of human treatment that the Lord acted decisively. The medical treatment accorded to this man was that commonly used in a 'Bedlam' a few generations ago: he was loaded with chains, in a vain attempt to curb his inner violence by outward restraint. Not surprisingly, this proved quite futile (4). It was also probably part of the 'treatment' to drive him away from the homes of men, to find in graveyards on desolate hillsides his 'isolation block'. But isolation, whether self chosen (Lk. viii. 29) or enforced by others (as in the case of lepers, too), only meant that the destructive force of evil, instead of turning outwards in outbreaks of violence, vented itself on the wretched man himself, in acts of senseless self-torture, as stated here (5).

6–8. Strange that the insight of evil into the nature of Christ should be so clear and instantaneous while ordinary men were so slow to see His Godhead. Such great truths, as James tells us, 'the devils also believe, and tremble' (Jas. ii. 19); because for them these are not such abstract principles as at times they

97

seem to us. The demons knew Jesus from afar, for fear, as well
as love, sharpens the eyes: contrast the prodigal son's father,
who recognized his boy from 'a great way off' (Lk. xv. 20).
They ran and did their homage all unwillingly, confessing at
once the vast gulf between them, and the searing effect that
Good has on evil. A better reply to the Pharisaical accusation
that the Holy Spirit resting on Christ and the spirit of evil were
fundamentally one (Mk. iii. 22) could hardly be found: here
was evil itself refusing to acknowledge the Christ as in any way
akin to itself.

9, 10. The Lord had already spoken a word of quiet authority (8) which had apparently provoked this demonic outburst
(7); now He asks him his *name* (9), in order to make apparent
to all the man's need, and perhaps to bring home to the man's
own clouded mind the awful plight in which he stood. Of
demonic powers, as of God, it is equally true that in the Bible
name stands for 'nature': so the man was virtually asked to
confess the nature of the powers of evil by which he was en-
slaved. His reply is not only a confession of human impotence,
but a vivid expression of the might and destructive force of the
demonic powers by which he was gripped.

11–13. There are several puzzles to us here: why did the
Lord allow the demons in this case to manifest their destructive
force on the herd of pigs? Sometimes the expelled demon spent
his force in a last attack on the patient (e.g. ix. 26, the epileptic
boy), but sometimes we have no record of any special manifestation on exit. We know so little in this realm that we do
well to tread reverently: it may be that such an outward sign
was required in this case to convince men of the reality of the
expulsion. The size of the herd would in turn fittingly correspond to the number of demons possessing this wretched
man, and make plain to all by symbol that he was distraught
by countless evil impulses: he was not even 'integrated' in
evil. It may well be that, in some way that we do not understand, this was some sort of 'safety valve' or lightning conduc-
tor, to avert great spiritual violence from the patient. It is
sometimes half-humorously suggested that, if the owners of

the pigs were Jews, presumably engaged in selling ceremonially unclean pork to the indiscriminating Gentiles of the district, then this was by way of being a punishment to them as well. But it seems unlikely that the Lord would take such pains to punish a breach of ceremonial law, when He Himself constantly faced the charge of breaking it (Mk. vii. 5).

Note that the Bible differentiates between degrees of demon possession: ordinarily it is 'a demon'; 'seven devils' is a stage worse, seen in Mary Magdalene's history (Mk. xvi. 9), and in the parable of the one devil expelled, who returns with seven comrades (Lk. xi. 26): but this man is filled by a veritable 'brigade' of militant devils. No-one used to the biblical use of symbolic numbers would press the details; seven is continually used as symbol, not so much of 'divine perfection', as is often said, but of completion and totality (e.g. Gn. xli. 2). Yet the inference is quite plain: there are varying degrees of control by Satan just as there are varying degrees of control by the Holy Spirit. This man of Gerasa was utterly bound by Satan as he had never been by the chains and fetters. Hence, at his healing, equally drastic manifestations of divine power are not to be wondered at.

14–17. The immediate reaction of the swineherds, at this very obvious exhibition of supernatural power, was fear (cf. iv. 41, the same reaction of the disciples at the stilling of the tempest). They seem to have scattered in their flight: both city and country nearby heard the news, and came to see for themselves. As soon as they had been convinced that the demoniac was indeed healed, they shared in the fear. When they had heard the whole story from eyewitnesses—'and heard about the pigs, too', adds Mark drily, alone of the Evangelists —they begged Him to leave their area. To their terror (Lk. viii. 37) was added the thought of financial loss possibly mixed with uneasy consciences, if they were in truth Jewish pig-breeders. The saddest thing in the whole story is that the Lord listened to their request, and left them: there are times when the worst possible thing for us is that the Lord grants our prayer. Compare Psalm cvi. 15, 'He gave them their request;

but sent leanness into their soul', of Israel. But when Peter prayed a similar prayer (Lk. v. 8) after the miraculous catch of fishes, it was because his own consciousness of sin and unworthiness overwhelmed him, in a new recognition of the Godhead of the Christ: and such a prayer the Lord would not hear—and well for Peter that He would not! Gerasa, on the other hand, desired only to be left alone by this frightening supernatural Christ: and it was to be her judgment that the Lord left her, to return no more, for there is no biblical evidence for any later ministry by Christ in this part.

18, 19. There is a striking and deliberate contrast here between the attitude of the men of Gerasa and the attitude of the healed demoniac. The Gerasenes had begged Jesus to go, and He heard them: the healed man begged to stay in the company of Jesus, and his request was refused. There is another paradox: the cleansed leper (i. 44) had been strictly forbidden to tell anybody about his healing, but this healed demoniac was ordered to return home and bear witness (v. 19). There are good reasons for what might at first seem arbitrary and inconsistent. For Christ Himself to continue preaching in the Gerasene country was clearly impossible: therefore, in refusing the man's request, the Lord was ensuring a continuity of witness in a needy area.[1] When the leper of i. 44 had been healed, there were already well-nigh unmanageable crowds milling about Christ for healing: there was no need for spreading the tidings. Christ never healed just for the sake of healing: this healing was selective (cf. Lk. iv. 25–27).

20. The man was called to a peculiarly lonely and difficult task, which he fulfilled faithfully and with success, as can be seen from the summary account here. We might have thought his understanding of the gospel inadequate: but he had recognized the Person of Christ (even if it was initially by demonic agency) and experienced His saving and cleansing work: and that, in the early Church, was ever held sufficient.

---

[1] Cranfield further suggests that this was a largely Gentile area, where there was the less need to suppress news of a miracle, in that there was the less danger of men misunderstanding the Christ.

He had made the equation of God ('how great things *the Lord* hath done for thee', 19) and Jesus ('how great things *Jesus* had done for him', 20) and knew himself to be the recipient of the divine mercy. Cf. Acts viii. 37 for what was probably the earliest baptismal creed of the Church: no man could make such an equation save by the Holy Spirit (1 Cor. xii. 3) and so, upon such terms, the early Church was happy to accept members, or rather to acknowledge them.

iii. Two more healing miracles (v. 21–43). The next two miracles continue with the theme of man's despair and helplessness as being the dark night, out of which God's light of salvation springs (cf. Lk. i. 78, 79).

25–29. The woman suffering from haemorrhage is the centre of a minor miracle of love and mercy set in the context of the healing of Jairus' daughter, but it, too, makes plain in the bluntest language (not surprisingly, this is somewhat softened down by the doctor; cf. Lk. viii. 43) that earthly doctors and treatment were powerless to aid her. The doctor, like the fisherman, must learn that without Christ he can do nothing (cf. Lk. v. 5 with Jn. xv. 5). It is easy to trust God at our 'weak points'; we must learn that we have equal need of faith, as being equally inadequate, at what we consider our 'strong points'.

She heard of Jesus (27) and she acted on what she had heard, by thus coming to Him. She showed the greatness of her faith, not merely in that she believed that Jesus could heal her, but in that she asked so little contact with Him: merely to grasp the fringe of His robe would be sufficient. The centurion's faith was even greater; 'Speak the word only, and my servant shall be healed' (Mt. viii. 8); he required no touch, not even a visit from Jesus. But then he was a soldier, and recognized the ring of military authority in the words of Jesus: and the Lord marvelled at such faith in a Gentile, unequalled even in Israel (Mt. viii. 10). Such faith on the woman's part was at once rewarded by a healing of which she was instantly conscious (29).

30. This is an interesting verse, in that it shows that the Lord was conscious of the flow of healing power from Himself to the sick individual; it may have been that such healings cost Him much spiritual energy, for we read of Him being wearied, and escaping from such things for times of recuperation and prayer (Mt. xiv. 13, etc.). But in apostolic healings there is no hint of any such cost to the healer (Acts iii. 7, etc.). Perhaps we may see the key where Matthew saw it, in the application of Isaiah liii. 4 to the Lord's healing ministry: 'Himself took our infirmities, and bare our sicknesses' (Mt. viii. 17).

31–33. Here is yet another instance of the disciples' expostulation with the Lord for what they regarded as His unreasonableness: compare Mark vi. 37 and the indignant 'shall we go and buy . . . and give them to eat?' But the Lord quietly ignored them in both cases: for here at least, the meaning of His question was at once apparent to one hearer, the woman herself (33). It was not enough to believe in the heart: the woman must as well confess with the mouth (Rom. x. 9). She must confess in front of all men her prior need of healing, and then the glad fact of her salvation. That it was a costly confession we can tell from her *fearing and trembling* (33). For a woman to speak at all before an Eastern crowd, and above all of such matters, would be very humbling for her.

34. She was already healed, but confession brought the word of assurance from the Master, and a fuller understanding of her own experience. This brought a realization of the means by which she had entered into this experience (*Thy faith . . .*), an assurance of God's peace, and a sense of security for the future: confession thus brought to her, not conversion, but assurance. This woman is a good 'type' of healing of the soul. She suffered from a disease which, to a Jew, was ceremonially unclean (like leprosy) and which, again like leprosy, barred her from access to God in His Temple and fellowship with God's congregation in worship. Conscious of her need, she had made many costly attempts to remedy it: but the human help, sought and given in all sincerity, was in vain—indeed, it only worsened her situation. Her sense of need, coupled with the glad news of Jesus (for both factors were present), led her to come, although at first only as a nameless cipher, one amid the throng. Her faith was at once exercised and displayed in the direct contact with Christ. The exact nature of the contact was, it seems, unimportant: it is the greatness or littleness of our faith that dictates the mode. Little faith (like Naaman in 2 Kings v. 11, or Thomas in John xx. 25) would have insisted on a close personal contact, but the greatness of this woman's faith lay precisely in the fact that she asked so little in the way of a 'sign'.

35. This verse brings us back again to Jairus, whose story begins in verse 22. He is a man in need, unashamed to make that need known publicly ('he fell at his feet', 22). His faith may not have been as great as that of the woman with the haemorrhage, but yet it was saving faith: if Jesus only came and laid His hands on the girl, all would be well, though she might be at death's door already. There was a purpose in the very delay of that slow push through the crowds, which must have irked Jairus sorely; and there was a purpose in the turning aside to heal one woman in the midst of a multitude, which must have tried the patience of Jairus still further. Verse 35 seems to show that such impatience was justified. In this time so spent, the opportunity of healing was past; the girl was dead, and there was no need to worry the Rabbi now, they said. But man's despair was God's opportunity. Christ had already been shown as Lord of nature; it was necessary that He here be shown as Lord of life. This was an important proof of Godhead, for it was supremely fitting that He, who created life first, before sin and death entered the world, should show Himself now Master of death and the grave. More, this was an important piece of preliminary evidence for His own resurrection: He who could thus conquer death in others could burst its bonds Himself. The central miracle of the Bible is ever resurrection, because it must be the central fact of all true Christian experience.

36. And so to Jairus comes the command to abstain from

fear (the biblical opposite to faith) and, instead, to *believe*. The one condition of God's working for us is that we trust Him: nor is this an arbitrary demand, but one springing from the very nature of the relation between Godhead and manhood. We are called to trusting, dependent love and obedience, and this is the biblical meaning of faith, not merely intellectual assent. Such faith is the only fitting expression of our helplessness, and only fitting acknowledgment of God's might; and thus it is an essential to salvation.

37. Peter and James and John (but never, curiously enough, Andrew) were alone chosen on this and other occcasions, as at the transfiguration (Mk. ix. 2). It may have been because of their responsiveness to what they had already received that they were trusted with more. This certainly is the principle of God's spiritual dealing with men, already laid down in iv. 25. To judge from all biblical evidence, John was closest of all to the Lord, the apostle of love; then came blustering Peter; of James we hear hardly anything, but that may be due to his early death (Acts xii. 2), at the hands of Herod, which meant that one line of apostolic tradition was cut off. We have virtually both a Gospel of Peter and Gospel of John, whoever the final authors be: but we have no Gospel of James, or the picture might be different.

38–40. The weeping and wailing (38) may not have necessarily been exclusively that of hired mourners: such an influential man would have many who would come to share his grief. But the scornful laughter (40) with which they greeted the words of Jesus would seem to show that there was little real grief there, for all the noise. This unbelief (for such it was) excluded them from seeing the miracle to which the parents were admitted. The pity of it was that it was their superior 'knowlege' which excluded them (cf. Lk. viii. 53, which adds 'knowing that she was dead'). In point of fact, the girl was dead, by all earthly standards: but Christ, knowing that He would raise her from the dead, properly described her condition as a 'sleep', because from sleep comes wakening. So, too, the Lord described the death of Lazarus as a 'sleep', and

His mission as that of wakening him from sleep (Jn. xi. 11). So, too, the early Church described the dead as 'asleep in Jesus' (1 Thes. iv. 14) and so, too, in later days, they used the word 'sleeping place' for the burial ground—though 'cemetery' in modern English has lost the original associations, through very familiarity. To the pagan Anglo-Saxon, such a spot was a 'graveyard', a place where holes were 'graven': to his Christian brother it was God's Acre, where the metaphor is slightly different—a joyous harvest was to come (cf. 1 Cor. xv. 37).

41. The Lord never feared to contract ritual defilement by touching of leper, or blood stains, or the dead, precisely because His touch at once cleansed and revived, and thus, as it were, removed the source of pollution. But further, in the Old Testament, 'holiness' as well as 'defilement' could be contagious: so they contracted life and purity from Him, and not He the impurity from them. This, too, explains His readiness to eat and drink with 'publicans and sinners', the morally defiled (Mt. xi. 19). His very words to the girl, *Talitha cumi*, in her own Aramaic mother tongue, are preserved in Mark alone of the Gospels: if, as tradition has it and internal evidence confirms, Peter was Mark's informant, then it is obvious that the scene made such an impression upon the apostle that the Lord's actual words were remembered long after.

Space does not permit a long discussion on the linguistic situation in Palestine at the time: but everywhere Greek would seem to have been understood, with Aramaic as the usual speech of the home, especially in Galilee, while Hebrew may well have lingered around Jerusalem, as a semi-artificial survival. Every appearance is that the Lord and His disciples were bilingual, though, as coming from strongly nationalist Galilee, surrounded by the Gentiles of Decapolis and Syro Phoenicia, their mother tongue would seem to have been Aramaic: witness specifically the nicknames 'Cephas' and 'Boanerges' given by Christ Himself—both in Aramaic form. Other fossilized pieces of Aramaic preserved in the Gospels are the '*Ephphatha*' to the dumb man (Mk. vii. 34) and the '*Eloi, Eloi, lama sabachthani*' on the cross (Mk. xv. 34). *Abba*, as a cry to the Father, is common to both Gospels and Epistles (Mk. xiv. 36 and Rom. viii. 15): while *Maranatha* as a watchword of the early Church is found in 1 Corinthians xvi. 22. Whether or no the Lord ever taught in Greek (as Mahaffy stubbornly held) is very doubtful: but even if He did at times, there would be a special appropriateness in using her own mother tongue to the little girl, as the risen Lord conversed with Mary in her own tongue (Jn. xx. 16). Perhaps the emphasis laid on the fact that Aramaic was used on these occasions suggests that it was not so common on other occasions. Those brought up in bilingual parts of the 'Celtic fringe' will appreciate to the full the emotive value of such a use of the mother tongue, even if the tongue of the stranger be well understood.

42, 43. At once the Lord proved Himself stronger than death: other similar miracles concern the widow of Nain's son (Lk. vii. 15) and Lazarus (Jn. xi. 44). The Lord's loving care is shown in the command to give the girl something to eat. His care lest idle sightseers throng Him as a miracle worker is shown by His strict commands to the parents to tell nobody of the miracle (cf. His similar words to the healed leper of i. 44, on a similar occasion, when the crowds were also thronging Him).

iv. Christ's own city rejects Him (vi. 1–6). Jairus had been a synagogue elder in one of the small lakeside towns of the western shore, to judge from the various topographical details: but now the Lord and His disciples seem to have moved inland from the lake to the highlands of Galilee, and He is found teaching in the synagogue of Nazareth, which is always His 'native place' though He may live and work from Capernaum. To the last He is 'Jesus of Nazareth', for all His birth in Bethlehem and domicile in Capernaum (cf. Mk. xiv. 67 with Lk. iv. 16; Mt. iv. 13).

2. Even in Nazareth, the effect of His teaching was startling: no man denied His wisdom and the insight displayed in His doctrine. Nor did they deny He had elsewhere done mighty works: but instead of laying either of these to heart, they were simply concerned as to what their source was. In this, they were not unlike our modern scientific age, which is much more concerned with the mechanical question 'how' than the theological 'why'. And yet the question in itself was a good one: it was the question that was to exercise the scribes and Pharisees (Mk. xi. 28)—what was the source of the Lord's authority? Like John's baptism, it could only be 'from heaven, or of men'. For although the scribes suggested a third possible demonic source, it is doubtful, from the sternness of the Lord's reply, if even they themselves took their bitter suggestion seriously. So the question of the men of Nazareth was good, had they only been ready to accept the obvious answer: while from Mark i. 22 onwards the *fact* of the Lord's authority had been obvious to all men not already blinded by theological prejudice.

3. They were right in rejecting the human work or relationships of Jesus as the source of His power. It was not as Mary's son, nor as elder brother of Joseph's family, that He did such works: nor was it as the village carpenter (Mt. xiii. 55, 'the carpenter's son'), as they would have considered Him. One can sense the slow bewilderment in the listing of His brethren by name (also in this parallel from Matthew). But, having rightly rejected any human source, they boggled at attributing them to a divine source: they were staggered by such an equation—they *were offended*, or 'stumbled', at it, as the Bible says. The men of Nazareth 'knew all the answers' about the Lord: they were not prepared for any fresh revelation. Familiarity, as we say, had bred contempt—as apparently it also had among His own brethren, who failed to believe on Him till after the resurrection (Jn. vii. 5; Acts i. 14).

4–6. And so it was that, in the very place where He had been brought up as a boy, the only exhibition of divine power that He was able to give was to heal a few sick folk who were humbled enough by pain and sense of need to believe in Him (5). He who marvelled at the faith of the Roman centurion (Mt. viii. 10) marvelled at the lengths to which unbelief could go in His own people (6). They might be staggered at Him: but not more than He was staggered at them.[1]

v. The sending out of the Twelve (vi. 7-13). Christ's earthly ministry seems to be roughly divisible into periods of intensive localized teaching and periods of more general peripatetic evangelism. The sending out of the Twelve (or of the Seventy, as in Luke x. 1-16) was a logical multiplication of His own ministry. It was indeed the very purpose for which He had called them (iii. 14), both that they should abide in His presence (intensive) and that He might thus send them abroad (extensive).

Both in this case and the sending out of the Seventy, the Lord never seems to have sent out a disciple alone: they went in groups of two. Perhaps this constant association in small groups may account for the set associations in which the lists of names have come down to us, apart altogether from the teaching needs of the Church. They had again the authority over demons: Matthew x. 8 adds that they were to heal generally as well, and Luke ix. 2 reminds that they were to act as heralds, proclaiming the advent of God's reign.

8, 9. It may be that here we have a programme of 'village evangelism', after the larger population centres of Galilee had decisively rejected the Lord. This demanded a scattering of forces, a peripatetic ministry, and a deliberate renunciation, a studied simplicity of life, designed to encourage and to demonstrate trust in God. But we have no reason to suppose that this renunciation was a universal rule, binding on all His disciples at all times, while such a simple faith is indeed the rule, in whatever way expressed. Indeed, in Gethsemane's hour, the Lord, having first ascertained that His disciples had learned this lesson of not trusting to material helps, bade them take all they had—coats, money, sword (Lk. xxii. 36). He reminds them in the context that this shows no lack of faith, for they have already proved that none of these was necessary for the

---

[1] Cranfield *ad loc.* well points out that these are indeed the only two places where the verb *thaumazō*, 'wonder', 'marvel', is used with Jesus as subject.

man who goes in simple faith, obedient to his Lord's command, and looking to that to supply his needs.[1]

10, 11. The disciples were to be marked by a gentle persistence: they were to try to get a hearing by all means, but not to force themselves on places unwilling to have them. Such a rejection they were not to treat lightly, knowing the condemnation that comes to those who refuse the gospel of life: and hence it is that to preach the gospel is ever a joyous task, but not one to be entered upon light-heartedly, in view of the eternal issues with which such teaching is fraught. The latter part of verse 11 is omitted by RV, RSV, NEB, following the principal uncial MSS. It was no doubt added here because of Matthew x. 15.

12, 13. Today we speak of 'spiritual' and 'medical' work as two distinct missionary channels. It is very doubtful if the early Church made such a distinction, the more so as they saw disease as one manifestation of Satan's power, though not necessarily to be connected directly with sin on the part of the individual (contrast Jn. ix. 2 with Jn. v. 14). Anointing with oil, as here, was not a medical treatment, though it appears to be so in the case of the good Samaritan (Lk. x. 34). It is the anointing of James v. 14, which, accompanied by prayer, can heal the sick. Oil is a biblical symbol of the Holy Spirit's presence, and thus the very anointing is an 'acted parable' of divine healing.

vi. Herod's estimate of Christ (vi. 14–16). This preaching tour in Galilee brought Christ for the first time to the notice of Herod, in whose jurisdiction Galilee lay (Lk. xxiii. 7). The last mention of 'Baptizer John' was a brief note (in i. 14) of his imprisonment, as marking the end of his preaching ministry, and the beginning of that of Jesus. Verses 17–29 below will give, in a parenthesis, the reason for John's arrest and subsequent execution: but at this point, the death is assumed, and

---

[1] This seems more likely than to explain by the rabbinic prohibition of staff, sandal and wallet on the temple mount, with T. W. Manson. The Talmudic passage is quoted in Cranfield, p. 200, and, more fully, p. 358.

the chief interest lies in the instant psychological reaction of Herod to the tidings of Christ. True, he had killed John, but that he had not silenced his own conscience is clear from his equation of Jesus with a John 'Redivivus', raised from the dead. It is strange that, though John had done no miracles of any kind—he had been but a truth-teller (Jn. x. 41)—yet Herod evinced no surprise at the thought of this greatest of all miracles, a rising from the dead, taking place in John's case. Even Herod had theological insight enough to see that, once granted a resurrection, any other miracle is not only possible but logical. Compare the way in which the Lord persistently refused to give any 'evidential' miracle to His foes save that of the resurrection (Mt. xii. 39, 40). It was from this time onwards that Herod wanted to see Christ, hoping to watch Him perform a miracle (Lk. xxiii. 8), but what may in origin have been genuine religious feeling had dwindled into a craving for the sensational. Such God never grants.

15, 16. As later, when Christ questioned His own disciples at Caesarea Philippi, there were various popular interpretations of Christ's nature and work (Mk. viii. 28): until then, none saw the true one. But Herod clung sombrely to the view suggested by his own uneasy conscience, and the very brutality of the words *whom I beheaded* (16) emphasizes his self-torture. The house of Herod was ever a strange blend of cold cruelty and religious interest: the wild blood of Edom ran strong in their veins, but the Herodian masonry of the great Haram at Hebron showed to all that Abraham was their father too.

vii. Martyrdom of John the Baptist (vi. 17–29). This insight was on a par with Herod's moral perception throughout. The Herods (cf. Agrippa in Acts xxvi. 3) were dilettanti in religion, and the tetrarch knew well enough the spiritual stature of John (20) and was afraid of his moral greatness. He not only gladly heard his preaching, but paid heed to it. 'He was much perplexed', the best reading in verse 20 (see RV), suggests that John's preaching put Herod into a great quandary: and so Herod temporized by doing nothing. But inexorably he was pushed to a decision—first to imprison John, then to execute him. The less likely reading in verse 20, *he did many things*, would make Herod actually respond to John's teaching in many points: and we have no evidence of that.

18-21. John's condemnation of Herod's incest brought him gaol from the tetrarch, who could not tolerate open criticism of himself in his own domain: but it also brought something far more dangerous, in the undying hate of Herodias. Even while John was in gaol, he was in no great danger of his life, as far as Herod was concerned: that is clear from verse 20. Herod wished only to stop John's mouth. A humiliating defeat by Aretas, the father of his rejected first wife, was doubtless punishment enough in his eyes, without John's condemnation. But with Herodias, it was different: she was but biding her time to kill John. She would have killed him at once, but there had been no opportunity (19); and now it had come, in the birthday feast of Antipas, as this member of the house of Herod is usually called. A glance at the family tree of the house will show the gloomy succession of murder and incest that tangles the branches.

22-25. It was Herod's infatuation with Herodias that had led him to imprison John: and so devotion to a wife can lead a man astray. Such is our distortion of values that we see his rash promise to a dancing girl as generosity, and his compliance with a wrong demand as faithfulness to his word given. Even the obedience of a daughter to a mother becomes here a sin: and so, outside Christ, all human, 'natural' virtues can become veritable vices. Jezebel, in the Old Testament (1 Ki. xxi. 7), is the eternal type of the woman who usurps man's place (as Eve did, Gn. iii. 6) and through devotion to whom a husband sins: so, in the New Testament, Jezebel becomes a term for woman heresiarchs (Rev. ii. 20).[1]

---

[1] Many modern editors have seen here a deliberate reminiscence of the Old Testament story, with Herodias as a sort of 'Jezebel redivivus', and Herod as an Ahab. This is *a priori* likely, but need not lead to distrust of the story before us here.

26–28. Unquestionably, Herod's grief was real (26); but he had already been trapped, and he knew it. It had been wrong to bind himself to such a promise. It was doubly wrong to keep it; but he was afraid to face the scorn of his own nobles, who had heard the royal oath. So John died alone in the dungeon of Machaerus, by the shores of the Dead Sea. One wonders whether even Herod's callous courtiers were used to such a banquet dish as this. Rash oaths are condemned by the Lord in Matthew v. 34: rash oaths brought Jephthah into agony (Jdg. xi. 31ff.) and nearly undid Saul (1 Sa. xiv. 38ff.).

29. This marks the end of 'John's disciples' as a coherent group, whose practice can be quoted against that of the Lord's disciples (Mk. ii. 18). Ever since early days, the disciples of John had been leaving him gradually and following Jesus: and John was content that it should be so (Jn. iii. 30). Now, when their leader was dead and they came to bury him, Matthew adds a significant clause, saying that they 'went and told Jesus' (xiv. 12), which probably points to a further mass amalgamation. Outside of Palestine, however, John's disciples still persisted as a separate group, as can be seen from Acts xviii. 23, xix. 3, where they are a 'sect' already prepared for the full gospel, but as yet without any knowledge of its richness. The very existence in the Church of the Holy Spirit is as yet unknown to them. John's disciples were fully orthodox Jews (Mk. ii. 18).

viii. The feeding of the five thousand (vi. 30–44). There is a delightful naïvety in the apostles' reporting to the Lord, not only what they have done, but also what they have said. This was the Lord's wisdom in allowing them thus to unburden themselves, before suggesting a time of rest. All those who have attended a 'News' period in the first hour of each day at an infants' kindergarten will appreciate the psychology. After the weariness and rush and strange faces of the mission, they craved solitude and rest in the company of Jesus; and while He did not seem to care that He Himself had no time to eat (cf. Mk. iii. 20 with Jn. iv. 32), yet He would not ask the same of His weary disciples. There had been a similar preaching tour in Galilee before (i. 39), but that had been in the company of Jesus; this was the first time that they had gone out alone, relying upon His word (cf. Lk. v. 5).

33. The short lake voyage, back to the old familiar surroundings of the sea (after tramping the dusty paths), must in itself have been a rest and relaxation for the Galilaean sailors. But the small size of the Sea of Galilee made it quite possible for the crowds, travelling along the shore, to outdistance the little ship, which doubtless had no favourable wind. Many a modern deep-water harbour is bigger than the whole Sea of Galilee, and the average harbour ferry-boat bigger than the Lord's craft on this occasion.[1]

34. It is easy to imagine the groan of despair that must have gone up from the disciples, when they saw, long before they had reached the other shore, that the inevitable Eastern crowd had forestalled them. It is probable that this natural weariness accounts for the note of irritation in their question to the Lord in verse 37, as well as their obvious hint in verse 36 that the crowds had had more than enough teaching already. But the Lord, doubtless as weary as the disciples and seeing the same crowds as they, *was moved with compassion* (34). But note that He preached Himself; He did not call upon His wearied disciples to join in the task now. (Compare what was said above about His anxiety to secure proper rest for them after their wearisome preaching tour, careless though He might be for Himself.)

35. The objections raised by the disciples were all eminently reasonable. It was indeed late, and the place was indeed uninhabited; and, if bread was to be given to the crowds, it would have to be brought in from a distance; and it would have cost, at the most conservative estimate, two hundred denarii to feed them. All their calculations were correct; but they had forgotten Christ, the incalculable factor. At the 'unreasonable-

[1] Nowhere is this better shown than in the many excellent photographs of the lake in Grollenberg.

ness' of the Christ their suppressed irritation grows, for God's way is ever folly to natural man (1 Cor. i. 18). This miracle is therefore an illustration of the central stumbling-block of Christianity: we all stand condemned with the disciples.

36–38. The sequence here is interesting: once the disciples have seen the need of the crowd (35, 36), then the Lord at once lays upon them the duty of meeting that need (37). Half angered, and half humiliated, they confess their own utter inadequacy to do so: and then He quietly reminds them that they can meet any emergency not of their own making (for we may not 'test' God, Mt. iv. 7) by the use of what they have, if it is seen to be inadequate, but offered in its totality to Christ to be used by Him. God does not lead us to see a need, unless it be in His mind to use us to meet that need, be it by prayer or otherwise.

39, 40. The disciples must have faith that the Lord could and would use their inadequacy, and this was to be shown by making the crowd sit down in expectancy. Perhaps it is not unfair, too, to see a hint that God is a God of order, One who in the dawn of time brought order out of chaos (Gn. i. 2), and would have order in worship, instead of the disorder that could so easily arise from unrestricted use of spiritual gifts (1 Cor. xiv. 40). It is not enough to have faith: it must be exhibited in active action that, as it were, implicates us. The disciples would indeed look foolish now, in the eyes of the expectant crowd, if no miracle took place; but this is the risk of faith.

41. The loaves were taken up, blessed[1] and broken, and finally given to the disciples to distribute to the crowds. Thus the disciples were, almost unwillingly, pulled into participation in the miracle. So, too, in a deeper sense, the Lord Himself took and blessed a human body. That Body was broken for us upon the cross; and so it is ours to feed upon. So,

---

[1] While it is true (with Cranfield) that the *berākāh*, 'blessing', had primarily God as object, not the loaves, yet, to the Jew, the broken bread was held to be hallowed by the glorification of the divine Name in it. This illuminates many New Testament passages.

too, He can take, bless and break our lives, to be a blessing to the spiritually hungry multitudes in the world around us (cf. Mk. xiv. 22, the Last Supper).

42–44. It is a mark of the divine provision that it is enough and more than enough for all our needs: and yet it is also typical of the divine economy that there should be no waste (43), and that we should learn to be good stewards of God's bounty. Of the Twelve, each disciple had gathered a basketful of pieces, and we may be sure that this was to be their food for the next day. They could not throw away the pieces and expect the Lord to work a great miracle like this every day. This was the sort of temptation that the Lord had rejected in the wilderness (Mt. iv. 3). Note that God guarantees to supply all our needs, but not necessarily all our foolish desires: here was a satisfying meal, but the fare was homely. There will always be some who grumble at the divine provision. Israel in the desert tired of the 'bread of angels' (see Ps. lxxviii. 25) and begged for more earthy sustenance (Nu. xi. 6). No doubt many a disciple was tempted to like thoughts as he chewed a stale crust next day.

ix. The walking on the water (vi. 45–52). A further touch of the Lord's understanding love was to send the overtaxed disciples on in advance, while He dismissed the crowd, giving them farewell counsel. Yet even after that, He turned not to rest, but to prayer on the hillside: indeed, it was only the sight of the storm-tossed disciples that brought Him from His prayer to their rescue (48). No supernatural vision is implied here: the little boat would have been clearly visible from the spot where the Lord was praying.

This episode is a good illustration of the life of discipleship seen as a constant experience of testing and deliverance; for it was not through stubborn self-will, but through direct obedience to the Lord's command, that the disciples found themselves in this plight. Thus the storm in no way showed that they had deviated from the path of God's will: God's path for them lay through that storm, to the other shore of the lake. Moreover, it appeared as if the Lord had forgotten them; they were alone, at night, and making heavy weather with the rowing. This storm, too, was no sudden lake storm, such as had preceded the calming of the waves (Mk. iv. 39), but a tiring, continuous head wind, necessitating steady, back-breaking rowing. Then, at the darkest hour, in their greatest need, and in a totally unexpected way, Jesus came to their rescue. In both storms at sea (cf. chapter iv) it must have seemed at first as if Christ was irrelevant: in one, He was asleep in the stern, and in the other, at prayer on the mountain. In both, it must have seemed as if He were careless of their plight, and yet the event showed that nothing could be further from the truth. Why the *would have passed them by* (48)? Perhaps a clue to the explanation lies in the 'made as though he would have gone further' at evening on the road to Emmaus (Lk. xxiv. 28). The Lord wanted His disciples to confess their need of Him before He came to their help: the disciples at Emmaus must 'constrain' Him (Lk. xxiv. 29). Jacob, too, is praised for this persistent refusal to desist from his clinging to God (Gn. xxxii. 26). It was not that the Lord intended to pass them by, for it was because of their need that He had come; but they must be brought to realize the need for themselves. If we would have the Son of David heal us, we must confess our need of healing and our faith in Him by crying for help (cf. Mk. x. 46, the healing of blind Bartimaeus).

49. Their cry was merely one of fear, and not even necessarily a cry consciously directed to Jesus; but it was enough to ensure His instant response. The Lord's power to answer is not limited by the inadequacy of our asking, and He is often contented with an initial response of what we would consider an inadequate nature.

50. As so often, the very exhibition of miraculous power by the Christ merely threw them into fresh fear and confusion. So the initial entry of Christ into their situation was marked by an increase in the tempo of the strife (cf. Mk. ix. 26).

51, 52. As before, at the storm on the lake (cf. chapter iv), the presence of the Christ brought peace to the disciples. But their fear then and their amazement here is alike traced by the Evangelist to their failure to learn the previous lesson of the feeding of the five thousand. Smallness of faith and hardness of heart are two constant sins of God's people. Hardness of heart is that lack of spiritual perceptivity, that lack of readiness to learn for which we are ultimately blameworthy ourselves, and in the extreme case of the Pharisees, could lead at last to the sin against the Holy Spirit. Smallness of faith is a failure to consider God's working in the past and to apply that knowledge of His nature to our present problems.

x. Healings at Gennesaret (vi. 53–56). This little cameo is a summary of what must have happened on many similar occasions: the spontaneous spreading of the good news under the stimulus of the presence of the healing Christ (in Old English 'the Healer' was the commonest title for Christ, as we say 'the Saviour' today). There was a recognition of the Christ, a realization of their own need, a belief that Christ could meet that need, and a determination to grasp the present opportunity afforded by His presence: all these are factors in every case of healing of the soul. The reaction was spontaneous and unselfish. There may have been many a paralytic carried in by friends, hidden in these short verses, and their faith, in requiring but to clutch at the fringe of His **clothing**, reminds us of the woman with the haemorrhage (cf. v. 28).

xi. Further clash with Judaism (vii. 1–23). This is presumably another fact-finding commission of theologians from Jerusalem, sent to investigate a campaign of healing and preaching that by now must have caused some stir—even the secular ruler Herod knew of Christ (vi. 14), let alone the religious authorities. Such a commission had come before, as the incidental reference in iii. 22 shows. There the bitter words about the Lord's casting out of devils through Beelzebub were spoken by the scribes from Jerusalem. That being so, it is probable that all the carping criticism with regard to sabbath observance came from the same source. A previous commission had similarly examined John as to his right to preach and baptize (see Jn. i. 19, 25). It thus comes as no surprise that the theological commission in this chapter is biased and suspicious from the start. This is apparent in their niggling, fault-finding attitude. They attacked Him, not personally, but through His disciples (verse 2), as in ii. 24 they had attacked His disciples for eating corn and in ii. 18 they had criticized the failure of the disciples to fast. They here attacked them on a point of ritual, not one of faith, and a point of ritual drawn not directly from the law, but from the body of explanatory tradition that was growing up round the law, later to form the Mishnah and Gemara, the modern Jewish Talmud. Of course, if the disciples were found ignorant of the 'oral tradition', the inference as to their Rabbi would be obvious. Mark thinks it necessary to explain the whole theory of ritual washing to his Gentile readers (verses 3, 4), though the sabbath, he assumes, will be familiar to them already. The Pharisees themselves betrayed their own position, for their indignant question was confined to the breach of *the tradition of the elders* (5).

6-8. No-one ever disputed the earnestness of the Pharisees in keeping these observances, nor disputed that such customs were genuine historical tradition, nor denied that they were aimed at the honouring of God, as being extensions, perhaps legitimate, of biblical principles given by revelation of God for the Jews. Why then is the strong word *hypocrites* (6) so frequently on the lips of the Lord with reference to scribes and Pharisees?[1] It is because He sees, in their attitude, a fulfilment of biblical prophecy, and a vindication of the authority of the very Scripture upon which they should have leaned. It is noteworthy that the Lord here both quotes Scripture and adds to it, thereby interpreting it. Indeed the whole of the New Testament is a wider illustration of this principle, for the words of Christ always stand on a par with any 'Thus saith the Lord' of the Old Testament, and thus the early Church

---

[1] This phrase is probably a hendiadys, and should be translated 'the scribes belonging to the Pharisaic party'.

treated them from the start. So Christ sees Pharisees as those who act a false part, who pretend to be other than they are: there is indisputably an outward honour for God, but this is directly and totally contradicted by the Pharisaic attitude of mind. This outward reverence does not correspond to any of that inward reality of which it should only be an outward expression and evidence. We may perhaps compare the prophetic attack on much of the meaningless and hollow religious ritual of the days of the kings.

That is the first 'prong' of the attack. But the second, in verse 7, is more serious still. Even were the Pharisees earnest in heart, yet their whole position is vitiated by the fact that what they teach depends entirely on human authority. Nor is that all, though it is bad enough in all conscience: this clinging to human traditions makes them neglect the plain command of God. Once again, note how the Lord answers on two levels those who criticize them: first, He answers on their level, using their premises: then, having thus demolished their position, He takes the argument to a far deeper level.

The latter part of verse 8 is not found in the best MSS. It may have been included, as an explanation of *tradition of men*, following Mark's own earlier explanation for Gentile readers in verse 4.

9–13. Such outspokenness may well have caused a murmur, so the Lord at once gives an instance of how obedience to the tradition means breaking a divine law—one instance chosen out of many, as He reminds them (13). At the very heart of the law, filial piety was enshrined: but by a typically rabbinic twist of values it was possible to vow to the Temple all the money that would normally have been expended on the maintenance of parents, and so to avoid the plain demands of duty, obvious enough to the pagan outside. This is a wise warning that the passage about hating parents for Christ's sake (Lk. xiv. 26) is to be seen in the context of genuine filial piety as a Christian duty: natural ties are not abrogated, though they may be overruled by Christ.

14. This seems to have silenced the scribes for the time being, but the major principle of the validity of the ritual law was still at stake. The disciples of Christ had, in point of fact, eaten with unwashed hands, and thus stood condemned, if the ritual law was valid. The discomfiture of the Pharisees in the last argument did not necessarily mean the acquittal of the Lord's disciples, unless the whole principle of oral tradition was to be attacked: and so it was, in this parable. It must have seemed to many Pharisees in early days that the Lord came near to espousing the Sadducean cause, with His firm rejection of the 'tradition of the Fathers'.

15. This ran contrary to all the rabbinic teaching: for all defilement there must be a 'mother of defilement', an external source, by contact with which defilement was contracted. They, in other words, assumed an initially pure state: not so the Lord. For Him, the source of defilement was not external, but within man himself. There is a world of difference between these theologies, as there is between the two views of sin.[1] To the Pharisees, lack of ceremonial purity, as in the case of the Lord's disciples above, was undoubtedly sin: whereas the Lord's list of sins below is one of moral defilements. What, then, are we to make of the apparent identification of ritual and moral in, say, Leviticus? Perhaps it is rather akin to the wise mother's insistence that her child be scrubbed and in clean clothes on Sunday, that by outward things the child's mind may appreciate at least something of the nature of God. Paul is clear that the ritual law—though not the moral law—belonged to God's kindergarten for His people (Gal. iv. 9).

Verse 16 is omitted by RV, RSV, NEB following the best MSS.

17. There must have been many other such occasions when we owe the explanation of a parable presented in the Gospel to the inability of the disciples to see its relevance and application in the first place, and to their coming to Jesus to ask for an explanation. The classic instance is the full explanation given

---

[1] Cranfield (p. 244) points out the fatal flaw. Instead of accepting the law's verdict on them as sinners, the Jews—as Paul says in Romans x. 1–3—are anxious to use the law to prove their own righteousness: and, to do this, man must always substitute human legalism for divine law.

of the parable of the sower in chapter iv. Naturally, an unexplained and thus meaningless parable would be of no value in the teaching programme of Peter or any other apostle, and thus would not be included. Therefore, even if we fail to understand a parable, we are not justified in saying that the early Church likewise failed to do so: if so, it would not have been preserved.

18. The unbelief of the disciples grieves the Lord: their hardness of heart amazes Him (Mk. xvi. 14)—the quality that also grieves Him in the Pharisees (Mk. iii. 5). But the chief thing obvious to a modern reader is their utter failure to understand even His simplest utterances. They consistently and crassly misunderstood Him, taking His words in the most literal sense (cf. Mk. viii. 16). Yet this was before the coming of the Spirit, the great Interpreter (Jn. xiv. 26): and the same blindness is still seen in natural unconverted man (2 Cor. iii. 14). We do well to search our own hearts rather than to condemn the disciples.

19. The Lord's outspoken words might be paraphrased as saying that 'the mind and not the stomach is the danger-point for man'. The last clause of this verse, *purging all meats*, is probably best taken as a comment on the Lord's words by the Evangelist: 'by saying this, the Lord was abolishing all distinction between ceremonially clean and unclean foods.' This interpretation is borne out by the clause in Matthew xv. 20 which does not appear in Mark: 'but to eat with unwashen hands defileth not a man.' If we see this interpretative comment as emanating from the preaching of Peter, then it takes a new meaning in view of Peter's vision before the visit to Cornelius (Acts xi. 5ff.).

20–23. The Lord here (as explicitly in Mt. v. 28) makes no distinction between sins of thought and sins of deed, unlike the law of the land, which can of course take cognizance only of acts, not the mental attitudes which ultimately find expression in such acts.

d. Ministry in Northern Palestine and back to Galilee (vii. 24–viii. 26)

i. The Syrophoenician woman (vii. 24–30). The previous activity had been on the lake shore of Galilee: now the Lord withdraws further north and west to the territory of Phoenicia, on the Mediterranean coast. Possibly it was for a time of rest and preparation, for He wanted His presence kept secret.

25. The story of the healing of the Syrophoenician woman's daughter reminds us that Elijah the prophet had, in roughly the same territory, worked a miracle for another widow (1 Ki. xvii. 2ff.). It may be a recollection of this that prompted Matthew to add 'and Sidon' (Mt. xv. 21) in his geographic note.[1] The two towns of *Tyre and Sidon* are often loosely linked together in the New Testament (cf. Mk. iii. 8). This in itself shows that Christ was known at least to the Jews settled in those parts, and it must have been in the home of some Jewish disciple of His that He was now staying incognito. That this miracle of Elijah was sometimes in the Lord's mind is shown by Luke iv. 25, 26, where, after His rejection at Nazareth, He gives clear warning of a coming mission to the Gentiles, using both the widow of Zarephath and Naaman the Syrian as illustrations. They also show that the Lord accepted without question what has been well called 'the stumbling-block of particularity'—that God should seemingly neglect many widows in Israel, but take the trouble to send the prophet to one widow in an alien land, of despised race. It was this aspect of the Christian gospel that ever infuriated the Jews (Acts xxii. 21, 22).

26. This woman was *a Greek*, or Gentile, as the woman of Zarephath of 1 Kings xvii had almost certainly been (cf. 1 Ki. xvii. 12, 'as the Lord thy God liveth . . .'). We are not told that this woman was a widow, but as no husband is mentioned, it is likely: and like the widow of Zarephath, it was the sore need of her child that brought her to God. The widow of Nain is a

---

[1] The better MSS omit *Sidon* in verse 25. It may have crept in by assimilation to verse 31 or because of the Matthew passage.

close parallel here (Lk. vii. 11–15) and it was fitting that both should receive help from a God who delights to succour widows and orphans (Dt. x. 18; Ps. cxlvi. 9, etc.).

27. The Lord's use of the conventional Jewish term *dogs* for 'Gentiles' (the late Greek diminutive is not in any sense affectionate, nor does it lessen the blow[1]) was not in any sense recognizing this description as accurate. He desired to see whether the woman was ready to take such a lowly position in order to win healing. But nevertheless, the Lord had a strong consciousness that, in His earthly lifetime, His immediate mission was restricted to 'the lost sheep of the house of Israel' (Mt. xv. 24). So He forbade His disciples, at this stage, to preach to Gentiles or Samaritans (Mt. x. 5). When He healed a Jewess, He saw it as very appropriate, because she, too, was 'a daughter of Abraham' (Lk. xiii. 17). It may therefore be that this woman, in claiming mercy from Him as 'son of David' (Mt. xv. 22), was standing on false ground, though even the smallest Jewish child might rightly welcome Him with 'Hosanna to the son of David' (Mt. xxi. 9). She must be taught that her only hope lay in the uncovenanted mercies of God. Unless she was prepared to approach the Jewish Messiah in the knowledge that she was indeed a Gentile, outside the old covenant, then her day of healing had not yet come.

28–30. But she had not only persisted when the Lord refused to answer (Mt. xv. 23); she now accepted this humble position gladly, and showed that, even on those terms, she still claimed healing for her daughter. God's abundance for His children was so rich that even the rank outsider could share in it. Paul seems to play with this idea when he says that even the rejection of Israel brought blessing to the Gentiles, and how much more their gathering in (Rom. xi. 15)! It is a great Old Testament truth that in Abraham, and thus in Israel, all nations will be blessed at the last (Gn. xxii. 18). It is a mis-

---

[1] See Arndt and Gingrich, last entry under the word: and compare the common linguistic phenomenon of the 'deterioration of diminutives' in the New Testament and Hellenistic texts generally: instances can easily be found by those interested in any collection like Wikgren.

understanding to say that the *dogs* are simply part of the back-cloth of the parable, the stage scenery, as it were: and that the whole point and stress is on the children of the house, whose the food is by right. It is true that in most parables there is a certain amount of back-cloth which is incapable of exegesis, but this ignores the express evidence of Matthew xv. 23, that the Lord at first refused to hear her, and also of Mark vii. 26, that she was a Gentile by race. This type of exegesis would make the healing a mere reward from the Lord, delighted by her quick wit. But Matthew xv. 28 shows that the Lord said to her, 'Great is thy faith': so to Him her reply demonstrated not her wit but the depth of her faith. As often in the Old Testament, what would pass as a pun or witticism nowadays had a solemn religious portent then.

ii. The deaf and dumb man (vii. 31–37). *Decapolis*, though largely a Gentile area, had considerable resident Jewish colonies, and was indeed the very region where the healed demoniac had witnessed so faithfully to what Jesus had done for him (Mk. v. 20). Even in early days, numbers of Jews had come across from Decapolis to hear the preaching of Jesus (Mt. iv. 25). There is thus no need to assume that this man was a Gentile, the more so as the Lord spoke the word of power to him in Aramaic.[1] Of course, throughout Syria many at least of the pagan population were originally Aramaic-speaking, under a superficial layer of Hellenism; there cannot have been many Greeks by blood in these backwood areas. But the constant use of 'Greeks', as the opposite of 'Jews', suggests at least a veneer of Greek speech (Jn. vii. 35, Greek text).

32–35. Here, too, in origin it was the faith of friends that brought the deaf mute to Jesus: but, as in the case of the paralytic (Mk. ii. 3), the Lord seems to have looked for at least some response in the man himself as well. All the actions of verses 33 and 34 were miming his present need, the course of healing, and the manner in which such healing alone could come, in a way which even a deaf mute could understand (i.e.

[1] See comment on v. 41 above.

the blocked ears opened, spitting an impediment away from the tongue, the upward glance and sigh of prayer). Thus there is no need to assume purely vicarious faith here, any more than there is in the case of the paralytic. Saving faith, however small, must be exhibited by the subject of salvation himself: but it is not irrelevant to point out that the faith of his friends came first. For comments on the use of the Aramaic *Ephphatha* (34), see note on Mark v. 41.

36. Presumably, the Lord had no wish to be known as a mere miracle-worker, unlike some of the early rabbis of the Talmud: for such had no necessary moral connotation, any more than magic would. That the result was notoriety, contrary to His command and expressed wish ('so much the more . . .'), is but an illustration of the strange perversions of human psychology of which Paul speaks (Rom. vii. 8), and which Augustine feelingly confirms from his own experience. It certainly does not prove, as is sometimes suggested, that the Lord had this result in mind when He forbade the spreading abroad. Such cheap-jack psychology is inconsistent with Christ's other methods of working, and so we may reject it.

37. The parallelism with Genesis i may have been unnoticed by the original audience, but can hardly have escaped unseen by the early Church. All God's creative works are perfect, and so is the manifestation of His Son's power. Not only God saw that it was good (Gn. i. 4), but even, on this occasion, man also.

iii. The feeding of the four thousand (viii. 1-9). By no process of the imagination can the feeding of the four thousand be regarded as a mere 'double', a variant account of the feeding of the five thousand. There are too many differences of detail for this view: and both Matthew and Mark contain separate accounts of the two miracles in close juxtaposition, which shows that the early Church had no such doubts. Even if Matthew, as we have it, is dependent on the Marcan account, the argument is not lessened: for the Greek word *palin* (RSV, 'again') of this verse draws specific attention to the fact that this is another instance. A little reflection will show that, in oral tradition, it is far more likely that originally dissimilar traditions should be assimilated, rather than that parallel accounts of the same event should be later 'dissimilated', especially when on the lips of those who were not themselves primary witnesses. Further reflection will show that if we find two vaguely similar stories of miracles, there is no need to assume that they are necessarily variant accounts of the same miracle. The Lord performed many unrecorded miracles, as the early Church knew (Jn. xxi. 25; and for one non-Gospel example of a 'Saying', Acts xx. 35). There must have been several similar original incidents in many cases, of which one would live on in one apostle's memory and one in another. It is interesting to note that one of the modern theories of textual criticism (the Fragmentation Theory) is broadly similar: it postulates multiple early variant sources, only later to be 'ironed out' into the great so-called Textual Schools of later days.

2, 3. There is a tendency today so to spiritualize the miracles that we lose sight of their primary meaning, which is that, whenever the Lord saw a man cold, hungry, ill or in distress, His heart went out to that man in love and pity: and so should ours (1 Jn. iii. 17). In other words, although the miracles of the Lord were used to point a spiritual message, the recipient was not made a spiritual stalking-horse. The root of all ministry, be it physical or spiritual, is this genuine inner constraint, which the New Testament writers unanimously see as the love of God, at work in us (2 Cor. v. 14).[1] But He did not miraculously heal every sick person in Israel, nor feed all the hungry: there was a curious 'selectiveness' which He Himself explained by pointing to Old Testament exemplars—there had been many widows and many lepers in Israel in days of old, but the mission of the prophet was but to one in either case, and a Gentile at that (Lk. iv. 26, 27). Nevertheless, this particular

[1] See Cranfield on vi. 34: he sees in this yearning of the Lord over the multitude the key to the understanding of the Lord's mission. For a Jewish definition of this sort of love see *Pirqe Aboth* v. 19 (Singer, p. 206).

group of earnest hearers had a special claim on the Lord's
provision in that they had not sought Him for food, like those
of John vi. 26. This audience had proved their right sense of
spiritual values by three days of eager listening to the Lord's
preaching. It is not just that they were hungry, but that they
were hungry in God's service: and so theirs was to be an experience of 'seek ye first the kingdom of God, . . . and all these
things shall be added unto you' (Mt. vi. 33). Like the Lord
Himself, in their hunger to know and do God's will, they had
scarcely been conscious of physical hunger up to this moment
(Jn. iv. 32–34).

4–7. This time the disciples' question (4) was one of sheer
bewilderment. Their own resources were so small that they
never even thought of them. So little had they learned from
the feeding of the five thousand, and so little were they to
learn from this new miracle, as we see from verse 20 of this
same chapter. This in itself is the strongest possible confirmation of the veracity of the statement that the first miracle
had meant so little. There is still a puzzle, it is true; but it
becomes now the puzzle as to the reason for such hardness of
heart. Modesty and self-distrust, even a shrinking from the
task, is an essential preliminary to all Christian service: but,
once we are convinced of God's call, to persist in such an
attitude betrays lack of faith in God's power, and is culpable
(Ex. iv. 14).

8, 9. It has often been pointed out that *spuris,* the word used
for *basket* here, is quite different from the *kophinos,* or beggar's
sacks, used to store the fragments in the former miracle (vi. 43).
These little differentiations of vocabulary must go back to the
preaching of Peter; otherwise it is hard to account for the
fixity of the tradition in either case in the Synoptists. There is
no need to see spiritual symbolism in the numbers. The twelve
beggars' wallets would doubtless be those carried by the
twelve apostles, hence the number. The seven wicker baskets
borrowed (it is unlikely that peripatetic preachers carried such
around with them) pin the story to history as surely as does
the unusual 'four thousand' for the crowd, which could in no

sense be used metaphorically for any large number as, say, 'ten thousand' could have been. Unfortunately, in the western world, 'beggar's sack' contains all sorts of connotations unknown to the ancient world, where beggary was a respectable profession. To an Australian, 'swagman's roll' would give a truer picture.

iv. The Pharisees seek a sign (viii. 10–13). As it stands, this is a pathetic little account of a mission to *Dalmanutha* (or the territory of Magadan, Mt. xv. 39, RV; but certainly on the opposite shore of the lake). It might have been as spiritually fruitful as any, but failed to achieve spiritual results, because it was met from the outset by a stubbornly 'theological' attitude on the part of the argumentative and unbelieving Pharisees. Compare the attitude in Nazareth, where no exhibition of divine power was possible because of their stubborn unbelief (Mt. xiii. 58). It is striking that in either case the stumbling-block to faith was knowledge—theological knowledge here, knowledge of the Lord's local origin in the case of the men of Nazareth.

11–13. This 'seeking for a sign' is so significant that it is recorded in all four Gospels. The Lord's reaction (*he sighed deeply* (lit. 'groaned') *in his spirit*, 12) is that divine impatience which He showed towards lack of faith in those who might be expected to possess it: compare His reaction towards the powerless disciples, at the foot of the mount of transfiguration (Mk. ix). Thus it is clear that unbelief lay at the root of the Pharisaic attitude. To those in such a state, even a sign given would not convince: 'If they hear not Moses and the prophets, neither will they be persuaded, though one rose from the dead' (Lk. xvi. 31). The difficulty lies in the will, not in the intellect, as far as acceptance of the claims of Christ is concerned (Jn. vii. 17 and v. 40).[1]

---

[1] Many modern editors have pointed out that the Johannine use of *sēmaion*, 'sign', is different to that of the Synoptists. The key surely is that in John it is a sign granted by God to belief, while in the Synoptists it is one asked by unbelieving man.

But even apart from the impossibility of convincing men by signs, such an attitude of sign-seeking strikes at the root of the biblical concept of the nature of faith. 'Except ye see signs and wonders,' said the Lord, 'ye will not believe' (Jn. iv. 48). The biblical order of events is 'these signs shall follow them that believe' (Mk. xvi. 17). In other words, to the Christian, 'believing is seeing', not 'seeing is believing'. Hebrews xi. 1 presses this still further: the eye of faith sees here and now what actually has yet to be realized in the future, and thus obtains strength to endure. Matthew and Luke add that such a cold calculating generation are 'wicked and adulterous', i.e. faithless to God, as the generation of the wandering were in Old Testament days (Dt. i. 35). They also add that the sole sign to be vouchsafed to such a generation was the sign of Jonah the prophet (see Mt. xvi. 4; Lk. xi. 29). This is explained by the Lord as having direct reference to His resurrection (Mt. xii. 40). That the Jews failed to believe this sign adds peculiar point to the words of Abraham to the rich man mentioned above (Lk. xvi. 31). They had failed to hear Moses and the prophets (Lk. xxiv. 27): now they failed to be persuaded when Christ rose from the dead. In the Marcan account, a literal translation of verse 12b would be 'Amen I say to you, if a sign will be given . . .'. This has, in Semitic speech, the full force of an oath, as even a double 'Amen' had to a Jew (cf. Jn. i. 51, etc.). It was a firm refusal on the Lord's part to take a line of action that He had decisively rejected at the temptation (Mt. iv. 6)—that of compelling men's allegiance by a spectacular sign. Matthew and Luke add the dry comment that, for men so shrewd in weather-lore, the Pharisees and Sadducees were peculiarly blind to the 'signs of the times': to men thus wilfully blind (Jn. ix. 40), a further sign would have been useless.

v. Beware of leaven (viii. 14–21). In this section, again, the lack of spiritual perception of the disciples is brought out: but the outline loses some of its angularity when we realize that the story owes its preservation to the recollections of one at least of this very group. Here we have not merely a condemnation of the disciples by the Lord, but a condemnation of the disciples by one of themselves.

14. It does not appear that the Lord was in the least interested as to whether they had brought bread or not: but the disciples certainly were. Probably they had a guilty conscience about their oversight. This can be seen both from the use of the word *had forgotten* (14), and from the way in which, when the Lord mentioned *leaven* (15), their minds at once flew to this point. Psychologically, this is very true to life: they expected to be blamed for their culpable lack of foresight, and so they saw reproof where none seems to have been intended. They were not blamed for their lack of foresight, but for their lack of faith. We look for good businessmen within the Church, but God looks for saints (in whom businesslike qualities are of course encouraged: Rom. xii. 11; 1 Cor. xiv. 40).

15. The Lord, in His use of *leaven* here, was using a pithy one-word parable for unseen pervasive influence. This was of a kind that unfitted for the service of God, if we are to judge from the analogy of the use of unleavened bread in Old Testament religious festivals (see Lv. ii. 4, etc.) and Paul's 'purge out . . . the old leaven' (1 Cor. v. 7), referring to the well-known Jewish custom in both biblical and modern times of clearing the house of leaven before Passover can be celebrated. Leaven is thus here clearly a biblical symbol of sin: but the clarity with which it bears that meaning in this context is due to the direct association with 'Pharisees' and 'Herod'. In itself, the thought of 'leaven' is merely of unseen spreading, as in the parable of the kingdom (Mt. xiii. 33). Here some have been forced, by a false ideal of consistency, to see the picture as one of the spreading of evil within the Church: but the natural meaning called for by the context is simply the spreading of the Church within the world.[1] Luke xii. 1 makes plain that this 'leaven' was the Pharisaic hypocrisy, their 'playacting'. Matthew xvi. 12 equates it with their 'doctrine', and says that the Twelve so understood it ultimately. What was

[1] It is, however, true that this is the only New Testament context (with the parallel in Luke) where 'leaven' has a good sense (Cranfield).

this insidious danger that lay before the little band of disciples, the proto-Church at that time? It was that of allowing their thinking to be approximated and assimilated to that of the world about them, the world of Pharisees and Herodians, the main religious and political circles respectively of their day (Sadducees are included in Mt. xvi). In the Old Testament, men were warned of the gulf between God's thinking and men's (Is. lv. 8), and Christ's words of rebuke to Peter underlined this in the New Testament (Mk. viii. 33). The Pharisaic sin was hypocrisy (Lk. xii. 1), while Herod's leaven may have been that procrastinating time-serving which had led him first to imprison the Baptist, then to execute him, though fighting his conscience all the time. Matthew xvi. 6 has 'Sadducees' in place of *Herod* here: they were the shrewd, wealthy, priestly aristocracy, with a leavening influence at least as dangerous as that of the hard religious formalism of the Pharisees. But at each stage of the history of the Church, the exact nature of the danger changes, while the danger itself ever remains. In the Church as in the world 'the price of liberty is eternal vigilance'. 'Watch and pray', said the Lord (Mt. xxvi. 41).

16. The Greek *hoti* (AV, *because*) might be used here merely to introduce a direct quotation. A free translation would then be: 'They reasoned "But we have no bread at all".'

17. 'Why are you reasoning?' The Greek word *dialogizomai* represents a mental activity condemned in the Gospels, akin to *meteōrizomai*, 'to be of doubtful mind' (Lk. xii. 29), and close to *tarassomai*, 'to be troubled, or confused'. But Matthew xvi. 8 makes it clearer by the addition here also of 'among yourselves'. Unanswered problems should be taken directly to the Lord Himself, rather than bandied about among the disciples.

18-21. They credited the Lord with spiritual insight, yes, and saw in His remark supernatural perception, but limited that perception to material objects. They were so blinded by their immediate bodily needs that they had again forgotten to seek first God's kingdom, in the knowledge that, as they did this, their bodily needs would be met. Yet, in spite of their lack of spiritual perception, at the last these very disciples could give glad witness to this providing care of God (Lk. xxii. 35: 'lacked ye anything? . . . Nothing'). Every Christian is called to such a faith as this.

vi. The blind man of Bethsaida (viii. 22–26). The disciples had been blinded to spiritual truths by their constant pre-occupation with their immediate bodily needs. It is thus fitting that the next miracle should be the opening of the eyes of the blind man of Bethsaida. John ix. 1–7 may be compared for a similar miracle, again with the laying of clay on the eyes, but this time performed at Jerusalem. Of course, we are specifically told that the Lord healed many blind in the course of His ministry (Lk. vii. 21, etc.): but this particular miracle is recorded only in Mark—naturally enough, as it occurred in Bethsaida, the home town of Peter (Jn. i. 44)—another touch of the Petrine witness to Christ.

22. It is clear from the *they bring* and *they . . . besought* in this verse that, as in other miracles, the faith of others besides the afflicted man was involved: here is the great Gospel warrant for intercessory prayer to God on behalf of others.

23. The taking *by the hand* is an eyewitness touch, peculiarly apposite in the case of a blind man, as is the leading *out of the town* appropriate to the sightless man, bewildered by the noise of the crowd, to a place of quiet, where he may hear and understand the Lord whom he cannot yet see. The saliva is unlikely to have been used for any supposed therapeutic effect. It was simply dumb-show to draw the man's attention to what the Lord was about to do. The laying on of hands would have the same effect: touch means more than sound to a blind man, and only by touch could the Lord's meaning be conveyed. There must be an understanding by him of the Lord's act before that act could become revelation: unexplained miracle, unrelated to God's loving purpose, is too close to magic, and of such we have no instance in the Bible.

24. The point seems to be that he saw, but indistinctly: there are non-biblical parallels to this sort of phrase (see

Arndt and Gingrich), but the contrast with *tēlaugōs, clearly*, below, makes the meaning abundantly clear in any case. We must not blame the excited man for inaccurate description: after all, he had seen neither man nor tree before until that moment, though he was doubtless familiar with both by touch. Our use of the word 'trunk' for the body of both tree and man does denote a basic columnar similarity when mistily seen, and any who have been betrayed into apologizing to a lamppost, bumped in a London fog, will appreciate it at once.

25. Scripture does not make plain why two applications of the Lord's hands were necessary here: was it a lack of faith on the recipient's part? Nowhere else is such twofold action recorded of the Saviour.[1] But the important theological point is not how hard the task, nor wherein lay the peculiar difficulty, but that the Lord did not desist till the man was completely healed (cf. Paul's belief, expressed in Phil. i. 6). The very fact that the Lord asked the man whether he could see 'anything at all' suggests that He was conscious of some lack of faith in the recipient: of others, there was no need to ask such a question.

26. The Lord will not be known as a mere miracle-worker; and so (as in Mk. vii. 36) He forbids the man to tell others of his healing. He is to go straight to his home: he is not to go even into his own home village first. Is there a touch of love there? Must there not have been wife or children at home, to whom the man's healing would mean everything? and was the Lord desirous that theirs should be the first joy?

IV. HE STEDFASTLY SET HIS FACE: THE ROAD TO JERUSALEM (viii. 27–x. 52)

a. Confession and transfiguration (viii. 27–ix. 10)

i. Peter's confession of Christ (viii. 27–33). Next comes the great confession of Christ by Peter on the road to Caesarea

---

[1] This in itself is proof positive of the genuineness of the story: such an unusual detail would never have been invented (Taylor, *apud* Cranfield).

Philippi, and the first clear prediction to the disciples of His coming death. It is of course no accident that these two are joined; for if the disciples see Him as the Christ, it is essential that they see Him as God's Christ and not man's, and that they understand the path of Messiahship. Natural man never objects to the concept of a Messiah, provided it be a Messiah who commends himself to natural man. This careful explanation was so important, not only that they might be kept from nationalistic or other misconceptions of Messiahship, which the Lord had resolutely put from Him at the temptations in the wilderness (Mt. iv), but also because Christ's path determined theirs: like Master, like servant (Mt. x. 25). It was by a prophetic overruling that the light-hearted city wits of Antioch called the 'followers of the Way' by the coined name 'Christian', that is, 'the messianic people'. It is also appropriate that such a revelation should now be brought to the spiritually blinded disciples by Him who had so recently proved His power to open the blind eyes.

28. It is always easy to answer in the third person, and give the views of others as to the nature of Christ. We have seen that Herod saw Him as a 'John redivivus' (Mk. vi. 16), and it seems from this passage that he was not alone in this belief. Others saw Him as 'Elijah redivivus', a common Jewish concept of the day, derived from Malachi iii. 1, iv. 5, and endorsed by the Lord as having reference to Baptizer John (Mt. xvii. 13). The interesting thing is that both Elijah and John were, by definition, forerunners of the Christ, and not the Christ Himself. Thus none of the outside world had as yet guessed His true nature as Messiah. Others could not make so definite an identification, but agreed that clearly Christ was a prophet. The Emmaus Road conversation witnesses to the persistence of this 'minimal' view of His Person and nature, even among Christians (Lk. xxiv. 19); and the *nabi Isa*, 'prophet Jesus', of the *Qur'an* bears witness to its use in Mohammed's days among the decayed Christian churches of Arabia. A reduced Christology can ultimately lead only to even grosser heresy: for it inevitably makes Christ only a forerunner and not God's last word to rebellious mankind. Matthew xvi. 14 adds that some identified Him with Jeremiah. It is interesting to speculate what spiritual qualities, seen and noted in the Christ by outside observers, led them to these identifications. Jeremiah is the heart-broken prophet of love, meeting with little response; John is the stern eschatological prophet of doom; Elijah is the fearless wonder-worker, appearing and disappearing from the desert, the great example to New Testament saints of the power of prayer (Jas. v. 16–18). All of these prophets differed individually, yet each found a place in the portrait of the Christ. As often, if we would understand His Person and work, we must draw into one the several threads of Old Testament revelation, for all lines of revelation meet in the Christ. Thus, while they were inadequate, these views expressed above were not entirely wrong.

29. But now, as it continually comes to us, comes the rapier-thrust that transfers theology from an armchair discussion to an uncomfortable dialogue between God and us. Are His own disciples, then, as blind as the others? The rest maybe, but not Peter: impetuously the answer was made—had the great discovery only come in that moment? *Thou art the Christ*, 'the Anointed, the Messiah'. The weight of MS evidence seems to point to this wording as being the full Marcan statement: the addition 'the Son of the living God', with poorer MS evidence, is almost certainly an assimilation to the text of Matthew, where it properly belongs in any case. Simon Peter's similar declaration (Jn. vi. 68, 69) should be compared. Here, then, was the identification of Jesus with the Christ that made a man a Christian: no man could make such an equation without the inner illumination of the Spirit (Mt. xvi. 17). Matthew, at this point, continues with the Lord's blessing of Peter, His declaration that this is none other than the Spirit's revelation, and the Petrine promises: these pose some problems of interpretation into which we need not enter here. But one difficulty is apparent: if Peter is Mark's source, why does Peter say so little here? The answer may well be that, to him, the most vivid recollection was the Lord's stern rebuke which followed:

or he may well have shrunk from introducing into his preaching that blessing which must seem to aggrandize himself. But whatever the reason, it is surely a good commentary on later Roman claims that, by Church tradition, the one place where the Petrine promises were most certainly not preached was the very city of Rome, where we have good reason to believe Peter was an *episcopos*, or elder-bishop, before his death, possibly in the same persecution as that in which Paul died. We have seen, in the Introduction,[1] that Mark probably represents the Roman preaching of Peter: but if we want to find the Petrine promises, we must turn to the Palestinian tradition underlying Matthew.

30. Why were the disciples not allowed to tell others of the Messiahship of Jesus? Presumably because at this stage none of the disciples (not even Peter: see verse 32) understood what was involved in Messiahship, and thus those outside could not fail to misunderstand such a claim. But it may be that this was a discovery which each man must make for himself, as Peter had done, although in every case, as for Peter, this must come as the Spirit's revelation. Here, in a nutshell, is the mystery of the Gospel: we are very conscious of our human part in the process, at the moment of conversion, and yet, from the other side, we learn in reverent wonder that all was God's work (Jn. xv. 16).

31. This is the first of the three occasions on which the Lord carefully explained to His disciples the cost of Messiahship:[2] compare ix. 31 and x. 32, which seem to give a fuller picture, presumably as the disciples were better able to bear it. This in itself shows that none of the later Jerusalem happenings took the Lord by surprise. Indeed, as soon as He had accepted the vocation to Messiahship, so He had accepted the vocation to suffering. To 'suffer', when applied to the Messiah in the New Testament, seems a sort of 'theological shorthand' for His

[1] See p. 36.
[2] Although it is striking that the Lord does not say here 'the Messiah must suffer', but *the Son of man must suffer*, i.e. probably, 'I must suffer'. But for a summary of views on the meaning of His self-chosen title, see Cranfield, pp. 272–277.

death upon the cross (Acts iii. 18, etc.). But to *suffer many things* doubtless includes far more than His actual death, for Hebrews v. 8 makes clear that the cross was the culmination and supreme point of a life of suffering for the Lord. But it is only when men understand the Person of Christ that they can appreciate His work: that is the great theological lesson, and explains why the Lord made no attempt to tell of the cross until now. *Apodokimasthēnai, be rejected* (31), is an interesting word: it means literally 'fail to pass the scrutiny'. The thought is that the Sanhedrin, the priestly court of Israel, will scrutinize the Lord's claims, and then deliberately reject Him. But the true danger for all men is that of failing to pass the scrutiny of God, as Paul saw (1 Cor. ix. 27). The concept of resurrection is apparently unexplained to the disciples as yet, for much later they are still puzzled by it (Mk. ix. 10). Perhaps, like Martha (Jn. xi. 24), their trouble was that they boggled at a resurrection here and now, while accepting one 'at the last day' quite happily. Only Sadducees rejected the whole concept of resurrection: but that was on a par with their general anti-supernatural bias (Acts xxiii. 8).

32. Again, the same natural reserve may have kept Peter from quoting the terms of his remonstrance to Christ (see Mt. xvi. 22). It was enough that he failed to understand. It is hard to believe that the First Gospel is not using some Judaean source or sources here, apostolic in origin, but quite distinct, and parallel to the Petrine reminiscences in Mark. If Levi's tradition at least lies behind it, then that is very understandable; for all the apostles seem to have been present on this occasion, and each would have had his own recollections of it.

33. No sterner rebuke ever fell on any Pharisee than on this disciple of Christ, this first Christian. In so speaking, he was now voicing, not the mind of God revealed by His Spirit, but the mind of the enemy: and so Peter could be addressed directly as *Satan*. The avoidance of the cross had been a temptation faced and overcome by the Lord in the wilderness: and for Peter to suggest it here was to think in human terms, and not in divine terms. The form *Satana* suggests that here we

have another original Aramaic Saying of the Lord. Otherwise
the pure Greek *diabolos*, 'devil', might have been used (cf. Jn.
vi. 70). It is unlikely that there was any gradation in meaning
between the two words, which seem to be mere synonyms.

ii. The cost of discipleship (viii. 34-38). Now we see why
it was so essential that Peter should grasp the conditions of
Messiahship for Christ: otherwise, Peter could not grasp the
conditions of discipleship for himself. This correspondence was
fulfilled very literally if we accept the universal tradition as to
the manner of Peter's death at Rome. John xxi. 19 seems
clearly to have been written after Peter's death: on any dating
of the Fourth Gospel this seems highly likely, especially if
Peter died in the Neronian persecution at Rome in AD 64. So
the Lord warns all the crowd—not just His professed disciples
—that to follow Him means to deny all natural inclinations
and to 'shoulder one's stake' (cf. Lk. xiv. 27). 'Stake' keeps
better the association of shameful death than does *cross* in
modern English. Compare Mark x. 39 for His solemn words
to James and John as to the cost of discipleship. The thought is
simple enough, and plain to every child playing 'follow my
leader', of which there is only one rule—that no follower
shirks going to any place where the Leader has first gone.
Ultimately, to the Christian, this becomes the great hope of
heaven, since our Leader has gone there (Heb. vi. 19, 20).

35. The man who tries to live his life 'unto himself', who
hoards it jealously and selfishly, will lose it. This is true, not
only ultimately in the death that all must face, but moment by
moment, for such is no true life—it is but animal existence: it
is not *zōē* but *bios*, as John would say. Life, like sand, trickles
between our fingers whether we will or no, and to grasp it the
more tightly means that it merely flows the faster from us. So
a refusal to accept that 'death to self', that is the bearing of
Christ's cross and following Him, is a spiritual death; whereas,
by a divine paradox, spiritual life is only to be found by passing
through the gate of death to self. All men must one day die.
The Christian dies here and now, and so has nothing left to
fear; for him, death no longer has any sting (1 Cor. xv. 55).

Luke xvii. 33 is a similar Saying of the Lord rather than a parallel account of the same Saying (for this latter is found in Lk. ix. 23–27), and it makes the sense even clearer by the use of *peripoiēsasthai*: what man, in his folly, wishes to do is to keep his life eternally as a possession for himself, to have it 'remaining over and above' as it were, when all else of possessions is gone. Mark's explanatory addition *and the gospel's* makes plain the exact way in which life is to be spent for Christ, in His service, in the spreading abroad of the good news. The Christian has not two goals, but one.

36, 37. The metaphor here seems to be commercial rather than judicial. As usual, the Lord is meeting or anticipating man's objection on man's level, appealing, as it were, to the shrewd commercial instincts of these Galilaean tradesmen, as He appealed elsewhere to the common sense of fishermen (Mt. xiii. 48) or farmer (Lk. xiii. 15). The parables of the treasure hidden in the field (Mt. xiii. 44) and the pearl of great price (Mt. xiii. 45) seem to be of the same genre: in either case, the kingdom was a good 'buy' at any price, if only these hard-headed businessmen could see it.

38. But then, as usual, when man has been defeated at his own lowly level of thinking, the Lord takes the argument to a deeper level, with an eschatological reference. *Son of man* He has used as title before (e.g. verse 31), but now, through the great Petrine declaration, 'man's Son' has been definitely equated with 'Messiah'. The Lord has shown that the biblical interpretation of the anointed One is not initially at least the conquering king eagerly awaited by the Jews, but the rejected suffering Servant (Is. liii). Yet, for all this, as 'man's Son' He was still God's chosen instrument of judgment at His coming again (cf. Dn. vii. 13). The biggest puzzle for the disciples must have been how to relate all these different concepts to one another, and to the Jesus before them. The Christ of history is ever mankind's great stumbling-block, not only to their generation but to ours also.[1]

[1] That is, if *genea* is to be interpreted *generation* as seems probable. See Arndt and Gingrich, *sub voc.*, paragraph 2. The later Jewish use of *dōr*, in e.g. *dōr hammabbûl*, 'the generation that lived at the time of the flood', is in point here.

iii. The transfiguration (ix. 1–10).

To what does this prophecy in verse 1 refer? That depends on our understanding of the exact moment when the disciples saw *the kingdom of God come with power*. The parallel passage in Matthew (xvi. 28) makes the understanding clearer with its slightly different phrasing, 'the Son of man coming in his kingdom'. Now there are two distinct questions: the first is, what did the disciples initially think the meaning to be? The second is, what did the Lord Himself mean by the Saying? We know that many in the early Church expected the Lord's second coming to be in the lifetime of the first generation of apostolic witnesses: John xxi. 23 seems to be written as a cautious counter to that belief, and 2 Peter iii. 4 refers to it. The first apostolic generation may well, then, have thought that this Saying was a reference to the *parousia*, the second coming of Christ for judgment and establishment of His reign. This view could only nowadays be maintained if we understand *taste of death* in a mystical or Johannine sense (cf. 'shall never die', Jn. xi. 26), which is possible, but unlikely. In Semitic idiom 'taste death' is but poetic for the blunt 'die', and so the apostles themselves must have interpreted it. But the views of the first generation have only an archaeological value: by the date of the Gospel of Mark, even Peter had passed away, so this literal interpretation was no longer possible. Mark certainly would not have recorded a Saying which was meaningless to him and thus useless to the Church. The verse must, therefore, refer either to the transfiguration immediately after, which seems reasonable; or to Christ's triumph on the cross, confirmed by the resurrection (Col. ii. 15); or to the coming of the Spirit; or to the later extension of the blessings of the kingdom to the Gentiles. Of these, perhaps the complex event of cross and resurrection is the best interpretation. We are accustomed in hymnody to the concept of Christ reigning from the tree, for it was after the cross that He said 'All power is given unto me' (Mt. xxviii. 18) and sent them to further the great commission, conquering and to conquer (Rev. vi. 2). But Luke x. 18 associates this victory with the sending out of the Seventy, so perhaps we do wrong to associate it **exclusively** with any one isolated point of time in our human sense of the word.

2. There need be no theological reason for the precise *six days* of Matthew (xvii. 1) and Mark, though attempts have been made to connect them with the 'six days' of God's working in Genesis, followed by His sabbath rest. This is just one of the irrelevancies of the memory of any eyewitness, assuring us that the story of the Christ is pinned to history, firmly set in place and time, though we may not always be able to reconstruct these from the scanty data given. The phrase 'suffered under Pontius Pilate', in the Creed, is another continual reminder of how Eternity entered into, and thus ratified, time. Luke has 'roughly eight days' (see Lk. ix. 28); no Gentile would count in weeks, of course, since the seven-day 'week' was a specifically Jewish institution. So both Mark and Luke give an approximate number—'about a week', as we would say today.[1]

Why did the Lord take *Peter, and James, and John*? Why did He include James, who died so soon in the apostolic age (Acts xii. 2), and exclude lovable Andrew, who had brought Peter initially to Christ (Jn. i. 42)? God's sovereign choice is a mystery to us, but we can be sure that it is not favouritism, although these three men shared many experiences denied to the Twelve (e.g. Mk. v. 37). If such a question has any answer, it may be that these three had shown themselves especially spiritually responsive to what illumination they had already been given (cf. Peter's declaration in Mk. viii. 29). For it is an abiding spiritual principle that 'unto every one that hath shall be given' (Mt. xxv. 29). Yet in another sense, even this spiritual receptivity is a gift of God, and we are no nearer the heart of the mystery than before. But at least it is clear from the parable of the talents that we are responsible for the use or abuse of the spiritual privileges committed to us (Mt. xxv), quite irrespective of whether these are great or small.

---

[1] Although Cranfield may be right in seeing such precise dating as proof that Mark at least saw in the transfiguration the fulfilment of the Lord's promise in viii. 38.

We are reminded, perhaps deliberately, of the leading by Moses of Joshua up to the mount of revelation (Ex. xxiv), and of how Moses was there transfigured by the glory of God (Ex. xxxiv. 29), although Moses had but a fading and reflected glory, as the Bible makes plain (2 Cor. iii. 7, 13). Christ's glory was His own: He was but reassuming that divine glory which was His with the Father before the world began (Jn. xvii. 5). In a sense we do wrong to call this *the* transfiguration, as though it were unique: the true transfiguration, the *metamorphōsis*, had been at Bethlehem, as Philippians shows (Phil. ii. 6, 7).

3. The abiding impression was one of unearthly purity. So, too, when men see God's spiritual ministrants in human form, they wear white robes (Mk. xvi. 5). In spite of modern biblical illustrations, white was not a common colour for working clothes in biblical days: it soiled too easily in a workaday world. If it had not been somewhat unusual for a young man to wear gleaming white garments, the detail would not have been recorded, for the Bible makes but sparse reference to colour in any case.

4. We often loosely take the appearance of *Elias with Moses* as the witness of Law and Prophets to Christ: and so it is, but it is more. Moses had himself spoken of Christ prophetically (Jn. i. 45; Lk. xxiv. 27) and scribe and Pharisee alike looked for Elijah to come as Messiah's harbinger (Mk. ix. 11), on the authority of Malachi iii. 1, iv. 5. True, as the Lord said, there had already been a fulfilment of this prophecy at one level in the coming of John the Baptist (Mt. xvii. 13), but nevertheless there was a peculiar appropriateness in the presence of Elijah himself here. It is interesting that Abraham, for all his forward-looking to Christ (Jn. viii. 56), was not present: perhaps it was because Abraham was, even physically, the father of many a Gentile as well as Jews. We may all be children of Abraham (Rom. iv. 16) but scarcely of Moses: and the Lord's mission was, as yet, only to the lost sheep of the house of Israel (Mt. x. 6). Luke (ix. 31) adds the interesting detail that the subject of their consideration was the Lord's coming death in Jerusalem. His use of the Greek word *exodos* for 'death' is a deliberate reminiscence of God's initial triumph in Israel's history: and the verb that he uses, *plēroō*, 'fulfil' or 'accomplish', makes this even more plain. At the cross and resurrection and ascension there was a new exodus, a new 'saving act' of God; and only in its light can the first exodus be understood, just as the true meaning of the cross is only to be seen by studying the Old Testament 'types' of redemption.

5, 6. Luke also makes plain (ix. 32) that the disciples had been asleep, as in Gethsemane. This in itself, like the Lucan reason for the journey ('for prayer', see Lk. ix. 28), suggests that the transfiguration took place by night, either during a night of prayer such as the Lord observed at focal points of His ministry (e.g. Lk. vi. 12), or 'a great while before day', at one of the Lord's early risings (cf. Mk. i. 35, etc.). Compare the angelic glory at Bethlehem, shining out of the blackness of night for the shepherds (Lk. ii. 8, 9). There was a divine appropriateness that God's light of salvation should so shine. Peter, suddenly awakened from sleep in time to see the glory fade (Lk. ix. 33), was garrulous in his terror, as some men are. Now that they had seen the Shekinah-glory that had covered Israel's meeting-place of old (Ex. xl. 35), surely another such tent—nay, three such tents—was the answer. Peter did not know that the Shekinah-glory, the very manifestation of God's presence, was already 'under canvas' among men, in the body of Christ (Jn. i. 14). Peter does not spare himself in his own reminiscences, of which the use of *Rabbi* is another interesting original touch; Matthew (xvii. 4) has the usual polite *Kurie*, 'Lord', or 'Sir', and Luke the Gentile (ix. 33) *Epistata*, 'Master' or 'Overseer'; but Peter keeps the original Aramaic word.

7, 8. *Cloud*, as light, was the sign of God's presence in the wilderness (Ex. xl. 38); and, in true Old Testament style, there came a voice from the cloud (cf. Ex. xxiv. 16). It is at least a striking coincidence that it was also after 'six days' that the Lord called from the cloud of Sinai.[1] This time it strikes

[1] Oepke, quoted by Cranfield, has the interesting suggestion that *episkiazein* means 'conceal' rather than *overshadow*. When Moses ascended Sinai, he was lost to Israel's sight in the cloud (Ex. xxiv. 18). Even at the moment of revelation, there was concealment (Ex. xix. 21).

less terror into the hearts of the hearers (cf. Ex. xix. 16). Once again, as at the baptism, God the Father bore testimony from heaven to His Son (cf. Mk. i. 11). The Greek *agapētos, beloved,* almost certainly has the connotation of 'only begotten' here, as the Hebrew *yachīd* would have had. 2 Peter i. 17, 18 refers specifically to the evidential value of this voice, as 2 Peter i. 14 seems to refer to the saying about the three tents.

9. The full meaning of this vision would only be apparent after the resurrection, and so they were forbidden to tell others of it until then. Presumably this forbade even a sharing of it with their fellow-disciples. In any case, all three Synoptic accounts must go back to Peter's recollections, for Matthew had not been present, and James was dead long before Luke was interviewing his eyewitnesses (Lk. i. 2).

10. This is an interesting incidental confirmation that the disciples never interpreted literally the Lord's words about His coming resurrection. Thus they were amazed by the event (Lk. xvi. 8). The strange thing is that, on so many other occasions, they misunderstood His words by taking them with the crassest literalism (cf. Mk. viii. 16). The only answer to this problem is that given earlier: they lacked the key of faith (Mk. viii. 17, 18). Of course, resurrection at the last day was no problem to them: but clearly the Lord's words here referred to some other event.

b. The passion foretold (ix. 11–50)

i. 'Elijah redivivus' (ix. 11–13). The appearance of Elijah upon the mountain had raised another question in their minds: was not Elijah yet to appear, not in a vision, but in person, to usher in the messianic age? As they descended the mountain, they put this question to the Lord. This at least proves that all of them now believed in His Messiahship; otherwise the question has no meaning.

12, 13. To judge from the Petrine preaching, as preserved in Mark, the Lord not only agreed with this interpretation of

Malachi, seeing its fulfilment in John the Baptist, but showed the parallelism with His own case. The problem now was not whether 'Elijah redivivus' would come again or not, but 'when the Son of man cometh, shall he find faith upon the earth?' (Lk. xviii. 8). In rejecting John, Pharisees and scribes rejected God's counsel for them (Lk. vii. 30) and made it all the more sure that they would reject the Messiah. None of this took God by surprise, for all was as it had been written (see verses 12, 13). As Elijah's coming was a heralding of the Lord's coming, so Elijah's rejection was a warning of the Lord's rejection: and all alike was in fulfilment of Scripture.

ii. The epileptic boy (ix. 14-29). But sterner work than abstract theological discussion awaited the little group at the foot of the mountain, where spiritual failure had shamed the other nine apostles, and drawn a crowd, as failure will do as surely as success. As usual, those theological harpies, the scribes, were at the forefront, doubtless, in the face of this failure, questioning the theological credentials of the disciples or their Lord. One wonders why these same scribes, instead of further embarrassing the crestfallen disciples before the crowd, did not set about exorcising the demon themselves, as a proof of orthodoxy. Some orthodox Jews were exorcists: indeed, the Lord appeals to this to justify His own activity (Mt. xii. 27).

16. The Lord's first questioning words were not words of ignorance; they were designed to draw the attention of the crowd away from the humiliated disciples, and to Himself, as verse 19 makes explicit. Nor was this just to spare the feelings of the disciples; it corresponds to a deep spiritual principle. First, men must confess their own inadequacy, and then they must be brought to see the Person of the Christ. To concentrate on the person of His servants is irrelevant, as both John (Jn. i. 23) and Paul (1 Cor. iii. 5) saw clearly.

17, 18. The symptoms are certainly those of epilepsy, but we do well to observe a reverent agnosticism on matters of demon possession.[1] The very boldness of the man's answer emphasizes

[1] See note on p. 85.

his weary despair. The father has brought the lad to the disciples, hoping for healing, but *they could not*, lit. 'were not strong enough'.

19. The Lord's reaction is a half quotation from Psalm xcv. 10, referring to God's endurance of the faithlessness of the generation of the wandering in days of old. It gains in poignancy when we realize that the generation of the ministry was also the generation of the judgment, and that after the fall of Jerusalem, in AD 70, apart from the Christian Church which had fled to Pella in Transjordan (cf. Mk. xiii. 14), few of the Lord's hearers would be left alive: their bodies would lie in the wilderness, as had those of their forefathers (Heb. iii. 17). The Roman legionaries were terrible agents of the wrath of God on a stubborn rebellious generation. But whose was the lack of faith—the disciples', or the parents'? It seems from the wording of verse 23 that it is the father who is blamed for lack of faith, while the disciples are blamed for lack of prayer (verse 29). But prayer is of course one demonstration of faith, so that ultimately all stand under the same condemnation, and we with them.

20. The violence of the demonic onset corresponds, in the dumb man, to the confessional outcry wrung from the lips of the demon-possessed elsewhere (cf. Mk. v. 7). It was the impotent rage of the enemy, an unwilling acknowledgment of Christ's status.

21. The Lord is not just interested in a 'case history' of the boy. He is making the man confess how desperate his case is—making, as it were, faith as difficult as possible for him, and at the same time showing him that he has no other resource but the Christ.

22. It is a pitiful tale, but the telling of it works the desired purpose; for even though it be with little faith, yet the man who doubted the power of Christ never questioned His compassion. Contrast the robust faith of the leper of Mark i. 40: 'If thou wilt, thou canst make me clean.' He had no doubt of the Lord's power; all he doubted was His readiness to help a despised leper.

23. The Lord gently reproves the lack of faith. *If thou canst believe . . .*; lit. 'That "if you can"!' (quoting the man's own words). 'Why, everything can be done for one who believes.' This is a statement of the great biblical principle enunciated in Matthew xxi. 22 (cf. Mk. xi. 24). But we are not called to 'put God to the test' by irresponsible prayer for what is our human desire but may not be His will. We are free to ask what we will, but only if it be what He wills (1 Jn. v. 14). This is no mere theological quibble: it is a statement in another form of the need for the 'mind of Christ' in us. It is also a warning against taking a statement of Scripture in isolation, and basing presumptuous prayer on it.

24. The father cries for God's help, honestly confessing the paucity of his faith; and the Lord answers, not according to the poverty of the asking, but according to the riches of His grace. The man is doing exactly as the Gentile woman of Mark vii had done: he accepts humbly the Lord's estimate of him, and pleads for the divine mercy, not for his deserts. No better illustration of the doctrine of justification of faith could be found than the man's words here. This is clear from the fact that he uses the same verb, *boētheō*, as above (verse 22). He had said 'If you can, help me'. The Lord rebuked his first phrase, and so *with tears* (some MSS) the father said 'Then help me just as I am, a doubter'. In other words, the man was not praying that his unbelief might be 'helped' till it came to the point where it was worthy of meeting with a response from God. We do not need to ask God to increase our faith until it is deserving of salvation, as a sort of 'congruent faith'. That would be justification by works, not justification by faith. Instead, he was asking for practical help, to be demonstrated in the healing of his son, and confessing, deeply moved, that he had nothing to make him worthy of it. His very coming to Christ showed a trembling faith, and this was enough. This is justification by faith. A parallel would be the cry of dereliction on the cross (Mk. xv. 34). Even at that moment, a cry of seeming despair was in fact a cry of faith, for it was directed Godwards. Primarily, it was not the content of the cry, but the fact that the Lord cried, that is significant: although, at a deeper level, the quotation from Psalm xxii is highly significant, seeing that this Psalm ends as a note of triumph.

25–27. The Lord never encouraged crowds of idle sightseers, agape for the latest sensation. So at times He deliberately avoided crowds, when He thought their motives unworthy (cf. Jn. vi. 26), and He refused to perform a miracle for a jaded Herod (Lk. xxiii. 8). Crowds are not necessarily indicative of success in spiritual work. The Lord regarded crowds as a signal to move on (Mk. i. 37, 38), or to explain more clearly to shallow disciples the true cost of following Him (Mk. viii. 34). The test of success was the few who followed when the crowds had turned back.

28, 29. Note that the nine who failed were not the three who had been on the mount of transfiguration. We may, therefore, be justified in saying that these nine were less spiritually responsive than the three. It is noteworthy that in the parable of the talents the rule of giving is 'to every man according to his several ability' (Mt. xxv. 15). But if it was earnest prayer that was wanting, were the three who slept on the mount of transfiguration (as at Gethsemane) any further along the road, for all their greater opportunities? There is good MS evidence for the addition of *and fasting* (29).[1] Scripture does not condemn voluntary self-discipline as an associate of prayer (1 Cor. vii. 5). What Scripture condemns is the outward form that corresponds to no spiritual reality, and becomes matter for pride and self-glorification (Lk. xviii. 12). It is doubtful if the sub-apostolic age saw this as clearly as the apostolic, to judge from the Fathers.

iii. Second passion-prediction (ix. 30–32). The plain meaning of verse 30 is that the Lord wished on this Galilaean journey to travel incognito, because He desired to teach His

[1] Cranfield, however, rules it out, on the grounds that such an addition by the early Church was *a priori* likely. But to the Jew, fasting was a very natural adjunct to prayer: see both Old Testament and rabbinic literature: and *Didache* VIII shows how naturally this passed into Christianity (see Lightfoot).

disciples some important truths. It was in fact to be another period of intensive, not extensive, teaching: this distinction has been noted already (see comment on vi. 7). This is an example of how He could neglect one opportunity to take another, without feeling spiritually burdened. He had a quiet purposeful selectiveness, so often lacking in the fevered rush of much of our Christian work today, which produces nervous breakdowns as part of its bitter fruit.

31. This is commonly called the second prediction of the passion, and is to be found in all the Synoptic Gospels. In point of fact, the second prediction was on the path down from the mount of transfiguration, in answer to the question of the three about Elijah redivivus (see verse 12 above): this, then, would be the third such prediction.

32. What did they fail to understand? His own title 'Son of man' was by now familiar; 'betrayal' and 'death' were hard to accept, perhaps, but easy to understand as concepts; it must have been His reference to a resurrection after three days that baffled them. Of course it is clear from Luke xiii. 32 that 'the third day' could be used vaguely and metaphorically for 'subsequently' so that they are not to be blamed for failure to take it in a literal sense. The Old Testament use (Ho. vi. 2) would not help here in its original context, although the Christian Church later saw in it a clear prophetic foreshadowing of the resurrection. Where the Lord specifically used the analogy of Jonah, then it would be clearer (Mt. xii. 40), for He bluntly stated that the nature of the sign lay in the reappearance from underground after three days.

iv. Who is greatest in the kingdom? (ix. 33–37). But this sense of awe, induced by the Lord's as yet not understood words, did not last long. As they walked along, they were strung out in a long 'crocodile' behind their Rabbi. No Eastern pupil dares to walk abreast of his teacher, nor indeed would the narrow Eastern bridle-tracks allow it. They had been bickering up and down the line, and doubtless occasional angry words had reached the ears of the lonely figure, pressing resolutely on in front (cf. Mk. x. 32). So His question sounded natural enough, no doubt: but there was a hint of rebuke already in the use of the verb *dialogizomai* (*disputed*), which implies 'bickering' as well as 'reasoning'. But He did not wheel on them in public: they had been humiliated enough in front of crowds. He waited for the privacy of the evening halt.

35. *He sat down* implies more than a wearied traveller composing Himself: the teaching Rabbi is once more about to give instruction to His disciples. Compare Mary, who 'sat at Jesus' feet, and heard his word' (Lk. x. 39), and by so doing humbly accepted the place of a disciple. One interpretation of this Saying is the spiritual principle that those who desire or grasp at spiritual position condemn themselves automatically to the lowest place in the kingdom. This is true; and the song of Mary (Lk. i. 46–55) makes plain that it is as much part of God's strange work to 'put down the mighty from their seats' as it is to exalt the humble and meek. But the true key is perhaps to be found in the *ginesthō* of Luke xxii. 26, 'let him become', in place of the *estai*, 'he shall be', of the Marcan passage before us. Mark's use of the future may then reproduce a Semitism of Peter's original preaching, where a future form may also be an imperative or jussive. In that case, the deeper principle will be that, if we desire spiritual greatness, then what we desire is the place of service to others, and so we must deliberately choose the lowliest and most humble place. This is the whole key to the Lord's life, for He came, not to be served, but to be a Servant (Mk. x. 45). This is at least one point of the enacted parable of the foot-washing (Jn. xiii. 5), whatever deeper meanings its symbolism conveys.

36, 37. The picture is a beautiful one. It is evening, and the meal is doubtless over; the Lord calls to Him (cf. Mt. xviii. 2) one of His host's children and takes him *in his arms* (Gk. *enagkalisamenos*, lit. 'holds him in the crook of His arm'). But the exact connection of this Saying (37) is not clear in Mark. Matthew xviii. 4, the parallel passage, makes it clearer by amplifying: 'Whoever humbles himself like this child, he is the greatest in the kingdom of heaven' (RSV). This, then, makes plain that to accept the kingdom like a child means to accept it in humility: and this, says Christ, is the great law of entrance (Mk. x. 15). So it is in this humility, knowing no respect of persons (Jas. ii. 1), that we treat a child as we would the King of kings, if that child be indeed an ambassador of the King (*in my name*). Our Christian greatness lies not in ourselves, but in the greatness of the One whom we represent, in whose name we come. So even the Lord is to be understood in the light of God, His Sender (cf. Jn. v. 43).[1]

v. The man casting out devils (ix. 38-40). But now, as Moses had suffered from the over-zealous partisanship of Joshua (Nu. xi. 28), so the Lord was to suffer from the quick temper of one of the 'sons of thunder' (cf. Mk. iii. 71). Later, they were to suggest calling down fire from heaven on the churlish Samaritan villagers (Lk. ix. 54). Now, it was to forbid exorcism in the name of Jesus by one who was not a professed disciple, like the Twelve. Compare Acts xix. 13-17 for others who used the name of Jesus in exorcism without themselves being followers of Him. David's sufferings from the misdirected zeal of the sons of Zeruiah may also be compared (2 Sa. iii. 39): there was the same passionate personal loyalty, combined with the same failure to discern their master's true nature and purpose. Later, the Master was to tell Zebedee's sons roundly that they did not understand the nature of the very Spirit that infilled the little band (Lk. ix. 55). Now, all that He did was to rescind their prohibition, and give the great 'minimal' condition, *he that is not against us is on our part* (40). That is the rule for judging those outside. For the disciple, the more searching word is 'He that is not with me is against me; and he that gathereth not with me scattereth abroad' (Mt. xii. 30). The whole theology of the Spirit was at stake here: the scribes had seen the work of the Spirit, yet deliberately misinterpreted it, putting it down to Beelzebub (Mk. iii. 22). But

---

[1] There has been much recent discussion on the relevance of the Semitic *šalîaḥ* in this context. Some such word probably underlies 2 Corinthians v. 20: but a study of the rabbinic use of *běšēm*, 'in the name of', would be equally rewarding.

here were His own disciples, seeing and admitting a work of the Spirit, and still forbidding it. Wherein was the difference between disciples and scribes, if both were to oppose the Spirit's working? Elsewhere the Lord uses the shrewd farmer's criterion of the nature of the fruit as the only safe means of judging a tree (Mt. vii. 16–20). There again speaks the countryman, and we can almost hear the Galilaean farmers in the audience guffawing and slapping their thighs at such a Saying, the salty common sense of which would appeal to them.

vi. On stumbling-blocks (ix. 41–48). If this is still the same context, then there is a return to the wide-eyed child, standing in front of the Lord, and verse 41 would be the bridge-verse with its *whosoever*. The link is the words *because ye belong to Christ* (41). If this belonging to Christ be such an important bond, then nothing is too precious to sacrifice in order that we may retain it. So Paul argues against unchastity, not on strictly 'moral' grounds, but because of our close relation to Christ (1 Cor. vi. 18, 19). In the kingdom, all rules of moral conduct are based on theological principles. Therefore to trip up or impede one who enjoys this close relationship to Christ is so terrible a crime and merits such a terrible punishment. The incidental touch of verse 42, *one of these little ones that believe in me* (cf. Mt. xviii. 6), suggests that the Lord was staying in the house of a disciple at the time. So, too, we dare not allow ourselves to be thus tripped: for a man's whole attitude to himself alters after redemption. Before, he may have loathed and despised himself. Now, he dares not: he is no longer worthless, but a man for whom Christ has died. So hand, foot or eye, the most important members, but also the members through which temptation might come, must be sacrificed, if need be, for the good of the whole. And yet, with all this knowledge of the infinite value of the human soul, there comes less temptation to pride than ever.

43, 45, 47. There can be no reasonable doubt here that two alternatives are set before man. The one is called *life* (which is thus not purely a Johannine phrase; cf. 1 Jn. iii. 14, etc.). The other is called *hell*, 'Gehenna', and explained as 'unquenchable fire' (Gk. *asbestos*), for which Matthew xviii. 8 has the adjective *aiōnios*, translated 'everlasting' in the AV. It is true that the primary thought of *asbestos* is not one of duration; but it does seem to be that of absolute immutability, and the two concepts are not far apart. No man ever spoke stronger words about hell than the loving Son of God;[1] but His words on this topic were addressed either to His disciples, as here, or to professed religious leaders (as in Mt. xxiii. 33). We never hear of Him expounding this topic to publicans and sinners, although Baptist John seems to have struck this note widely (Mt. iii. 7). The Lord spoke of hell to professed saints, and of heaven to acknowledged sinners; we often reverse the process today.

48. The Old Testament reference (Is. lxvi. 24) helps to elucidate this solemn phrase: it is a reference to 'the carcases of the men that have transgressed against me'. So Gehenna, the eternally smouldering rubbish-dump outside Jerusalem, is the final abode of those who have sinned against God. The parable of Dives and Lazarus brings out the same sobering truth of the eternal irrevocability of the choice of destiny made 'in the body' (Lk. xvi). Note that the better MSS (followed by RV, RSV, NEB) omit verses 44 and 46 which are identical with verse 48.

vii. The salt of the earth (ix. 49, 50). Verse 49 is the bridge-verse: all is to be tested and purified by fire (cf. 1 Cor. iii. 13). The concept of a refiner's fire is found in the Old Testament (Mal. iii. 2) also. It appears, then, that the verb *halizomai*, 'to salt', suggests the further Sayings about *halas*, salt. Whether of course these Sayings were used at one and the same time by Christ, or simply thus strung together for ease of memory in Peter's teaching pattern, we cannot now say. The words of Papias, quoted in the Introduction, suggest the latter as the

---

[1] It is true that this passage is cast in a Semitic poetic form, like, e.g., much of the Sermon on the Mount: but Cranfield wisely warns us not on that account to explain it away, although it may well be that not all the details are to be understood in a literal sense.

scheme of construction of the Gospel, rather than the chronological pattern so congenial to the modern Western mind.

50. Any who have lived in Eastern lands may not be able to
give the chemical explanation, but they will know how salt is
adulterated, as sugar is, and many another commodity, by
unscrupulous local retailers. But to enquire what process the
adulterated substance goes through, and how it results in
tastelessness, is beside the point, although interesting. The real
point is that such *salt*, salt only in name, is useless: and if the
very thing designed to bring savour to other things is itself
savourless, what way out is left? So here are the very Christians themselves, quarrelling with one another. How can such
be 'sons of peace' (see Lk. x. 6 for this as a Christian term)?
Christians are to be the moral preservative of the world; they
are to savour life, to season it, and also to stop it becoming
utterly corrupt.

c. Departure from Galilee (x. 1-34)

i. Local setting (x. 1). Hitherto, in chapters i–ix, we have
had the Galilaean ministry of the Lord. Now, from x to xv, we
shall have the Judaean ministry. In between the two Luke has
a great mass of material, covering roughly chapters ix–xviii of
his Gospel, and usually called the Lucan Travel-Narrative, of
which the mission of the seventy disciples and various parables (e.g. the lost sheep, the lost coin, the lost son) are the best-
known features. Matthew has parallels to numerous isolated
instances from this section of Luke, but Mark, as a rule, omits
them: and therefore, as much of the material is of specific
Jewish interest, it is reasonable to see here Luke's (and, to
some extent, Matthew's) use of a Palestinian Jewish source,
different in nature, scope and purpose from the western, and
therefore largely Gentile, preaching of Peter, which underlies
Mark's Gospel (see the Introduction).

The *coasts of Judaea* (RSV, 'region') is very different from the
Galilaean highlands in the North,[1] and even Transjordan is

[1] As a glance at the excellent physical maps in the *Westminster Historical
Atlas to the Bible* will show.

quite distinct, in nature and population, from rugged Galilee, with its uncouth and strongly nationalistic peasantry. Galilee was ever the most stubborn centre of Jewish revolts, possibly because the 'Circuit of the Gentiles', as its full name means, was surrounded by bitterly anti-Jewish populations. (See Lk. xiii. 1 for reference to Galilaean turbulence at festival time; and even in the AD 70 revolt Galilee was a hard nut for the Romans to crack, as Josephus shows.)

ii. Christ's teaching on marriage (x. 2–12). What was in the mind of the Pharisees, in asking this question about divorce? Their answer to the Lord in verse 4 shows that they were already well conversant with the law upon the score, as was natural enough. From the wording of verse 2 (*tempting him*, or 'testing' Him), it was obviously a trick question, designed not to obtain guidance, but to make the Lord compromise Himself. If they could trap Him into some blunt pronouncement, then He could be accused of having contradicted the law of Moses and its interpretative tradition. The Sadducean question about the resurrection (Mk. xii. 23) and the Herodian question about tribute (Mk. xii. 15) are examples of similar smooth-tongued attempts to make the Lord incriminate Himself, all of which failed dismally (Mk. xii. 34). Seen in this light, the heavenly wisdom of the Lord's answer becomes more apparent. This is not therefore Christ's teaching about divorce given *in vacuo*, as it were, to His disciples, although it did become a teaching occasion; it was primarily an answer to a test question, where, whatever He said, some party would seize upon it. If we follow Matthew's addition (Mt. xix. 3) 'for every cause', or 'for any reason whatsoever', then it may have been that the Pharisees suspected this Galilaean Rabbi, whose disciples broke sabbath so lightly (Mk. ii. 23), of lax views on marriage, and thus asked Him this question with a view to obtaining another handle for attack. John viii. 1–11, the forgiveness of the adulteress, shows how easily the charge of laxity could be levelled against infinite Love. If this was their object, they were sorely disappointed: the amazed reaction of the Lord's own disciples in Matthew xix. 10 shows how His strong views surprised even them. These disciples regarded such a high standard of marital faithfulness as so impossible that they despaired of marriage: if the bond is so indissoluble, better not to marry at all, they said. This is an interesting commentary on the married life of the disciples, of which we know so little.

3. As usual, the Lord answered men first at their level, by taking them to Moses, which they doubtless expected: this at once removed suspicion of heterodoxy or laxity. The Lord ever made clear that His function was to give a new depth of meaning to the law, not to dismiss it as meaningless (Mt. v. 17).

4. Nevertheless, the Pharisaic group had already been forced to yield ground, if, as is probable, the change from *eneteilato, command* (3), the Lord's word, to *epetrepsen, suffered* or 'permitted', the word they use in reply, is deliberate. They themselves do not dare to say that divorce is 'enjoined' in the law, even if it be allowed, and they have here shown some consciousness of the weakening of their position.

5. Then comes a further blow: this law of Moses was not only a permissive, instead of a categorical imperative; it was positively concessive, because of the unresponsiveness of men's hearts to God. Better, in the days of the law (we might paraphrase), easy divorce than open adultery and defiance of all marriage codes. It was the lesser of two evils in Israel, but its very existence showed a fatal flaw in mankind. Perhaps polygamy in Old Testament times is another instance of the outworking of the same principle, as being something tolerated in early days, but never praised.

6. But now comes, as usual, the deeper theological level, where the Lord goes behind the law, which was at a particular point in time, to God's timeless purpose as shown in creation. In another context Paul is equally clear that Israel's law was but an 'inset' into God's purpose, and could say neither yea nor nay to God's covenant with Abraham (Gal. iii. 17), which expresses His eternal purpose of grace for man. The inviolable sanctity of the marriage tie is not of course here based on the mere words of Genesis, which are a description and commentary on God's act, but on the very initial act and purpose of God, in so creating two sexes.

7. The natural phenomenon of a man voluntarily leaving the strongest social group that he already knows (his own kith and kin) to form a new and closer link with a woman previously unknown to him would be inexplicable, were it not seen to be another instance of the outworking of this purpose of God. As so often, the Lord is appealing to the common sense of ordinary man against the intricacies of Pharisaic theologians (cf. Mk. vii. 15).

8. Marriage is thus the closest human bond; though, being human, it is at heart a physical bond, and its physical nature cannot survive death (Mk. xii. 25). So close a bond is it nevertheless, and so deep in the purpose of God, that Paul can use it as a picture of the deeper spiritual union that exists between the Lord and His Church (Eph. v. 32), or Christ and the individual believer (1 Cor. vi. 17).

9. This close bond was divine: it was the aim of creation, whereas any divorce is purely human. Nothing else needed to be said to the Pharisees. Did they go away crestfallen? Or were there perhaps some who went away thoughtfully (cf. Mk. xii. 32ff.)? We are not told. They cannot have been pleased by the Lord's continual habit of going behind the law of Moses to God's timeless mind, as expressed in creation and covenant of grace. At the last, this was to be the great stumbling-block, for law, temple, and the very concept of the chosen people stood or fell together.

10. But we, as the Lord's disciples, have more amplification and guidance, which was denied to these Pharisaic religious strategists. Matthew xix. 10 amplifies the blunt Marcan statement that *his disciples asked him again* by explaining that they regarded marriage as quite impossible on these terms if it was to be so insoluble. As most, if not all, of the disciples were married men (1 Cor. ix. 5), perhaps we have here an interesting sidelight into apostolic home life, of which Peter's mother-in-law is the only concrete evidence in Scripture (Mt. viii. 14). It is interesting that the Lord spoke His most solemn words on celibacy, as a state opposed to marriage, in this context (see Mt. xix. 11, 12). If marriage be avoided, it is not to avoid such difficulties, but simply because celibacy and not matrimony is God's vocation for some individuals. Paul's position in 1 Corinthians vii does not seem to be substantially different, though he is approaching the problem from a slightly different angle, that of Christian service. The fact that the disciples found it necessary to ask the Lord this question suggests that this was the first occasion upon which He had dealt with the subject, and also that His teaching conflicted, in some respects at least, with generally accepted views. He who had seemed lax proved to make unbelievably rigorous demands; for God's standards are ever absolute, and will not tolerate accommodation to human weakness.

11, 12. Peter's report of the Lord's preaching is, again, of a skeleton nature, and by no means as full as the account in Matthew. This question is one which would have interested and exercised the Palestinian Jewish-Christian Church, peculiarly concerned with the Christian interpretation of the law of Moses, and so Matthew preserves much more material.[1] But Peter's is the blunt teaching formula for a Graeco-Roman Gentile Church, where immorality was a grave danger (cf. the Council of Jerusalem, Acts xv. 29, which seems to be quite literal, and not just another metaphorical reference to idolatry). It was also a milieu in which divorce was perilously easy. The Lord, it is noteworthy, assumes as a matter of course that a divorced party will, in either case, remarry, and such remarriage is branded as plain adultery. Perhaps, even without considering the parallel account in Matthew, this is the link between Paul's words (1 Cor. vii. 15) and this Gospel passage. Separation of the two parties is seen as a last resort, but remarriage does not seem to be contemplated. It is true that some commentators see a deeper meaning in 'not under

---

[1] In view of the well-known difference between the Schools of Shammai and Hillel on this point, the question would have great interest to Pharisee and Palestinian Christian alike.

bondage' of the Pauline passage, and thus think it permits remarriage, but that would be in direct contradiction to I Corinthians vii. II, and it is a fundamental principle of biblical exegesis that no one scripture may be expounded in such a way that it is contradictory to another. The so-called 'Matthaean exception' ('saving for the cause of fornication', v. 32, and 'except it be for fornication', xix. 9, lit. 'except because of immorality'), whatever its exact meaning, has no certain reference to remarriage, although certain Protestant divines have so used it.

iii. 'Suffer little children' (x. 13–16).

We have already seen, in the acted parable of ix. 36, that God's kingdom is composed of those who share in the qualities of little children; we have also seen that it is in our acceptance of, and entry into, the kingdom that we exhibit these childlike qualities.[1] In Matthew xviii. 3, 4 we are told to 'turn' (RV) and become childlike, and here we are told to emulate the lowliness of a child; but more than lowliness seems to be meant in this context. The usual interpretation is to see a reference to the trustfulness of a childlike, guileless faith in one it loves.

Apart from this, we may see in the anecdote the faith and love of the parents who brought their children. Whether they were actually *paidia* (*young children*, 13; cf. Mt. xix. 13, 'little children') or *brephē* (Lk. xviii. 15, 'infants') is uncertain and indeed immaterial here. Unaffected, too, by questions of interpretation is the brusqueness of the doubtless wearied disciples. Perhaps they were jealously trying to guard their Lord from what they regarded as another unwarranted intrusion upon His time. The disciples made their Lord by no means easy of access (cf. the coming of the Greeks, Jn. xii. 21, 22). This is a lesson and warning to us today, lest we stand between men and Christ, instead of leading them to Him.

Unaffected, too, is the Lord's grief (14) at this action of His disciples, as betraying their utter failure to understand His

---

[1] Cranfield refuses to allow this, saying that this would turn faith into a 'work': to him, the weakness and helplessness of the child is the point.

loving purpose (cf. His words of rebuke to James and John, Lk. ix. 55).

iv. The rich young ruler (x. 17–31). Next comes the story of the rich young ruler, who must have made a deep impression on the apostolic circle, for his story is found in all three Synoptics, with individual additions, as the memories of the various narrators recalled different points. It is from Matthew (xix. 20) that we learn of his youth, while the Lucan source records that he was a 'ruler' (Lk. xviii. 18). His orthodox wealth, so different from the 'evangelical poverty' in which the Lord's disciples lived, deeply impressed the naïve Galilaeans, as did the splendours of Herod's Temple (Mk. xiii. 1). He thus probably belonged to a social group as yet scarcely touched by the gospel (later see Acts xiii. 1 for Manaen, foster-brother of Herod the Tetrarch, a Jewish noble, yet a Christian; and compare the nobleman of John ix. 46, where the word might be translated 'of royal blood'). From the very start, some women of this circle were numbered among Christ's followers (Lk. viii. 3), and used their wealth to further His cause.

17. The youth's eagerness is shown by his running and kneeling in the public highway, if the *gonupeteō* is to be taken literally, and not merely metaphorically, as is possible. His spiritual yearning is shown by the application of the adjective *Good* to Jesus, and also by his very desire for *eternal life*. His impatient brushing-aside of the Lord's half-smiling suggestion, that the way to life was by keeping the Commandments, shows a spiritual perception far in advance of that displayed by the average scribe (but cf. Lk. x. 29). But his spiritual insight was not equalled by strength of character, and so he went away sadly. In this case, the impediment was his wealth; sooner than give it up, he gave up Christ; herein he becomes a continual warning to us all.

18. The Lord, as usual, tries to draw from the man the full implications of his own words. He had come to the Messiah for help, but had he yet made that identification of Jesus with God that would enable him to recognize the true nature of the

Messiah, as Peter had in Matthew xvi. 16? For only such a divine Messiah could give to him that which confessedly by nature he could not have.

Matthew (xix. 16) makes the question slightly clearer with the words 'What good thing shall I do, that I may have eternal life?'; but the sense is not altered. In either case the main basic error was the same; he assumed that he, already the heir to possessions, could win by his own exertions the right to possess everlasting life. He saw salvation as something to be attained by works. Until he was ready to receive it by faith, he could not enjoy it (Eph. ii. 9).

Corresponding to this difference, Matthew xix. 17 has the Lord's question as 'Why question Me about the One who is good?' (a preferable translation to RV 'Why askest thou me concerning that which is good?', in view of what follows). But the main sense remains unaltered, and both could be loose Greek paraphrases of the same original Aramaic Saying.

19. The Lord sums up the 'categoric' commandments that deal with duty to man's neighbour; He does not as yet bring in the more searching question as to man's duty to God. If He can induce a sense of inadequacy on this lower level, then so much the better. It was as if the Lord had said, in answer to the youngster's eager question of 'What shall I do . . .?' 'Do! if that is to be the way, then you must do all that the Law commands.' Paul had discovered the futility of striving to win life by keeping the law (Rom. vii. 24), but had this young man as yet? If 'ruler' (Lk. xviii. 18) is to be taken as a member of the Sanhedrin, the religious council of Israel, then his position becomes even more like that of Saul of Tarsus, the brilliant young theological student, doubtless from a wealthy merchant home.

20. His spiritual experience had not been as deep as that of Paul. He spoke only of the outward observances of the law, and not of the inward breach (which the Lord saw as equally important, Mt. v. 28), but he doubtless spoke in all good conscience when he said he had kept them all. So Paul before the Sanhedrin (Acts xxiii. 1) could make the same claim for his outward behaviour, whatever the inner spiritual torment of an awakened conscience (Rom. vii). Yet at least, even if outwardly self-satisfied, he realized that he still lacked something (as Mt. xix. 20 makes explicit). Otherwise why did he come at all?

21. What were the lovable qualities which the Lord saw in this young man? It is clear from the *emblepsas autō* (*beholding him*, lit. 'gazing at him') that He saw something attractive at that moment in him. Was it his quick spontaneity and earnestness, the very qualities[1] that seem to appear in single-minded David, the man after God's own heart (Acts xiii. 22)? John was the beloved disciple (Jn. xiii. 23) and he certainly shared this warmheartedness in early years. John's title of 'thunder and lightning' shared with his brother James (see Mk. iii. 17) was not given for nothing, as Luke ix. 54 shows. Peter, too, was always one of the three; and this above all was his characteristic, even to excess. But not even for one whom He loved, and whose discipleship He desired, would the Lord lower the demands of discipleship to make an easy convert.

The Lord plays on the youth's words (to judge from a comparison of Matthew's account with Mark's) in a way hard to reproduce in English. 'In what am I lagging behind?' 'One thing keeps you lagging behind . . .', playing on the verb *hustereō*. There is a probe at a deeper level, too, for here was a young man who had never lacked anything (doubtless this was why he had never been tempted to kill or rob, as a poor man might, Pr. xxx. 9), but the Lord was seeking to bring home to him that the 'poor rich man' had a great unseen need (cf. Rev. iii. 17).

This demand for physical renunciation of earthly wealth and comfort is made potentially of all of us, and may be made literally of some. Christ demands of us an initial renunciation of all, when we follow Him (Lk. xiv. 33). What He then hands

---

[1] Cranfield again will have none of this: to him, the biblical *agapaō* is to display self-giving love, irrespective of the worthiness or unworthiness of the object. But (a) while this is true of Christ, it does not seem capable of linguistic proof in later Greek. See Arndt and Gingrich; (b) it would evacuate the previous clause of meaning.

back to us is completely at His disposal; henceforth, we but hold it as stewards for Him; it is His to give or withhold at will (Jb. i. 21).

22. Here is the only man in the whole of the New Testament of whom it is said that he went away *sad* from the presence of Christ, though many were sad when they came (cf. the 'sour-faced', *skuthrōpoi*, disciples on the Emmaus Road, Lk. xxiv. 17). He had been weighed in the balances, and found wanting (cf. Dn. v. 27). He could not, by definition, be a disciple of Christ (Lk. xiv. 33), for this demanded a total committal, which he was not, as yet, ready to give. His reaction shows only too clearly that the Lord had laid His finger on the spot; his wealth was indeed the thing that was holding him back from the kingdom of God.

23. It is well to remember, lest we congratulate ourselves on not being rich, and thus as not coming within the scope of this Saying, that a literal translation would run 'How hard it is for those who have things .. . .'. Television, record player, projector—these are some of the 'things' that may occupy first place in the life of men today, in our civilization of expensive gadgets and 'things' (*chrēmata* to the New Testament). One is tempted to wonder how much of the original sense of *duskolōs*, (*hardly*, lit. 'with difficulty') is intended by the Evangelist here; how unsatisfied, with how ill a grace, do rich men enter the kingdom, seeing that for them the cost is so great! This linguistic possibility is heightened by the fact that just above we have a reference to the sorrow of the rich youth, expressed by his fallen countenance. But one who finds the pearl of great price joyfully sells all that he has, to buy it (Mt. xiii. 46). Since each must give all that he has to follow Christ, who of us is to say which of us gives up most?

24. The disciples were thunderstruck; they had assumed that just as all other things were easier for the rich ('those with advantages', as we tactfully say nowadays), so entry into the kingdom must also be easier, whether their riches be intellect, personality, or other talents apart from money. This is the ordinary viewpoint of 'natural religion', doubtless shared by the worldly Jewish Church of the day. Apparently it was also shared by the Lord's disciples, as they looked wonderingly at the receding figure of this young man, so blessed with advantages, and ideal for the kingdom in so many external ways. But Christianity makes all men equal; none starts with the balance loaded in his favour when it comes to entry into the kingdom of God.

But there is a truth at a deeper level, which must have crossed the minds of some at least of the disciples; all of us are 'rich' in something—who then *can* be saved? This is the true puzzle voiced wonderingly in verse 26; if it is hard for the rich, then it is hard for all.

Whether or not the Lord actually said the full *how hard is it for them that trust in riches*, lit. 'those who are leaning on their wealth' (the MSS are fairly equally divided), this is obviously the meaning. But the shorter textual reading 'How hard it is to enter the kingdom' makes equally good sense, for it at once removes the 'rich men' from being in a class by themselves, and shows that entry is hard for them, not because they are rich, but because they are mortal men. This is a great theological truth, but perhaps the generalization is not so suitable here; for verse 25, immediately following, resumes the 'special' subject of the rich man, and the 'general' does not reappear till verse 26 and after. The fuller reading, then, seems preferable in verse 24.

25. It is tempting to read the homophonous—in the days of *koinē* Greek, that is—*kamīlos*, 'rope', for *kamēlos*, *camel*, but there is no good early evidence for what may just be a popular misspelling of the same word. Likewise, it makes somewhat banal a palpable folk-proverb of impossibility; compare the juxtaposition of 'gnat' and 'camel' in Matthew xxiii. 24, for the same connotation of ungainly bulk. The camel was by now the largest animal found in Palestine.[1] Elephants were long ex-

---

[1] True, 'elephant' is humorously used with the same nuance in Strack-Billerbeck's rabbinic saying, quoted by Cranfield; but elephants, known only by hearsay, had no place in Jewish folk-proverb, while the camel had, exactly as in Arabic.

tinct, even in the bend of the Euphrates, and the hippopotamus rare, if not extinct, in the sub-tropical Jordan valley. Even the great wild ox of Bashan was now but a memory. In spite of its beautiful imagery, there does not seem to be good early evidence for the view that the *eye of a needle* is a postern-gate in the city wall, with a consequent need for the camel to kneel and be unloaded if he is to be pushed through. It is better to regard this forced explanation as a piece of Christian 'midrash' rather than exegesis, and see the metaphor as one of sheer impossibility. May not the choice of the camel, worst-tempered of all beasts, be suggested by the *duskolōs* (23, 'hardly') above, and the 'sadness' of the rich young ruler?

26. The indignant *Kai* (lit. 'and') at the beginning of the disciples' question almost defies translation; it implies exasperation and indignation rather than despair—not by any means the first time that the Lord's seeming lack of 'realism' drew this response from His impatient disciples.

27. The answer is another divine paradox. Hard? no—it is quite impossible; but God is God of the impossible, and so the impossible can be. He creates from nothing (Gn. i. 1; 1 Cor. i. 28). Christ makes no concessions to our stumbling faith; instead, He warns of even greater stumbling-blocks ahead (cf. Jn. iii. 12, in the interview with Nicodemus). To the last, we fail to realize how great a stumbling-block to natural man is God's way of dealing with him, and that this is no accident, but must of necessity be so (1 Cor. i. 23).

28. Is Peter slightly jealous of all the attention paid to the young man: jealous, it may be, not so much for himself alone as for the whole band? Faced with one from another social group, there has been an instinctive closing of the disciples' ranks; they cannot forget those miserable little nets they left by Galilee. It is a psychological fact that those who have left least are the most conscious of their sacrifice (contrast the recklessness of true love, Lk. vii. 38). Yet Peter was not wrong in what he said. Every man who follows Christ makes the same sacrifice, for every man must give all that he has, and the Lord does not reckon the sacrifice as great or small by the amount

given, but by the amount withheld for ourselves. This is the
lesson not only of the widow's mite (xii. 42), but also of
Ananias and Sapphira (Acts v. 3). Hence the Lord does not
rebuke Peter, for what Peter says is true; in the words of the
Evangelist, at the call of Christ they had indeed 'left everything and followed him' (cf. Lk. v. 11). It may be that some
among the apostolic band, awed by the wealth of the young
man and his refusal to give all he had as the price of Christ (cf.
Mt. xiii. 46), were ruefully rethinking their own initial sacrifice
and sorely needed this reassurance that the Lord saw and
valued. This Saying must have left a deep impression on
Peter's memory, reproduced as it was in his preaching. In true
humility he was always ready to preserve and retell anec-
dotes where he himself appeared in an unfavourable light.

29. Here it is Mark who has the fuller text with *for my sake,
and the gospel's,* lit. 'because of me, and because of the good
news'; he thus makes the goal clearer. The disciple makes such
a sacrifice for his Lord, and that the gospel of his Lord may be
spread. So Paul (1 Cor. ix. 23) can almost personify the
gospel.

30. To every Christian worker this verse comes as a ring of
triumph, but to none more than the missionary, who finds
countless ties of love in the land of his Lord's choice to take the
place of those temporarily sundered in his homeland. But there
is always the gentle hint contained in the *with persecutions,* to
remind us that the cross is not merely an initial burden, but a
constant one ('each day', see Lk. ix. 23). Finally, compensa-
tions though there are in this life, yet fundamentally the
Christian's hope is other-worldly (cf. 1 Cor. xv. 19).

31. This may be a quiet word of reassurance to the disciples
that God does not see as men do; the young man might be a
ruler in this world, but the disciples who had stayed faithfully
by the Lord, in His time of testing (Lk. xxii. 28), would be
'rulers' in the world to come. The widow with her mite gave
more than any rich man (Mk. xii. 43); the disciples, with their
nets, had left all their livelihood, too.

v. Third passion-prediction (x. 32-34). Now comes the third passion-prediction—or the fourth,[1] if we take into account the Lord's words to the three on the road down from the mount of transfiguration. This is the fullest warning yet given of all that was to come; but it is clear, both from subsequent events in Mark, and the explicit statement of Luke xviii. 34, that the disciples still failed to understand. Why did they fail to understand such bold statements? Perhaps because of the reference to the resurrection; if they did not take that literally, then there was no clue to the other enigmas. The Bible is clear that the resurrection is *sui generis*—that, in fact, the resurrection is to be understood only in the light of the resurrection.

32. What was it in the acts or attitude of Christ that filled them with wonder and fear?[2] It cannot have been this going to a hostile Jerusalem, for this He had done before; nor was it that He walked in front of His disciples, for so, by definition, a rabbi should do (though on less momentous occasions He might send them before His face, cf. Lk. x. 1). It is unlikely that it was a memory of the two former passion-predictions, for these the apostles had failed to understand and utterly failed to remember, so that the Lord judged another and sterner reminder necessary here. It must have been either a vague sense of foreboding, or else something in the Lord's face and manner, that awed the noisy quarrelsome band. Compare 'he stedfastly set his face to go to Jerusalem' (Lk. ix. 51), which seems a reminiscence of 'therefore have I set my face like a flint' in Isaiah l. 7. It is certainly a Semitism in any case, and, as such, has a ring of the Old Testament prophet.

33. The bitterest sting of all is not even the rejection of her Messiah by Israel, but that Israel, to reject Him, will betray her Messiah *to the Gentiles*, the outsiders. This is probably the full force of *anomos* in Acts ii. 23; the Jews were guilty of the

---

[1] See comment on ix. 31 above.
[2] Cranfield tries to distinguish between two groups—the *wondering* Twelve and the *fearful* others: but this distinction seems untenable.

death of Christ, but they caused it by the hands of those who were 'wicked', or 'without the law'.

34. Here Peter's memory is more vivid than that of Matthew's Jerusalem source, and small wonder; the patient suffering of his Lord had left an indelible impression upon the one who had denied Him (cf. 1 Pet. ii. 23). As Peter saw the horseplay and spitting and flogging, each detail of the passion-prediction must have recalled itself to his mind. Strange that the Lord's last clause, *and the third day he shall rise again,* was utterly forgotten in the black days between death and resurrection—unless indeed the plaintive words of the disciples on the Emmaus Road contain a bitter memory of what they may have regarded as an unfulfilled, albeit uncomprehended, promise (Lk. xxiv. 21).

d. The sons of Zebedee (x. 35–45)

But although the disciples may have failed to understand the passion-prediction, yet at least something in the Lord's manner warned them that the hour of the establishment of His kingdom was near; and so each disciple is quick to strike for his own hand. Ironically enough, although the request of the 'Thunderers' was wrong-headed, yet at least it denoted faith in Christ's ability to establish His kingdom. So the Lord dealt gently with them, more gently than the ten would have dealt, as we see from verse 41 below. The petty selfishness of His followers at a time like this, when His mind was full of all that lay ahead at Jerusalem, must have cut Him to the quick; but compare their sleep in the Garden of Gethsemane (xiv. 37). Are we, today, blind also?

35. They sought a monarch's boon, a sort of 'blank cheque' upon His favour. This was the way of kings; it befitted their majesty; it is not by accident that Latin *generosus*, 'highborn', has come to mean 'generous', i.e. open-handed, in modern English. Nevertheless a wise king would put a top limit on such blank cheques; witness Herod's 'unto the half of my kingdom' to the dancing girl (vi. 23). Thus, no doubt, they would have interpreted the Lord's question in reply; they would have seen it as natural caution, not spiritual insight. Matthew (xx. 20) adds the interesting point that it was Zebedee's wife who was behind this request. Was it from a masterful woman that James and John took their fiery nature? Old Zebedee quietly fishing by the Sea of Galilee, alone with the hired servants (i. 20), may well have been but a cipher in the home. Certainly we hear no more of him, while the wording in Matthew suggests that his wife was one of the circle that ministered to the Lord (cf. Lk. viii. 3). The Shunammite of 2 Kings iv seems another woman of this type; and one wonders also about Deborah's husband (Jdg. iv. 4).

36. The Lord, as usual, allows men to display their own spiritual depth or shallowness by disclosing their aims; for it is by his aims rather than by his achievements that a man stands judged. In verse 38 below, the Lord will gently show that if they realized the true meaning of their request, they might have refrained from making it. (Cf. 'If thou knewest the gift of God, and who it is . . .', Jn. iv. 10.) At times this lack of knowledge is pure tragedy, as in the Lord's weeping over Jerusalem (Lk. xix. 42, 'If thou hadst known').

37. It was not a mere desire to be near their Lord at the moment of triumph that moved them to this request; they wished for themselves the post of Grand Vizier in the new kingdom. It was ambition, not loyalty, that moved such a request; and for John, at least, it must have seemed a natural extension of his position as 'beloved disciple' (cf. Jn. xix. 26). James and John were, after all, not only of the Twelve, but of the three (ix. 2, etc.). Had not King David had his three (2 Sa. xxiii)? They were also known to the high priest (Jn. xviii. 15), so doubtless 'well connected'.

38. There was a double irony in their request, in that those on the right and left of the Lord at the great moment of His triumph were two crucified thieves (xv. 27), making plain in vivid parable that closeness to Him meant sharing in His *cup* and in His *baptism.* In that sense, the day would come, whether in Jerusalem or on Patmos, that the brothers would be on Christ's left and right hand. *Cup* has been an Old Testament symbol for suffering, especially one for enduring the wrath of God, as well as for joy (contrast Is. li. 17 with Ps. xxiii. 5). The Lord explicitly uses it in the first sense in the Garden of Gethsemane (xiv. 36). *Baptism* is again an Old Testament picture of one undergoing the wrath of God (see Ps. lxix. 15), although, of course, in later Judaism it took on other meanings of a purificatory nature (Mk. vii. 4). The Lord used it in the first sense in Luke xii. 50, and although the New Testament concept of Christian baptism is rich and many-sided, it is still nevertheless 'into Christ's death' (Rom. vi. 3). So both baptism and the Lord's Supper remind us forcibly, by their symbolism, of the cost of following Christ; the servant must be like his Master (Mt. x. 25).

39. Whether their brief reply *We can* (one word in Greek) represents a thoughtless braggart spirit, or the quiet answer of a pair suddenly sobered, we have no means of telling. But it brings the equally quiet assurance from the Lord that this price they will in any case pay, for this is not the price of Christian greatness but the price of following Christ at all. He who follows Christ cannot haggle at terms, for there are no two levels of Christian discipleship.

40. This is a reminder that even the Son is in loving subjection to His Father; it is not even for Christ to dispense honours at His will but only at the Father's will. So, too, the last hour is hidden deep in the counsel of God (xiii. 32); and yet this is not 'Subordinationism', for it is voluntary.

41. *The ten*, in turn, betrayed their spiritual shallowness by being indignant at the spiritual shallowness of the two, who had thus skilfully stolen a march on them. They were 'righteously indignant', as we say, thus condemning ourselves, too. The verb *aganakteō* is the same as was used (x. 14) of the Lord's reaction to the disciples when they summarily dismissed the mothers of Jerusalem. A man's character is shown by the things that provoke his strongest reactions; and so the Lord justly rebukes both the two and the ten at once, by showing to them their common ignorance of the very nature of Christian leadership. The Lord shows that all such leadership is humble service, for it takes its colour from His example, who is, above all, the suffering Servant. Thus closeness to Him is not something at which to grasp thoughtlessly; while Christian position is only a prize to be grasped at by those ignorant of its nature and cost (see Phil. ii. 6).

42–44. 'Lord it over them' is a good philological translation of the Greek *katakurieuō, exercise lordship over them.* But for the Christian, such an attitude becomes a contradiction in terms, for his understanding of such a verb is derived from the meaning to him of *Kurios*, 'Lord', the underlying noun, uniquely a title of Christ.[1] It is the whole concept of the nature of lordship that has changed with the stooping of the Christ, who is Lord of all. The main argument is the same as that of ix. 35 above; but the clinching word comes in verse 45.

45. This is an argument *qal w'chōmer*—as the rabbis said—from major to minor premise. Even Christ came not to enjoy the service of others, but to accept a lowly Servant's place for Himself, and *to give his life a ransom for many.* This last saying is pregnant with meaning; the Son of man concept, found in the Psalms, Ezekiel and Daniel, is linked with the Servant concept of Isaiah and both are here linked with the great ransom concept of Old Testament days (Ps. xlix. 7). Even the *for many* is a memory of Isaiah liii. 11, 12. The New Testament gathers into one, as it were, all these strands of Old Testament thought, and uses all in combination to explain the full meaning of Messiahship. This ransom-price metaphor was one greatly beloved by the early Church, and although we may not like to follow them too far into unprofitable speculations (such as the question as to whom the price was paid), it remains a strong statement of the purpose and efficacy of the atonement, and of its cost to God (cf. 1 Pet. i. 18, 19). Of course, no one line of explanation is in itself exhaustive, nor can any one line do justice to all the biblical evidence.

[1] See the instructive article in Arndt and Gingrich, *sub voc.*

e. Blind Bartimaeus (x. 46–52)

46. *Bartimaeus* is an eternal picture of the man in need, who fights his way to Christ, though all Christ's disciples try to turn him aside (cf. their attitude to the mothers of Jerusalem, Lk. xviii. 15; the Greeks at the festival, where consent is grudging, Jn. xii. 22; the man casting out devils, Mk. ix. 38). In spite of all, Bartimaeus had the grace of perseverance—a reminder in Christian work that we do not well to be over-anxious, however great our yearning over souls. 'All that the Father giveth me shall come to me' is a great biblical truth (Jn. vi. 37).

47, 48. There is a world of insight in the use of the one word *heard* of the blind man; more he could not do, but the ears of the blind are necessarily quick. Only the Petrine preaching has preserved the name of the blind man—an interesting eye-witness touch.

Jesus of Nazareth is interesting as contemporary evidence for the terminology used to describe Christ; compare 'the carpenter's son' (Mt. xiii. 55), or even 'Joseph's son' (Lk. iv. 22). These were, no doubt, later discarded by the Church as untrue and misleading, though the old Syriac retains traces, which need not be heretical.

Son of David is not so much a name as a messianic title[1] (cf. for the Old Testament, Je. xxxiii. 17; and the cry of the multitudes, Mt. xxi. 9). The meaning of this title was in dispute between the Lord and the Pharisees (xii. 35). But at least Bartimaeus, as a Jew, had a right to appeal to the Son of David, whereas the Syrophoenician, and therefore Gentile, woman (Mt. xv. 22) had no such right, and, as such, was gently rebuked by the Lord. Further, this blind man begs for pity; he throws himself upon the Lord's mercy.

49. The disciple that impedes the way to his Master is a contradiction in terms; but the disciple is true to his own inward nature and calling when he says, as here, to the soul in

---

[1] This seems abundantly clear, in spite of arguments by modern editors that it may be only a polite form of address to one of Davidic descent: but to this 'son (or daughter) of Abraham' would be the only near-parallel.

need: 'Courage, up you get, He is calling you.' When Andrew tells the Lord of the desire of the Greeks to see Him (Jn. xii. 22) he is fulfilling a similar task.

50. Everything suggests expectant faith: the impeding garment is tossed aside, he bounds to his feet. There is a joyous extravagance and recklessness of response, when the soul becomes suddenly responsive to the call of Christ; so the woman of Samaria forgot her waterpot as she ran (Jn. iv. 28).

51. Here is a man who knows what he wants; no wavering in prayer for him (Jas. i. 6). The title he uses for Jesus, 'Rabboni' (RV), is one of even greater respect, if anything, than the common 'Rabbi', 'great one', i.e. 'teacher'.

52. It was the man's faith, evidenced by his persistence, that had saved him; and so James ii. 14 and Romans iv. 16 alike find fulfilment in him. The onomatopeia of the Greek phrase *hē pistis sou sesōken se, thy faith hath made thee whole*, has often been noticed. It probably dates only from the Western preaching form, with its continuous repetition, rather than the original Saying, which was almost certainly in Aramaic; if Bartimaeus was Jew enough to call Jesus 'Son of David', he was unlikely to converse with Him in Greek.

V. THE ZEAL OF THINE HOUSE: THE JERUSALEM MINISTRY (xi. 1–xiii. 37)

a. Entry into Jerusalem (xi. 1–14)

i. The entry (xi. 1–10). Now with chapters xi and xii come the Jerusalem days. Mark gives a graphic account of the triumphal entry, the deep impression of which upon the apostolic band may be seen by its recording in all three Synoptics, as well as in John xii. 12–19. The triumphal entry of the Messiah into His capital city was a fit fulfilment of many an Old Testament prophecy; here at least was nothing to stumble the disciples. This mission of the two disciples (was it Peter and John?) was a 'Faith Mission', for they went forth in simple obedience to their Lord's word, and in complete dependence upon Him (cf. Lk. v. 5). It was, further, like all such missions, 'of faith unto faith' (see Rom. i. 17), for naturally their faith for the future would be immeasurably strengthened by finding that every detail was as the Lord had said. The Lord, be it noted, ever sent His disciples out in fellowship, even if it be only 'by two and two' (vi. 7). The solitary Christian is never a biblical ideal; it was left to later Christian ages to introduce the concept of the *monachos*, the 'on-his-own', giving 'monk' in modern English, and the *erēmitēs*, the 'hermit', literally meaning 'living in the wild', where no other men live.

2–5. This is but one instance out of many where the Lord clearly shows supernatural knowledge of what will afterwards befall; cf. His words to the two disciples who go to make ready the Passover (xiv. 13). Admittedly, in both cases, the individual to whom the disciples were sent must have been friend or follower of the Lord, or the words, put by Him into the mouth of His disciple, would have fallen upon deaf ears. But the actual contingency described in either case required divine foreknowledge, of the type so often vouchsafed to prophets of Old Testament days (cf. Samuel's detailed predictions to the young Saul in 1 Sa. x).

6. Here is a good instance of the power committed to the disciple of lovingly 'commandeering' in his Master's name[1] and at his Master's bidding. At His word, we may do as Elijah did for Elisha, and claim another for the Lord's service (1 Ki. xix. 19, 20). The sole justifying principle needed is that the Lord needs such a one (verse 3). Compared with the claim that the Lord makes, the rights of all those who stand in the position of the 'owner' in the text shrink into insignificance; not even father and mother have the right to withhold one whom God calls.

7, 8. The first few pieces of clothing laid on the donkey's

[1] This is assuming that *ho Kurios* (3) refers directly to Christ (or at least to God) and that we are therefore justified in translating 'The Lord needs it'. To take, with Taylor, quoted by Cranfield, as 'Its owner needs it' seems banal.

back were no doubt strictly utilitarian, to serve as a rough
saddle, but those hurled recklessly on the road, like the leafy
branches, were purely honorific. So a Jewish conqueror should
be greeted, on his triumphal ride into his capital. All had a
share, however small, in the sacrifice associated with such a
ride; for if one man gave the donkey, yet others sacrificed
clothing; and, on this day at least, none spoke of such sacrifices
as being waste. Love's extravagance in self-giving ever goes
unrebuked by God, though not always by men (xiv. 4). Sir
Walter Raleigh would have understood those Jews, poles
apart though the Elizabethan was in all other ways.

9, 10. The song of the pilgrim throngs (not necessarily the
same as the Jerusalem mob that howled for the blood of
Christ within a few short days, Lk. xxiii. 21) made the meaning
of this identification clearer. To them Jesus was 'the Coming
One' (cf. John the Baptist's wording, Mt. xi. 3), the expected
King of David's line, about to establish His earthly kingdom
there and then. This was still an expectation of the disciples
even after the resurrection (see Acts i. 6). If the word *hōsanna*
was more than a pious liturgical exclamation at that time (cf.
'amen', 'hallelujah', for similar words), then it was a cry to
this Davidic King, pleading for immediate salvation: 'save,
we beg.'

That certain of the Pharisees took grave exception to the
theological implications of such an attribution is clear from
Luke xix. 39. The Lord's refusal to silence His disciples was a
tacit acceptance of the position accorded to Him; and this the
Pharisees must surely have seen. Matthew xxi. 14–16, in a
slightly different context, betrays their growing irritation
against Him, for not only refusing to silence the childish voices
in the Temple, but for gravely accepting the homage that they
gave. In the Lucan context, He goes further, and tells the
Pharisees that to silence such homage would be a crime
against which dumb nature would protest audibly (Lk.
xix. 40).

ii. The return to Bethany (xi. 11). Mark alone makes clear
that there was a preliminary inspection of the Temple on the

evening of arrival in Jerusalem, but that, probably owing to the lateness of the hour, nothing was done until the next day. This, again, is a small piece of factual information, doubtless derived from the Petrine reminiscences, which was lost in the other traditions, being overshadowed by the magnitude of the actual cleansing of the Temple. It also gives one of the little touches of the Lord's domestic life; He did not sleep in Jerusalem, crowded for the festival and full of His enemies, but at the welcoming home of Bethany[1] (presumably that of Mary and Martha, Jn. xi. 1). Even Bethany, with all the other surrounding 'outer suburbs', was probably crowded with pilgrims over festival time, so that the presence of the Lord and the Twelve would not arouse particular comment.

iii. Cursing the fig tree (xi. 12–14). Were the resources of the Bethany household somewhat strained by this hungry band of healthy Galilaean fishermen and peasants? To be hungry at such an hour in the morning (Mt. xxi. 18) was unusual. Unless we realize that this was an acted parable of Israel, we shall be puzzled by all sorts of irrelevant questions. The tree gave outward promise of fruit but disappointed the Lord; so its punishment was to remain eternally fruitless—in a sense this was but a perpetuation of its present condition. The fig tree and the vine are two time-honoured symbols of Israel (cf. xii. 1–12 for the vine), to whom God's Son had now come, looking for fruit and finding none, though there was outward religious profession and promise. Henceforth Israel was to be blasted and fruitless; and the physical judgment of AD 70 was but an outward token of this. So in Luke xix. 41–44, which is roughly a parallel passage, we have in this context the prediction of judgment on Jerusalem; and immediately below the Marcan fig tree passage, in verses 15–19, there comes the acted parable of the cleansing of the Temple. God came to His Temple looking for fruit and found none; and so it was inevitable that the predictions of Mark xiii. 1, 2 be made: that, of the Temple in all its splendour, not one stone would be left standing upon

[1] Cranfield points out that this does not contradict Luke xxi. 37, for Bethany could be regarded as lying on the slopes of the Mount of Olives; see Grollenberg, p. 115.

another. Like tree, like temple, like nation; the parallel is exact. But Paul warns us that all this is to make us to tremble and search our own hearts (Rom. xi. 21), lest God have cause to do so to us as well.

The time of figs was not yet (13). As it stands, the Greek simply says 'It was not the right season for figs', and it is unfair to translate '*its* season for figs', to avoid a difficulty. But it is fair to say that presumably the Lord was looking for the small early ripe figs, that ripen with the leaves, before the main crop.

The Greek particle *ara* suggests that the finding of figs was an unlikely possibility contemplated by the Lord; He was thus in no sense surprised by the tree's unfruitfulness, as He would have been had it been the time of the regular fig crop.

b. The cleansing of the Temple (xi. 15–19)

In a context like this, it is important to notice how different were the aspects that angered the Pharisees and priests from those that angered Christ. Both had a high concept of the nature of the Temple; but their concepts were fundamentally different. The Pharisees had been shocked beyond measure by the blasphemy of the children shouting in the Temple (Mt. xxi. 15), but were not perturbed by the uproar of the merchants and the money-changers. After all, they may have reasoned, these were for the furtherance and convenience of the cere-monial worship, that outward religious form which meant everything to them. There is plenty of early evidence to sug-gest that the priests benefited financially by this traffic; the high priest seems to have owned shops. They were doubtless shocked by the Lord's prediction of ruin to the holy place (xiii. 2), and certainly scandalized by His prediction, so they thought, of raising it again in three days (Jn. ii. 19). But for Him, the supreme blasphemy was that this place, which was to have been in God's purpose a place of prayer for Gentiles of every nation, and not merely a Jewish national sanctuary, should have become a business-house (Jn. ii. 16)—and dis-honest business at that (Mk. xi. 17). Those familiar with Eastern markets can easily imagine all the petty cheating and haggling, in the very shadow of the Shekinah. The steps and courtyard of any Chinese temple are the same today, a patent contradiction to the high moral ideals flaunted abroad on the painted tablets above.

15, 16. The violence with which the Lord dealt with these apparently harmless retailers and financiers left an abiding impression not only on the Pharisees, but also upon His disciples; to them the 'wrath of the Lamb' was a new experience (Rev. vi. 16). John ii. 17 gives the only explanation to which the wondering disciples could come; they found it, as usual, in terms of the Old Testament: He was jealous for the honour of God's house, for therein God's very name was involved.

The Lord's attitude to the Temple is an interesting study; at the age of twelve He treats it as a place of instruction (Lk. ii. 46). He may even have described it 'my Father's house' (Lk. ii. 49), though 'my Father's business' is a safer translation of the Greek. In the present context it is described as a *house of prayer* (17), as any synagogue might be described (see Acts xvi. 13, where the name *proseuchē*, 'prayer-place', is used, not even *sunagōgē*). In the parable of the publican and sinner (Lk. xviii. 10) it is again a place of prayer, though some have seen a subtle reference to the temple sacrifices in the word used by the publican, *hilasthēti* ('be merciful' or 'propitiated', Lk. xviii. 13). From the Saying forbidding oaths (Mt. xxiii. 16ff.) it is clear that heaven, earth or Jerusalem only gained their sanctity to Christ by virtue of their relationship to God's plan and purpose, whether in creation (as heaven and earth) or revelation (as Jerusalem). So the Lord's view of the Temple was not primarily as a place of sacrifice, still less as a static dwelling-place, but a place of prayer and teaching and an outward reflection to mankind of God's very nature. Christ neither despised nor minimized the Temple, as we can see from the wrath that its profanation aroused within Him. It is in the light of this unexpected side of His character that we can see how to some He appeared as 'Elijah redivivus' (vi. 15).

It is not thus strange that this concept of the Temple is exactly that of the early disciples in Acts; they go to the Temple at what is described as the 'hour of prayer' (Acts iii. 1), though it is actually the hour of the evening sacrifice. The colonnades of the Temple are where the rabbis of the new 'sect' sit expounding their 'Way' (Acts iii. 11), until expelled by the parent body of Judaism. This concept is, indeed, far closer to that of the synagogue than that of the Temple proper; for synagogues were, by definition, places for prayer (Acts xvi. 13), and instruction (Acts xiii. 15). The modern Ashkenazi Jew will say *Schul* ('school') for synagogue in Yiddish, without any consciousness of how his speech betrays his theological position. Seeing that, while the Temple gave a picture of the Church universal, the synagogue was almost certainly the pattern upon which the local church was organized, this point has vast theological implications.[1]

17. The Greek verb *edidasken, taught* (lit. 'was teaching'), implies more a deliberate teaching programme than a casual pronouncement, uttered in the heat of anger, amid the wreck of the temple stalls. This Galilaean Rabbi is giving scriptural justification for His action, as any rabbi would. The Scripture is Isaiah lvi. 7, telling how Gentile proselytes are to be welcomed to the Temple. It is noteworthy that the Lord quotes only the clause about prayer, and omits that about sacrifice, for He Himself was to be the sacrifice that would unite Jew and Gentile in one (Jn. xi. 51, 52). With this is joined Jeremiah vii. 11, a verse which comes in the midst of a searing indictment of the Jews of Jeremiah's day, whose lives were in utter contradiction to the outward worship which they offered. The quotation would gain force from the fact that Jeremiah, too, had preached it in the Temple of his day, as the Lord did. To the Jews of Jeremiah's day it came in the midst of the warning about Shiloh, and the prophecy that, as God had abandoned Shiloh, so He would abandon Jerusalem (Je. vii. 14). This helps in turn to understand how some saw the Lord as 'Jeremiah redivivus' (Mt. xvi. 14), and indeed His tears over Jerusalem must have lent further colour to this belief (Lk. xix. 41).

[1] For a detailed examination of the whole question, see the present writer's *The New Temple*, Tyndale Press, 1951.

18. Small wonder that the chief priests and scribes now began to plot His death; His meaning was only too plain (cf. Lk. xx. 16) and they *feared him*. The amazement of the crowds of pilgrims as they listened to His teaching was not without terror, too, to judge from the *exeplēsseto*, *was astonished*. Not since the days before the fall of the first Temple had they heard such explicit words of doom; one wonders how many of them lived to see the great stones topple over, one by one, into the fire in AD 70. Few of the generation who heard the Lord preach would outlive that carnage, except the infant Church, which took its Lord's advice and fled to Pella in Transjordan (xiii. 14).

19. It would scarcely have been safe for Him to have spent the night in the city now, with so many foes actively plotting His death; but quiet Bethany was safe, and so thither He went.

c. Exhortation and debate (xi. 20–xii. 44)

i. Meaning of the withered fig tree (xi. 20–26). Christ does not explain why He cursed the barren fig tree; that we must infer from the passage above (verses 12–14). Instead He uses it as an illustration of the effectual nature of prayer. Only the Marcan account records that it was *Peter* who observed and related the fact; this is a natural point in a Petrine source.

The disciples did not, as some might today, find any moral problem in the cursing of the fig tree; for if this is seen as an acted parable with reference to Israel, it drops into place at once. Their remark was amazement that the Lord's cursing was so effectual (Mark) and immediate (Mt. xxi. 20). Blessing (Mt. v. 3ff.) and cursing might both come fittingly from the lips of the Lord, but not from ours (Jas. iii. 10). Our cursing would be light and unthinking; His was of the nature of a solemn sentence. Yet in James v it is noteworthy that the two chosen illustrations of the efficacy of earnest prayer are one in cursing and one in blessing. Elijah prayed and there was a drought; he prayed again and rain came (Jas. v. 17, 18). This is a solemn reminder to us that prayer is not simply asking God for the pleasant things we desire, but an earnest yearning for, and entering into, the will of God, for ourselves and others, be it sweet or bitter. Such was the prayer of the Lord in Gethsemane (Mk. xiv. 35, 36).

22–24. The Lord is, in addition, gently rebuking their lack of faith in Him, for they obviously were astonished when His cursing of the fig tree produced such sudden and drastic results. He is also using the incident as a general illustration. Wither a fig tree? Why not? Given faith, they could uproot mountains (a rabbinic phrase), and hurl them into the sea. There are other similar Sayings (Mt. xvii. 20; Lk. xvii. 6), one dealing with the moving of a mountain, and one with the uprooting of a mulberry-tree, but both introducing the concept of faith like a mustard seed. It is obvious, then, that this was a point of the Lord's teaching which He reiterated on several occasions in variant forms to fit different occasions. As in so many of the Lord's Sayings, the parable is designed to illustrate one great point, the need for faith in prayer. We may not generalize, and think that we can remove all mountains and wither all fig trees at our will. Mountains will truly be removed, but at God's will, not ours. If we would move mountains we must have this faith. Nor is this an arbitrary choice of faith as a necessity; it is because no man may be saved without faith. Faith is the initial rule of acceptance of man by God; and the expression of this in the New Testament becomes the doctrine of justification by faith (Rom. iv. 13–25). As faith is the beginning, so faith is the rule by which we must continue (Gal. iii. 1–6).

25. But there is another 'condition' of prayer, if it might be so phrased; and that is our forgiveness of fellow men. This, too, is not arbitrary; we have no inherent right to be heard by God; all is 'the measure of grace', as rabbinic theology would say (cf. Rom. xi. 6). Unless our Father condescends to hear and forgive, we have no hope. But, unless we forgive our fellow men freely, it shows that we have no consciousness of the grace that we ourselves have received (Mt. xviii. 32, 33), and thus that we are expecting to be heard on our own merits. This would be a complete denial of the great principle of justification by faith; and so we cannot be heard.

26. This verse is omitted in several important MSS and may be by 'attraction' from the very similar Saying in Matthew vi. 15. If so, it is an interesting example of the assimilation of two manuscript traditions originally quite different, as mentioned in the Introduction.[1] In any case, whether properly belonging here or not, the verse not only expresses a logical deduction from verse 25, but also a solemn theological truth, which is certainly to be read in the Matthean context. This is not an arbitrary refusal by God to forgive us. We in our own unforgiving spirit have made it impossible for ourselves to accept the forgiveness freely offered by God since we refuse to adopt the only attitude in which it can be appropriated.

ii. By what authority? (xi. 27–33). The rumblings of the coming storm grow louder. As He continued to teach the crowds in the Temple (Lk. xx. 1; Mt. xxi. 23), the authorities came, angrily demanding to know 'in whose name' the Galilaean Rabbi taught; whose disciple was He, or what official commission had He to show? Only such commissioning could warrant and justify to them His cavalier way of dealing with the temple vendors.[2] The Lord tacitly agreed; true, He taught in His own name, unlike the scribes, with their eternal quotation of precedent (i. 22). But He also claimed, and clearly manifested, God's direct authority (Lk. iv. 32). It was a realization of this fact that drew His disciples to Him; and failure to see it—which is also an unwillingness to see it (Jn. vii. 17)—that condemned the Pharisees. So the Lord, instead of a direct answer, virtually tells them that His authority stems from the same source as that of John the Baptist. Their greatest condemnation is that they do not seem to have considered the Lord's question as a moral probe, but purely as an intellectual 'catch'. Their query was not 'true or false?' but 'safe or unsafe?'. It seems, in point of fact, from the order in which the alternatives come into their minds, that they did now consider (after his death, vi. 29) that John's mission had

---

[1] See p. 45.
[2] Cranfield claims, perhaps rightly, that their question is not limited to such rabbinic authorization: but surely, in view of official scorn of the 'unlettered Rabbi', this would be a natural taunt to use.

had a heavenly source, although he, too, was an unlettered rabbi, unattached to any great name, like his Galilaean cousin. (Contrast Saul, of Gamaliel's school, Acts xxii. 3.)

Likewise, although they were conscious of their failure to hear John (Lk. vii. 30), their concern was not so much over their spiritual blindness in the past which, had they once admitted it, would have been no sin (Jn. ix. 41), but merely lest the Lord should score a verbal triumph. Similarly, the popular conviction (verse 32) that John's authority was of God was seen, not as an example of a truth hidden from the wise but revealed to the simple (Mt. xi. 25), but only as a possible personal danger. Luke xx. 6 shows that the priests feared stoning; they never paused to see in this danger the irritation of the simple folk, provoked by such an obvious reversal of all moral values. So, a crowning irony, they blandly said they did not know; and the Lord quietly showed what He thought of such deliberate ignorance by saying, 'In that case, I, too, refuse to tell you . . .'. The root of the trouble lay not in their intellects, but in their stubborn wills. They stood self-condemned. The Lord's question was not a trap; it was yet another opportunity for them to realize and confess their blindness, and ask for sight. Theirs was the unforgivable sin, that constant wilful opposition to the Spirit that is the sin against the Holy Ghost. If it is true that there is a way to hell from the gates of heaven, as Bunyan has it, then it is equally true that there is a way to heaven from the gates of hell: yet here were men who contemptuously refused to take it.

iii. The wicked husbandmen (xii. 1–12). The parable of the wicked husbandmen follows very naturally upon the final refusal by the Pharisees to consider the source of the Lord's authority. In so doing, they refused to admit the palpable fact that they knew its source already. This is, in consequence, a parable of doom. It is more properly the parable of the rejection of the Son, than the parable of the wicked husbandmen, although His rejection is at once the logical result and the supreme proof of their wickedness.

1. As soon as the Lord began to speak, seeing that the Old

Testament 'back-cloth' of the parable was Isaiah v, all men would know that He referred to Israel—referred to them, in fact—and that this was yet another parable of judgment. All the marks of the landowner's care and protection are borrowed from Isaiah, though the concept of the tenant-farmer is new. Whatever the mistakes of the Pharisees, one common mistake of ours they failed to make; their very anger showed their realization that the Lord's words were directed to them personally (12) and not innocuously aimed at some third party.

2–5. Even the maltreatment of the prophets by their forefathers was readily admitted by that generation (Mt. xxiii. 30), for this did not compromise them. Indeed, they prided themselves on their superior spiritual insight, and on showing their piety by building fine tombs for these ancient worthies. As the Lord drily said, this only showed their identification with their forefathers—one generation killed the prophets, while another generation buried them, as if sharing in the crime (Lk. xi. 48). We can always see the spiritual blindness of our forefathers, but never our own, by the very perversity that is the great irony of human nature.

6–8. As often in New Testament days, *agapētos* (AV, *well beloved*) probably has the force of 'only', which is more specifically brought out in this context by the *hena, one*. The uniqueness of the Lord's position, and the unique exhibition of the grace of God in sending Him, are alike manifested in this. There is a pathos in the *They will reverence my son*, but it also contains a great truth, for the one who would receive the Father not only will but must receive the Son (Jn. xii. 44). The Lord's position is both analogous to, and yet very different from, that of the prophets, for there is a finality in His coming. God can, as it were, do no more. Christ is God's last word to men. Thus judgment is at once passed on the evil 'tenant-farmers', although its execution may be stayed as, in a sense, it is throughout this present age, in spite of its falling upon the Jerusalem of that generation. Henceforward, the demand is one for repentance for our share in that crime (cf. Acts ii.

23, 38). This is very different from the message of the former servants, whose demand was for that spiritual 'fruit', which alone could justify the tenant-farmers in the landowner's eyes. Of course, in full New Testament language, even good tenant-farmers should have learnt that no fruit could justify, and should have thus gathered their need to throw themselves on the Landowner's mercy, as we Gentile sinners do; but they never got as far as that. It was not through their failure to recognize the Son that they killed Him; that would have been pardonable. It was, as in the parable, precisely because they recognized Him for who He was that they slew Him. 'This is the heir to the estate; come on—let us kill him—and the property will be ours' (see verse 7). We reject the claims of Christ not because we misunderstand them, but because we understand them only too well, in spite of all our protestations to the contrary.

9. Matthew xxi. 41 contains a graphic addition, making clear that the judgment on the tenant-farmers was the spontaneous verdict of the crowd, carried away by the Lord's graphic parable. This is very true to life in the East; in open-air preaching, the missionary soon learns not to ask rhetorical questions, in Western fashion, or he will assuredly get rhetorical answers from his uninhibited Eastern congregation, as here. Once again the spontaneous moral judgments of unsophisticated man are vindicated (Rom. ii. 15). This, after all, is exemplified in modern life in our trust in trial by jury, rather than by professional lawyers. Luke xx. 16 makes clear that the leaders of Jewry, at least, saw the full meaning of the parable, from their involuntary but fervent ejaculation of 'God forbid'. It was in answer that the Lord quoted Psalm cxviii. 22, 23. The item in the condemnation that seems to have enraged them beyond all bounds, as when Paul (Acts xiii. 46) mentioned it, was the giving of the vineyard to others, a granting of the kingdom to a people who bear its fruits (Mt. xxi. 43). This struck a blow at 'the most favoured nation', Israel; the reference to the Gentiles was plain, and they could not stomach it, as is shown by their reaction in verse 12.

10. This quotation is from Psalm cxviii, the very Psalm from which the triumphal cry of 'Hosanna' had been taken[1] (verse 25, 'Save now'), as well as the 'Blessed be he that cometh in the name of the Lord' of the triumphal entry (verse 26).

The Lord is Himself the rejected stone, now become, in God's good purpose, the keystone of the building that is the new Temple, the Christian Church, that is also His body. But in a sense the Gentiles too, despised by Israel, yet finding a place as 'living stones' in God's plan (1 Pet. ii. 5, RV), may also be included in the wider meaning. Contemptuously rejected by Israel they might be, but yet they were chosen of God. This was the miracle that the Jewish writers of the New Testament Epistles never tired of explaining to their Gentile converts (e.g. Rom. ix. 25), lest we Gentiles take for granted our position in grace.

11. All that man can do, as always, is to bow his head in reverence and to marvel at the plan of God (so Paul in Rom. xi. 33). The quotation from the psalter shows us that this plan is nothing new, but God's eternal strange way of working. There is a massive consistency in God's dealing with men (Mal. iii. 6). Of course, as a Hebrew Christian pointed out to the present writer, to rejoice in God's strange dealing is easier for Gentile than Jew in this present dispensation. Yet Paul the Jew found a twofold answer; first, God's rejection of Israel was fruitfulness for the Gentiles; and there will yet come a glad gathering-in, a harvest-home for Israel (Rom. xi. 15). He also uses the downfall of Israel to warn us Gentiles to humility, now that we know the awful dangers and responsibilities of God's choice (Rom. xi. 22).

12. The Pharisees must have regarded Him now as a dangerous revolutionary and as one intent on arousing the crowds against them. Witness the same accusation brought against His disciples by the Jews after the crucifixion (Acts v. 28, xxiv. 5).

---

[1] Of course, as a regular Passover Psalm, it would be much in men's minds at this season: but for another interesting and possible reason for the exclamation at the triumphal entry, see Cranfield, p. 357. For the philology of the word, see Arndt and Gingrich, p. 907, and articles quoted there.

iv. Tribute to Caesar (xii. 13–17). Now begins the terrible game of diamond-cut-diamond, the endless Pharisaic manoeuvring that ends in the Lord's death. The question about the source of His authority had left them helpless (xi. 33), but perhaps He can be caught in the same snare Himself, and thus be condemned on a political charge. If He had placed them upon the horns of a dilemma, where either answer was unsafe because of the crowd, they will do the same with Him. The *Herodians* were not a coherent sect in the sense that Pharisees or Sadducees were, but rather a political group, cutting across all other divisions, made up of those who saw in the support of the unscrupulous but outwardly orthodox Herod the hope of Israel; and that meant acceptance of Rome as overlord.

14. Nothing is more horrible than the smooth plausibility of the beginning, as though they could flatter the Lord into abandoning all caution and compromising Himself. The contrast between this and the similar but heartfelt remark made by Nicodemus (Jn. iii. 2) could scarcely be greater. The point is that any religious teacher who was a 'respecter of persons', who looked on outer show and not inner reality, would certainly be afraid to say or do anything that could be construed as *lèse-majesté* towards Caesar. Into this trap they sought to lead Him. Yet if He avoided this, and lent His authority to the payment of tribute to the hated Roman, the Zealots of hot-tempered Galilee would certainly take it ill; and did not the Lord number at least one such among His disciples (see comment on iii. 18)? More, the bulk of the non-Judaean pilgrims, who had tumultuously escorted into Jerusalem their homespun Nazareth prophet (Mt. xxi. 11), were likewise Galilaeans— dreaded at festival time (Lk. xiii. 1; Acts v. 37) as perennially turbulent elements.

15. Such *hypocrisy*, or play-acting, did not deceive Him, and He did not conceal it from them. From such insincerity the Son of God must have turned with loathing; the strongest charge that He brought against scribe and Pharisee was that they were insincere (Mt. xxiii. 13). Yet we are never called by the Bible to third-party judgments of others, but to examine

ourselves soberly, lest we ourselves fall under the same condemnation (1 Cor. x. 11).

16. The production of a coin was a typical rabbinic touch
(compare, too, the Emperor Vespasian's famous '*non olet*', said
of the Roman coin won from Government sewerage contract-
ing), but the use made of it was new. By the acceptance of
Imperial coinage ('whose is the head and title?') the Jews had
already shown their acceptance of Imperial rule, albeit unwillingly. There is a world of bitterness in the terseness of their
one-word reply, *Caesar's*. Compare their goaded reply to
Pilate, 'We have no king but Caesar' (Jn. xix. 15). Even that
admission must have tortured the proud Jews (Jn. viii. 33).
The Pharisees who so replied were certainly no Herodians,
with their contempt for the Edomite jackal (cf. Lk. xiii. 32).
Had the reply to Pilate reached Herod's ears, some learned
heads would have gone rolling; for Herod, though Caesar's
man, was king in his own right.

17. So came the quiet reply, with its irresistible logic; the
coin belongs to Caesar—give it back then to him. Translated
into Christian terms, it becomes the Christian doctrine of the
State, as an institution ordained by God; this is strongly
advanced by Paul (Rom. xiii. 1, 2). If we accept the amenities
of the State, in law and order, expressed in a guaranteed
coinage as in other things, then we have no right to seek to
escape the burdens imposed by the State (cf. Rom. xiii. 7). But
this lesson the Lord would leave His audience to infer; had He
spoken so plainly here, the Pharisees would have used it as a
handle against Him, to stir up the Zealots. To His own disciples, He might and did speak much more freely, notably on
the subject of temple tax (Mt. xvii. 24–26), which was a
strictly Jewish and religious impost. Nevertheless even there,
lest He should give men needless grounds for stumbling, He
told Peter to submit to that tax also (Mt. xvii. 27).

To the listening Zealot, 'Give back to Caesar that which
belongs to him' may have been the sting in the Lord's answer.
But the true sting for the Pharisee was in the tail, *and to God the
things that are God's*, for no man would dare to say that he was

giving God His due. Even those trained lawyers were baffled by such an answer; there was even here no handle that they could use against Him. And yet it may be that we have here the reason why the Galilaean crowd made no attempt to rescue their prophet later; was He pro-Roman after all?

There may well be also a quiet note of rebuke addressed to the political aspirations of the Herodians, who had been so occupied with their little local 'Caesar', the temporal power, that they had altogether forgotten God and His prior claims. In that case, as often in the New Testament, the *kai* is not so much a conjunctive as an adversative 'and yet, for all your doing the first—do the second as well'.

A balancing of these two clauses explains the apparently different attitude displayed toward the Imperial power in, say, the Pauline Epistles (e.g. Rom. xiii. 1) and the Apocalypse, where the Empire had ceased to be a restraining power, but has instead become a harlot, drunk with Christian blood (Rev. xvii. 5, 6). State persecution of the Church had come in between; and when Caesar asks for those things that are properly God's, then the Christian may refuse out of that very conscience to God that normally makes him obey Caesar. But Caesar can scarcely be expected to appreciate this.

v. The Sadducean question (xii. 18-27). So the political attempt to snare Him failed; but perhaps a theological question would fare better. For different reasons both Pharisees and Sadducees saw in the Lord a dangerous enemy, although it is unlikely, owing to their antagonism (cf. Acts xxiii. 6), that they acted in conscious collaboration. They were attempting, in this instance, to make spiritual truth look ridiculous by interpreting it with the grossest of literalness (as some today do with the harps and palms of heaven, in a similar attempt). Thus they hoped that the whole concept of the resurrection would be laughed out of court. The case they presented was a 'man of straw', since they themselves believed in no resurrection. To present a caricature of a view, and then to demolish it, is an old pastime. Nevertheless they held as strongly to Moses as any others in Jewry, and so they began with the

Mosaic principle of Levirate marriage.[1] In a sense the Sadducees were the most conservative group of all. They had refused
to go on with God, as He unfolded His revelation. Christian
history is littered with groups that have ceased to respond to
the continual stimuli of the Spirit of God.

In spite of the addition of the 'with us' in Matthew xxii. 25,
this is but a hypothetical instance; the symbolical number
seven (20) in itself suggests this, although 'seven sons' seems to
have been far more common in New Testament times (e.g.
Acts xix. 14) than in our day of small families. But Ruth iv. 15
(cf. Jb. i. 2, xlii. 13) certainly suggests a figurative use, meaning
a good round number.

24, 25. The Lord's reply is a marvel of patience and for-
bearance, although He stigmatizes them for two things. The
first is their failure to understand the very revelation of God
upon which they appear to lean by quoting Moses; the second
is their failure to appreciate God's power supremely manifested
to Bible writers in the resurrection of Jesus Christ from the
dead (Rom. i. 4) and ultimately in a general resurrection
(1 Cor. xv. 20–26).

The Lord first, then, demonstrates the patent absurdity of
their hypothetical case, showing that the question in the form
in which it is put by the Sadducees is meaningless, because
marriage ceases to have any sexual significance in heaven.
There is a gentle irony in the way in which He shows that the
question of resurrection cannot be conceived apart from a
whole 'universe of belief', rejected by the Sadducees, which is
the spiritual world of which angels form part. In other words,
such a question is a problem only to the Sadducees and that
because they have already in advance rejected the only terms
upon which a solution could be found. The Lord might have
added (see Acts xxiii. 9) that, to the Pharisee, such a problem
would not have existed; but, as sinless, He forbore. It is hard
to envisage either Pharisee or Sadducee being strong-minded
enough to pass by such an opportunity of 'splitting the vote';

---

[1] This rule of marrying the childless wife of a dead brother was of course
Mosaic (Dt. xxv. 5–10): they were thus in no sense attacking it, although
they adduced an extreme instance.

certainly Paul was not proof, but his conscience later troubled him about that worldly-wise interjection of his (cf. Acts xxiii. 6, xxiv. 21). There is thus a gentle subtlety in the *as the angels* (25), which does not appear on the surface, but which would scarcely be lost on either Pharisee or Sadducee, for different reasons. At times the better type of Pharisee could only agree with the Lord (Mt. xxii. 34 suggests that there was some thigh slapping over the neat way He had muzzled the Pharisees, and Mk. xii. 32 makes the approval explicit).

26, 27. But having answered the Sadducees on their own terms, the Lord as usual proceeds to give a far deeper proof of the resurrection, one which would be incapable of being thus caricatured. This takes up the first clause of the original answer to them. He has already explained what He meant by their ignorance of God's power; now He will explain what He meant by their ignorance of the Scripture, by basing Himself upon that very Moses on whom, rejecting traditional accretions, they relied. In God's self-revelation made to Moses at the burning bush (Ex. iii. 6, 15) God describes Himself as the God of Abraham, of Isaac and of Jacob. Now to talk of Himself as being a God of the past experience of these men, as a Westerner might describe Him, is nonsense to an Easterner; for where is the experience apart from the man? Assuredly it is not with God; were it so, He would have but said simply 'I AM', as He did elsewhere (Ex. iii. 14). But to describe Himself as Abraham's God, Isaac's God and Jacob's God is obviously felt to be adding some further knowledge to this. Therefore if God can still so describe Himself to Moses centuries after their death, this experience must still be valid. If so, these three patriarchs must still be in existence; and the guarantee of their 'eternal life' is not the nature of their experience of God, but the nature of the God whom they experienced. He is the *God of the living* because He is the living God Himself; and so Christ could describe Himself as 'the life' (Jn. xi. 25). Thus, too, it was that, even in the physical realm, contact with Him brought new life to the dead (cf. Mk. v. 41); thus to know God, and the Christ whom He sent, is itself life eternal

(Jn. xvii. 3). Here is a great bridge-point between Gospel and Pauline theology (Rom. vi. 1–5).

vi. The greatest commandment (xii. 28–34). Now comes the question as to which is the greatest commandment of all. The first questioner seems to have been a Herodian (13f.), the second a Sadducee (18ff.). Mark simply tells us that this third questioner was a scribe, while Matthew xxii. 34 makes the position clearer by telling us that this was a Pharisaic move. It is hard to believe, as above, that the Pharisees did not feel some pleasure at that; and certainly of all the three questioners this scribe was the most honest, and alone received commendation from the Lord. It appears from verse 28 that this scribe was already conscious of the theological strength of the Lord's reply to the Sadducees; and from His words in verse 32, he was even more deeply struck by the Lord's words here. The 'Christian scribe' was a group not unknown later within the Christian Church. Indeed, it is arguable that Matthew's Gospel was written both by and for such men. See Matthew xiii. 52 for the double richness of such a man; but the Judaizers in the early Church showed the dangers inherent in such an amphibious position (Acts xv. 1, xxi. 20). After the destruction of Jerusalem in AD 70 this group, while still existing (see Eusebius), do not seem to have been a danger.

29–31. The Lord's summary of Israel's faith was a junction of the *Shema*, the credal statement of Israel (Dt. vi. 4, 5), joined to the 'manward' command of Leviticus xix. 18. It has often been remarked that many of the Lord's most telling Sayings (as in the temple cleansing) were derived from a creative combination of two or more different passages from the Old Testament. So, indeed, His understanding and explanation of His own work was by a combination of the widely separated images of Son, Servant, Son of man, Messiah and King as well as of the sacrificial Lamb. In this junction the heart of true religion is seen, not in negative commands, but in a positive personal attitude to God and man. This is the Pauline 'liberty' of the New Testament (Gal. v. 1). This is the patristic 'love and do as you like'—for such love towards God and man will in itself keep us from licence. If we love men we will do nothing to work them hurt and, if we love God, what we like and choose will be to do God's will and pleasure (Ps. xl. 8).

32, 33. The law, the Temple and the election of Israel were the three great 'planks' of Judaism, as we can see from Jewish reaction to Christian preaching (Acts xvii. 13, 14, xxi. 28). The second and third had already been challenged; this scribe had intended to test Christ's orthodoxy on the first and greatest, the law. This was no doubt the point where He was most suspect by the Pharisees ever since the earlier controversies (see xi. 23-28). One can almost hear in these two verses the trained lawyer weighing the Lord's answer clause by clause, with that pedantic repetitiveness characteristic of the legal mind that can be so trying to others. 'A good answer—a true answer—a scriptural answer', he agrees, perhaps not without a slightly patronizing air towards this layman. Yes, he gives a verdict finally; in Scripture, obedience is better than sacrifice (1 Sa. xv. 22), and thus to love God and one's fellow men is more than all the observances of the law.

34. The lawyer had weighed and appraised the answer that the Lord had made; but to his horror and the terror of the bystanders, he found that, even as he answered, the Lord had been quietly appraising him. When mortal man sits in judgment on the claims of Christ, he little knows that the Christ (or the word of revelation which He brought, Jn. xii. 48) is sitting in judgment on him. Man thus stands self-condemned or justified by his attitude to the Word of God and the Person of Christ (cf. Lk. vii. 29, 30). We are nowhere told that this scribe, so close to the kingdom, ever actually entered the door. There were many secret believers on Christ, even among the ruling group at Jerusalem (contrast Jn. vii. 48 with Jn. xii. 42), of whom Nicodemus and Joseph of Arimathaea came into the light of day (Jn. xix. 38, 39). Later (Acts vi. 7) there are still Jewish priests within the Christian Church; and the believing Pharisees gave trouble even at the time of the Council of Jerusalem (Acts xv. 5). Later some, as the Judaizers, were to become Paul's bitterest enemies; but doubtless many others were absorbed into the main stream of orthodox Christianity.

vii. Who is the Son of David? (xii. 35-37). Now follows the last of the series of 'hard questions'. It can be no accident that the Queen of Sheba thus tested Solomon (1 Ki. x. 1), in view of the New Testament statement that a greater than Solomon was now on earth (Mt. xii. 42). As the series had begun with a baffling question put by the Lord (on the source of John's authority; see xi. 30), so it would end with an equally baffling question about the Son of David.[1] The Marcan context aims this question directly at *the scribes*, as being propounders of the last conundrum, while Matthew xxii. 41 makes plain that it was still aimed at the strong Pharisee group. Of course 'scribe' did not denote a separate 'party', as Pharisee did, but a function; this can be seen from the Lucan parallels of 'law-teacher' (Lk. v. 17), and lawyer (Lk. x. 25). It may be that the triumphal cry of the children in the Temple, to which the priests took such strong exception (Mt. xxi. 15, 16), brought this particular messianic title into prominence. It was widely agreed that the Messiah was to be David's son; but this would have been understood as being by strictly physical descent, and applicable to the earthly deliverer, for whom all Jews looked, and for whom Zealots at least worked actively.

36, 37. Yet this, obviously, could not be the full biblical meaning of the title, as the Lord proves by an argument which they could not well refute. As usual, He first shows men that, even on their own premises, they are inconsistent. Psalm cx was accepted as a messianic psalm by every scribe; the Authorized Version verse-summary at its head, 'The kingdom, the priesthood, the conquest, and the passion of Christ. A Psalm of David' is fully traditional in attribution and exegesis. But if David is speaking here, and speaking of the coming Messiah, how can he call Him 'my Lord'? How is this con-

---

[1] There seems, in the light of this, no need to assume that here we have only the end of a last conflict-story (as Cranfield, following Gagg), rather than a topic introduced *de novo* by the Lord Himself.

sistent with David's occupation of a superior position, as that of physical ancestor to physical descendant? Matthew xxii. 46 makes plain that the scholars could find no answer, and that this marked the end of all attempts to trap the Lord in His speech, at least until His trial (see Mt. xxvi. 59ff.). We who are 'in Christ' can see clearly how the Christ might well be born of David's physical line, and yet still be David's Lord, because identical with God Himself; but the Lord made no attempt to explain this truth even as yet to His disciples. This was doubtless one of the truths whose meaning they realized only after the resurrection (Lk. xxiv. 32), though told to them long before (Jn. x. 30). Whether or no this Psalm is patient of other interpretations is beside the point; this interpretation was accepted by every orthodox Jew, and so the Lord's answer was unanswerable.

viii. Woe to the scribes! (xii. 38–40). The scribes had now been effectively silenced themselves, as the politically-minded Sadducees had been before (xii. 34). Such preaching undoubtedly increased the antagonisms of the priestly circles, but it is unlikely to have been more unpopular with the crowd (cf. the end of verse 37). Matthew xxiii is a much fuller version, and makes plain that the Pharisees were included. Both these are aspects more likely to be of interest to, and therefore preserved by, a Jerusalem Judeo-Christian source, particularly if they were suffering persecution at the hands of the orthodox Jews at the time (Jas. ii. 6, 7). In the Petrine preaching to a Western Gentile audience these aspects would be irrelevant; even if such finicky theological distinctions were of interest to Peter himself, which is doubtful, they would not be to his audience. On the whole, only that of obvious practical value is likely to have been preserved.

To us, 'scribes and Pharisees' have become a symbol of hypocrisy. They liked all the notoriety and outward honour that their unquestioned intellectual mastery of Scripture brought to them. They were nothing if not biblical expositors and commentators, and devoted to the text as few others have been; they were conservative to the hilt, nay, positively fundamentalist in their approach to the Bible as they had it. But the simple Christian man is warned against them (Mt. xxiii. 3). Had they rejected the authority of Scripture, their conduct would have been explicable; as it was they were left without excuse. For those today who accept the Bible as a rule of faith and conduct, there is no excuse for disobedience.

The scribes not only love the outward show and empty glory of religious observance, which is the sin of pride; they love money, and that is another sin, the sin of covetousness. Yet all the time they do this under cover of lengthy prayers—which invests all their other sins with the new and awful quality of hypocrisy. The widow and orphan should above all have been the objects of their compassion and prayer (Ex. xxii. 22; Ps. cxlvi. 9) and instead, they rob them. It is just because they pray that their condemnation will be the more terrible, more than that of a rogue who robs outright without pretence of prayer or religion. So comes the irony that the Lord preached love to the sinner, but judgment to the religious —more toleration for the Amazon and the Congo, than for London and New York (Mt. xi. 20–24). Greater knowledge and greater opportunities bring greater responsibility (Lk. xii. 47).

ix. The widow's mite (xii. 41–44). Now comes, appropriately enough, the story of the widow's mite. Avarice and nominal religion, with all its pomp and show, have just been castigated. Here by contrast is one of the very group made a prey by the scribes, a widow who, out of poverty and true devotion to God, makes an offering unseen and unheralded save by One. Together, the pictures are a pair of vignettes, gaining by the strong contrast. The Lord, be it noted, did not deny that the rich gave much; He merely said that the widow gave still more, for theirs was but a contribution, generous though it might be, while hers was a true sacrifice. In days when Christian churches are dazzled by large incomes and ambitious blueprints, it is well to remember that the Lord measures giving, not by what we give, but by what we keep for ourselves; and the widow kept nothing, but gave all.

d. The Olivet discourse (xiii. 1-37)

i. Doom on the Temple (xiii. 1-4). With chapter xiii we come to the so-called 'Little Apocalypse',[1] the Gospel core of that which is amplified in the book of Revelation (cf. 1 Thes. iv. 13-17 for a similar passage in the Pauline Epistles). It is noteworthy that the Lord makes no attempt to gratify morbid curiosity; His aim is practical and ethical. Indeed, wherever the disciples expressed such curiosity, He at once heartily discouraged it (Acts i. 6, 7).

This opening section deals with the destruction of the Temple. The whole of the 'Little Apocalypse' seems designed to warn the disciples against four great spiritual dangers. The first danger is that of reliance upon the outward adjuncts of religion, venerable and loved though they be. The second danger (verses 5, 6) is that of deception by false Messiahs; the third (verses 7, 8) is that of distraction by world turmoil about us; the fourth (verses 9ff.) is that of being 'tripped' because of the unexpected bitterness of the persecution for our faith. To be forewarned, in each case, is to be forearmed.

1, 2. There is a ring of patriotic pride in the words of the Lord's disciple (was it Peter?). Built by Herod it might be, but the third Temple was one of the architectural wonders of the Roman world, and still unfinished at the date of its destruction. The 'old fox' built well; Herodian masonry is noted for its excellence elsewhere in Palestine. So, too, there is a note of sadness in the Lord's reply that reminds us of the lament over Jerusalem (Lk. xix. 41), or Paul's passionate outburst over his people (Rom. x. 1), or that of Moses (Ex. xxxii). The Lord was thus preparing His disciples for the days when every outward religious adjunct would be taken away, in the expulsion of the Christian 'sect' from the parent body of Judaism, and when the danger was great lest the infant Church should waver or even go back to the well-loved institutions of Judaism (see Hebrews *passim*). Those who have in wartime worshipped in

---

[1] The use of this convenient descriptive title does not of course convey a distrust of the dominical nature of the contents, although many modern editors take this position. But Cranfield, pp. 387-391, is a healthier approach.

schools and homes, while their church lay in ruins, will enter a little way into such an experience. Later still, the destruction of the earthly Temple, while almost a death-knell to Palestinian Judaism (the final blow came later, after Bar-Cochba's revolt in AD 135), had a great 'evidential' value to the Christian Church. After that, there was little danger of going back to the outward forms of Judaism, for there was nothing to which to go. No sacrifice has since been offered in Israel; how could there be sacrifice, without a temple?

3. This is an interesting verse, in that *Andrew* is joined to the usual three, even if as an ungracious appendix. The real problem is not why he was joined with them on this occasion, but why he was omitted on other occasions. John's Gospel makes more mention of Andrew than Peter's preaching does (see Jn. i. 40, xii. 22). Is this a typically brotherly trait? For in John's Gospel, James in turn is but a 'lay figure', ever present but never individually characterized. But it may have simply been that Andrew and James were less forceful characters; for Luke in Acts does not mention Andrew, and in spite of the cursory reference to James in Acts xii. 2, James the brother of the Lord far eclipses his apostolic namesake.

4. Perhaps this question of the four disciples is an example of that 'morbid curiosity' mentioned above; compare the statistical curiosity of 'Lord, are there few that be saved?' (Lk. xiii. 23), to which the Lord's sole reply was a warning to the disciples to make sure that they themselves were among the number of the saved. This is an example of the way the Lord at once translated all such abstract enquiries into the personal and moral realm. No theological problem may be considered in isolation, for it does not exist in isolation; it has immediate practical relevance to our present position, beliefs and conduct. Interest which is purely intellectual becomes morbid in that it is unnatural and divorced from reality. The Bible knows no solely intellectual truth; all is moral as well.

ii. Signs of the end (**xiii. 5–8**). But in reply the Lord does indeed give the disciples the signs of the end, although they are not signs that enable them to give detailed chronological predictions. Nevertheless some of them were precise enough to assure the survival of the Jerusalem church, in that it took warning and fled to Pella in Transjordan before the Roman ring of steel had tightened round the doomed city in AD 70. So, as a sign of the times, the Lord gives the second warning, against false spiritual leaders, whether or no they call themselves by the name of Christ. Of course, there were literal fulfilments enough of this in the next century; Bar-Cochba at least claimed full Messiahship. But if we follow the Old Testament analogies, to worship Christ with the wrong beliefs about Him is to worship a false Christ, by whatever name we call Him; for we, in so doing, falsely imagine Him to be other than He is, and other than He is revealed in Scripture to be. This alone makes sense of the prophetic denunciation of much of the popular Yahwism of their day as in fact mere Baal-worship.

Tacitly, then, a crop of false teachers are one sign of the end, as is a steady worsening of the political world situation. This introduces the third danger, and thus the third warning; we must not be *troubled* (RSV, 'alarmed') over international affairs, as the non-Christian may be. The Christian's heart must not be 'in a turmoil' (see Jn. xiv. 1), for these troubles are a necessary stage. All this is but the onset of the world's labour-pains; the *telos*, the goal and aim of history which is the final establishment of God's rule, is yet to come. Paul has a similar concept when he describes all creation as moaning in labour, waiting for God's consummation (Rom. viii. 22). He apparently sees it as a continuous, present, this-worldly experience, though aimed at one future point of time, an interpretation which may help our understanding of this passage. Hebrews, in turn, sees this shaking of all apparently fixed human institutions as a necessity, that God's unshakable kingdom may be revealed (Heb. xii. 26).

8. If a local and temporary 'primary' fulfilment is to be sought, as distinct from a continuous or even final one, then the year of the four emperors (AD 69), as the Imperial throne changed hands with astonishing rapidity while all the time the fortified cities of Galilee were falling, would fit well. In a wider sense, this is a continual picture of the present age of turmoil, in the midst of which the Christian Church must live and witness; this corresponds to at least one school of interpretation of the imagery of the 'Greater Apocalypse', that is the book of Revelation. It is to be noted that neither of these interpretations rules out a final eschatological fulfilment in addition.

iii. The beginning of the troubles (xiii. 9–13). The last great danger is lest the Christian be staggered or tripped up[1] by the bitter persecution he will assuredly suffer for his faith. At this time, as the disciples saw the mounting tide of hostility against their Lord, they must have begun to understand, although the full force did not strike the disciples until the days of Acts viii. 1. Each of these 'testings' cuts closer to the bone than that before it, for such is God's way with His children, and this last test is no exception; this persecution is to be so bitter that it destroys the closest natural ties known to man (verse 12). But even this must not make us stumble, for the Lord has warned us beforehand just so that this may be avoided (Jn. xiv. 29). He would have no man follow Him without counting the cost (Lk. xiv. 28).

9. The mention of *councils* and *synagogues* must have struck a responsive note in those early Christians, who remembered the bitter persecution of Saul of Tarsus (recorded in Acts viii. 1–3). It was surely of God that he who had thus unwittingly fulfilled the first half of the verse by his virulence, should also gladly fulfil the second by his witness before men in authority like Felix, Festus, Agrippa and perhaps even Caesar himself (2 Tim. iv. 16, 17). The Greek *hēgemonōn*, *rulers*, is almost a technical term in the New Testament, used of Roman officials from provincial governors to the lowly procurator of Judaea; while *basileōn*, *kings*, covers all 'native rulers from tetrarch to emperor'.

---

[1] This is the meaning of the Greek word *skandalizō* in the parallel passage in Matthew xxiv. 9, 10 translated by AV, 'offended'.

10. The AV *all nations* is apt to lose the point;[1] 'to all the Gentiles' is the true sense. Once again comes the axe-blow at Israel's position of 'most favoured nation'.

11. There are numerous instances of extempore Christian defence in Acts. The behaviour of Peter before the Sanhedrin, acknowledged as he was by all to be an unlettered man, is but one example among many (Acts iv. 8ff.). But we may not trade on this, and 'put God to the test' (cf. Lk. iv. 12, from Dt. vi. 16). This promise is for those who are haled unexpectedly into courts by their persecutors, not for those who have the duty of Christian instruction of others laid upon them, in set places and at set times.

12, 13. Here, in outline, is the great doctrine of *hupomonē*, often called 'the perseverance of the saints': the one who endures to the end will be saved (13). Now this cannot mean 'will be rescued from tribulation', for there has already been warning of 'death' in verse 12. 'By your endurance you will gain your lives' (Gk. *psuchas*, souls, selves: Lk. xxi. 19, RSV) shows that there is the same eschatological significance here as in Revelation ii. 10, 'be thou faithful unto death, and I will give *thee a crown of life*'. So the Christian must hold fast right to the end; but if he be truly Christian he will so hold fast, because God holds him fast (Rom. xiv. 4). Thus ultimate apostasy is the sign that the apostate never really belonged to Christ (1 Jn. ii. 19). Here is another biblical paradox which we do well to hold reverently; its solution, like that of all the others, is to be found not, as with mathematical problems, at infinity, but in eternity, which is God. Matthew x. 22 gives this same Saying in another context as well; it was therefore not merely an *ad hoc*, casual utterance, but represented an integral part of the Lord's set teaching. It is only fair to add that some have seen a further problem in Hebrews vi. 4; but a discussion of the peculiar circumstances there involved is not strictly germane to a commentary on Mark.[2]

---

[1] Though Cranfield so takes it, as indicating the *extent* of the preaching even if not the extent of the response.

[2] See T. Hewitt, *The Epistle to the Hebrews* (*Tyndale New Testament Commentaries*), 1960, pp. 106ff.

iv. The abomination of desolation (xiii. 14-20). Now comes the reference to *the abomination of desolation* (14), better translated 'the idol that profanes'. As in all apocalyptic, particularly that produced in troubled times (as most apocalyptic is), the wording was deliberately guarded, lest it fall into the wrong hands; the book of Revelation provides numerous instances of this. Daniel ix. 27, xi. 31, xii. 11 provide the phraseology; in origin it probably refers to the statue set up by Antiochus profaning the holy place and the sacrifice of swine's flesh to it; but here it fairly certainly refers to the encirclement of Jerusalem by Roman armies (so Lk. xxi. 20 turns the same Saying). The Roman eagles, standards of the Legions, were held by the Zealots to be just such an abomination (being images, and as such forbidden in the Commandments), and AD 70 was to show what desolation the Roman eagles could work. Later, of course, after the revolt of AD 135, when a statue and temple of Zeus stood in the holy place of Aelia Capitolina, as rebuilt Jerusalem was called, the horror was complete for the orthodox Jew.

The phrase *let him that readeth understand* cannot, by definition, be part of the original spoken Saying; contrast the frequent 'He that hath ears to hear, let him hear' (iv. 9, etc.). By its form as well as by its rabbinic ring, such a phrase belongs to the original spoken words of Christ. But the phrase before us must belong to an editorial in some early written collection, and as it is common to Matthew and Mark, poses an interesting question. Luke has not got the phrase, but then he has omitted the cryptic reference to Daniel, and speaks outright of the besieging Roman armies. This suggests that Luke was writing after the fall of Jerusalem, and for a Gentile church which had nothing to fear from such open statements. Mark is most cryptic of all, with his *where it ought not* (to stand) for Matthew's blunt 'in the holy place', i.e. in the Temple.

These verses supply a good illustration of prophetic 'foreshortening' of history. Prophecy is of course a forthtelling of God's ways and mind, as we are constantly reminded nowadays. But it undoubtedly includes foretelling of God's purposes (although this is not a fashionable view today) and this it does in a 'two dimensional' manner, in that the perspective of time is usually either lacking or vague. This may well be because time has no independent existence outside our temporal order; but to argue this would take us into philosophy. In any case, we can only argue from our world of experience, and, even if God be above and outside time, we are not. Thus we can only say that there is often discernible to us in the Bible this prophetic foreshortening, the ignoring, in the sequence of the several events, of vast stretches of time that separate them. Here God's judgment on Jewry is almost insensibly dovetailed into God's judgment on all mankind at the time of the end; and if both are but manifestations in point of time of God's continual attitude of judgment on human sin and rebellion, then the whole makes sense. Here, then, in the first place are portrayed the devastations of the Roman armies, and especially of the wild auxiliaries from Gauls to Edomites. Here, too, is the flight of the Church to Pella, as the Roman legions purposely delayed their attack on Jerusalem, hoping to persuade this stronghold to surrender voluntarily. It must indeed have seemed, in the mopping-up operations, as if the entire population of Palestine was to be extirpated; but God, *for the elect's sake* (20), would cut short those days. Imperial Rome had other interests, in the scramble to establish the new Flavian dynasty. The Christian Church would see a deep meaning in the use of *chosen* (20); for it could not now refer to Jewry, coming as it does in the context announcing Jewry's downfall. The infant church at Pella, in Transjordan, survived.

v. False Christs and false prophets (xiii. 21-23). *False Christs and false prophets* (22) will arise; this is really a return to the theme of verse 6 and the reference to *signs* may allude to Deuteronomy xiii. 1-3 with its solemn warnings. The primary reference may be to the numerous abortive pseudo-messianic rebellions that both preceded and followed AD 70. But for the Christian Church the relevance here seems to be that of Jewish-Christian (especially Gnostic) heresies of the first century; although the reference could be widened to 'the chosen ones', with an almost Johannine reminder that to succeed in deceiving *the elect* is a contradiction in terms (1 Jn. ii. 26, 27). Equally Johannine is the reminder that the Lord has warned us in advance of these things (cf. Jn. xiii. 19). Mark has fewer Johannine touches than either of the other Synoptists; he omits the Saying, for instance, found in Matthew xi. 25–27 and Luke x. 21, 22; but enough remains even in Mark to show that John is reproducing faithfully both thoughts and words of Christ.

vi. The coming of the Son of man (xiii. 24–27). Then comes a clear foretelling of the coming of *the Son of man* in a passage which is a jigsaw of quotations from the apocalyptic books of the Old Testament. Verse 26 seems to mark the real break, if there is a break, between the immediate judgment of God on Jewry and His ultimate judgment on all creation. Great world commotions are described in terms of astronomical phenomena, derived from the book of Isaiah (Is. xiii. 10, xxiv. 23). This is a typical eschatological use, and might refer just as much to toppling first-century Roman rulers as to the clash of East and West today. But verse 26, with the clear imagery of the return of the Son of man to judgment (Dn. vii. 13), can refer only to one event in history, the second coming of Christ. In view of His constant use of the title 'Son of man', His disciples cannot have failed to see that He refers to Himself here, although they may well have failed to understand how such a thing could be.

This was presumably the temptation brought before the Lord by Satan when he suggested that the Lord leap from the roof of the Temple and float down among the worshippers as a convincing 'sign' (see Mt. iv. 5, 6). This descent from the clouds would not only have suited the wording of Daniel, it would also have fulfilled the prophecy of Malachi iii. 1, if it indeed took place in the temple courts.

27. In Daniel vii, the coming of the Son of man immediately follows the judgment by the Ancient of days, and it initiates an everlasting kingdom. Daniel vii. 10 has reference to angelic bands of ministrants, and so the reference to angelic reapers here in Mark, while owing more to other Old Testament passages, is not unfair to the context of Daniel. Here comes the third reference to *his elect*, the 'chosen ones', in this passage (cf. verses 20 and 22). From the 'remnant' concept of the Old Covenant to the 'church' concept of the New Covenant is but a short step.

vii. The parable of the fig tree (xiii. 28, 29). It is probably unnecessary to read into the parable of the fig tree in this context a reference to the subsequent earthly history of the Jewish nation. It is true that vine and fig are traditional symbols of God's people in the Old Testament, and that the fig tree cursed by the Lord (xi. 12–14) seems to have been an acted parable of orthodox Judaism. Nevertheless that does not prove that every biblical mention of the fig tree conceals a reference to Israel, nor that every use of leaven as a symbol necessarily carries with it the hidden connotation of 'evil'. This Saying seems to be merely a good countryman's parable; compare the shrewd weather-lore of Matthew xvi. 2, 3 for a similar remark about reading the 'signs of the times'. Luke certainly saw it thus, or he would scarcely have added 'and all the trees' (Lk. xxi. 29) to the specific *fig tree* of the Marcan text.

viii. The date of the coming (xiii. 30–32). In the midst of many details that are puzzling, two main principles are clear. First, the Christian is to avoid unhealthy interest as to the actual date, and secondly, he is to see his very uncertainty as to the date as a strong stimulant to ceaseless watchfulness. In other words, like every other Christian doctrine, that of the second coming has a moral goal; it is designed to promote action more than contemplation, and that action is to be a growth in holiness.

This generation (30) must surely be the generation of the Lord's ministry, who would indeed have lived to see the awful days of the siege of Jerusalem. But the generation of the ministry could not of course see the second coming, so some have striven, rather unnaturally, to interpret *genea* as 'people', and refer it to the Jewish nation. Undoubtedly the delay in the *parousia* was a puzzle to the early Church, many of whom at least expected the Lord's return in their lifetime, and were saddened and troubled when, one by one, death carried them away (2 Pet. iii. 4). A similarly puzzling Saying about John is wisely explained in the Fourth Gospel (Jn. xxi. 23). But in seeing the Lord's return as always just around the corner, the infant Church was doing no wrong. So they should have done, and so should we; for every generation should be eagerly looking for and expecting the Lord's coming (2 Pet. iii. 12). It matters little whether or no Paul, for instance, believed the second coming to be a near event (1 Thes. iv. 15-17). If he did, in one theological sense he was right, for in the purpose of God no event stands between the ascension and the second coming, and thus it is eternally near. We see the two great mountain-peaks from afar; we have no knowledge of the extent and depth of the valley in between; and in one sense it is irrelevant.

Verse 32 contains a wise warning that, if we persist in pursuing a science of numbers, and calculate to our own satisfaction the date in time upon which our Lord will return, we shall infallibly be wrong. This should strike caution into the most daring exponent of prophecy. At a deeper level we find that there are certain things hidden even from the Son in the omniscience of the Father. Compare the Lord's statement (x. 40) that to sit at the right and left of Him was not His to give.

ix. The end of the discourse (xiii. 33-37). The final verses underline the moral and spiritual value of the doctrine. The price of liberty is indeed ceaseless vigilance, in things spiritual as well as temporal. Much of the parable appears to be 'back-cloth' in this particular context. Elsewhere (Mt. xxv. 14) we have the parable of numerous servants left in positions of responsibility. Elsewhere, too (Mt. xxiv. 45), we have the simile of the steward, put on test by his master's absence. Here, however, it is the watchfulness of the door-keeper that is the main point of the parable; he must stay awake and on duty, as must we.

There is some evidence to show that the simile of the *porter*

(34), or door-keeper, is peculiarly apt and indeed a chosen simile for the Christian ministry; it may even have been one of the early catechetical 'forms' (by which we mean the set similes and standard patterns used as instructional outlines by the first-century Church). Peter was granted the keys, as a spiritual door-keeper (Mt. xvi. 19); Christ is Himself the Door (Jn. x. 7); the maidens beg the Lord to open the door to them (Mt. xxv. 11); 1 Corinthians xvi. 9 and Colossians iv. 3 carry the metaphor into the Pauline Epistles. To the Lord of the house, when He arrives after long absence, the door-keeper will gladly open, for we will, in our turn, recognize His voice, although this is not a thought strictly expressed in the Marcan context (cf. Jn. x. 3 with Rev. iii. 20).

The Lord's last words (37) nevertheless show us that His command is generalized, not directed only at the ministry or indeed at any group or class within the Church. Further, it may be a hint that the Lord Himself did not expect that His second coming would be in the near future, as many modern expositors assume rather than prove. The whole tenor of this parable suggests a long absence. From this solemn last word, *Watch* (Gk. *grēgoreite*, 'be wakeful'), comes the later fondness in the Church for 'Gregory' as a Christian name, just as Anglo-Saxons called Hereward 'the Wake'.

VI. BEHOLD THE LAMB OF GOD: THE PASSION NARRATIVE (xiv. 1–xv. 47)

a. The Last Supper (xiv. 1–25)

i. Christ's death is decided (xiv. 1, 2). With chapters xiv and xv we come to the passion story in Mark; Matthew has various parables immediately preceding, some of which are also in Luke. This may be taken as showing that the Lord's teaching in and around the Temple was both more detailed and more extensive in those final days than we should gather from Mark alone. As usual Mark is a 'shorthand' for the whole story.[1]

[1] See Introduction (pp. 38f.) for note on *kolobodaktulos*.

Here we have the most definite decision so far made: Jesus must die, and as soon as possible; all that the chief priests now lack is opportunity. Even their objection to this judicial murder at a religious festival is not a moral objection because of its incompatibility with the nature of a religious ceremony, but purely prudential, lest a riot should break out among the excitable Passover crowds. The exact chronology of the crucifixion has long been in dispute, and the discussion has been revived with animation in recent years. At least it was clearly in the general period of Passover, whether or no it corresponded to the moment when the Passover lamb was killed.[1]

ii. The anointing at Bethany (xiv. 3–9). It has been seen in xi. 11 that the Lord spent each night among His friends in *Bethany*; the story of the anointing at Bethany makes clear that this was the home of Eliezer ('Lazarus' is the shortened Aramaic form), Miriam ('Mary') and Martha. Strong-minded Martha was clearly to all intents and purposes 'mistress' of this house, as indeed her very name means. But who then is *Simon the leper*, whose household it is, according to both Matthew and Mark? We may dismiss the suggestion that he was but a former owner of the house, giving his name to it even when it passed to subsequent owners. The survival of the name must have been a relic of the Petrine preaching; it may well be that the father of the house, though still alive, was well known as a leper, and that his household had therefore passed, for practical purposes, to his children. So Uzziah lived in splendid isolation in the basement of his palace, while his son Jothan ruled in his stead (2 Ch. xxvi. 21).

To equate this anointing at Bethany with that which is described by Luke (Lk. vii. 36–50) raises at least as many problems as it solves. The only real link is that the Pharisee host of Luke vii. 36 is also named Simon (verse 40), and that there is on that occasion a similar anointing by a street-woman. But the woman of Luke is not only sinful, but also a stranger in the house, while the lesson drawn from the act is completely different. It is best, as in the case of several of the Lord's miracles, to assume that we have separate

[1] So John undoubtedly seems to take it, from his careful dating.

accounts of two different though similar instances here. As stated in the Introduction,[1] later attraction or assimilation of text would be easy, e.g. in the names; while to account for the differences on any other hypothesis would be difficult.

4, 5. Matthew and John (Mt. xxvi. 8; Jn. xii. 5) are more blunt here than Mark. Those who objected to the wastefulness of the woman's loving act of devotion were the Lord's own disciples. John mentions Judas specifically. That Mark or his Petrine source cannot have been ignorant of this is shown by the fact that he moves straight from this incident to the offer of Judas to the temple authorities that he would betray his Lord (verses 10, 11). But Peter is scathing only when it comes to his own shortcomings and failings, not towards those of his fellow disciples. Judas obviously thought that the Lord's carefree attitude to money was quite inconsistent and unrealistic; first came the widow's mite (xii. 43), and now the alabaster jar of ointment—it did not make sense to him. Yet the Lord's attitude to this costly gift and to the widow's mite was fundamentally the same; He regarded both as priceless, but accepted such giving to God, either directly or in His Person, as right and natural. This was a strange reversal of earthly values; and even without the Johannine evidences as to the dishonesty of Judas (Jn. xii. 6) it is understandable that, as treasurer, he felt misgivings. The world despised the widow's mite as too small, while it criticized the anointing as wasteful, exhibitionist, unrealistic. This is a warning to us to beware of over-close, worldly-wise calculation in church affairs. What the disciples said about the value of the ointment and the need of the poor was perfectly true, but the Lord looks for uncalculating wealth of devotion to Himself rather than a fine wisdom and balanced judgment in giving. The Lord, in fact, loves a cheerful giver, not a careful one (2 Cor. ix. 7).

6. Their cruel criticism must have stung sensitive Mary like a whip-lash. Mark uses *enebrimōnto* (AV, *murmured against her*) which philologically means 'snorted at her', but in emotional content comes closer to modern English 'glowered at her'. The

[1] See p. 45.

Lord saw how troubled she was, doubtless wondering whether after all she had made a mistake, even out of love. Many young persons, harshly criticized for their self-offering for Christ's service, know a similar pang; and to them as well as to Mary comes the word of comfort. Ultimately the Lord looks, not at the human wisdom of our acts, but at the love to Him which prompts them; for note that He does not commend her for wisdom, though He is quick in her defence against the cruel taunts of the worldly-wise.

7. Here is the Christian sense of values, and that calm ability to choose out of many needs that which it is God's will that we should seek to meet. We cannot in person meet all the world's needs, nor indeed is it God's will that we personally should. This brings the tranquillity and divine selectivity that was Christ's amid manifold activity. There were many lepers and widows in Israel in Old Testament times, and yet God's blessing was restricted to one of each group, and not even one within Israel (Lk. iv. 25–27). This is the way of escape from the nervous restlessness of much modern Christian work; such nervous strain is, after all, only a symptom of that humanism which is ultimately lack of faith in God, for it springs from the belief that nothing will be done by God unless we do it ourselves.

8, 9. This does not necessarily mean that Mary had plumbed the whole secret of the Lord's death, although in Holy Week she may have heard some Saying that solemnized her. The Lord may have meant that, at His burial, loving hands would lavish costly spice on Him, as Mary had done; and if it were not waste then, it was not waste now. Both at the beginning and end of the Lord's life, such costly treasures were lavished on Him (Mt. ii. 11).

iii. Betrayal by Judas (xiv. 10, 11). With that, *Judas,* or 'Judah' (strange irony—his very name was taken as meaning 'praise'; see Rom. ii. 29, punning on Gn. xxix. 35, xlix. 8), went to the priests, determined to betray Christ. The Bible has no hint of the view, popular in some quarters today, that

Judas merely wanted to force the Lord's hand, to make Him exhibit His divine power, if He were unwilling to do it unprompted. The mention of the promised sum of money in verse 11 makes it clear that Judas was motivated by sheer avarice. He had decided that the poor play was played out—there would soon be no money to steal from the common purse, if the Lord continued to encourage 'wastefulness' like that of Mary. Matthew xxvi. 15 particularizes the sum as 'thirty pieces of silver', in prophetic quotation (Zc. xi. 12), a context which shows clearly how the early Church saw the deed of treachery. Exodus xxi. 32 specifies the sum of thirty silver shekels as the blood-price for the death of a servant—again appropriate for Him who came to serve. From that moment Judas, too, beside the priests, sought an opportunity to betray Him (cf. verse 1). How those worldly-wise priests must have nodded their heads, confirmed even more in their beliefs; even among the disciples of this other-wordly Galilaean, money talked loudly!

iv. The master of the upper room (xiv. 12–16). The story of the provision of the upper room bears many resemblances to that of the ass, used at the triumphal entry. The Lord must have had many unknown disciples, upon whom He could rely at such moments to render unquestioning service. This in itself is an encouragement to those with small or prosaic gifts; the Lord has need of them, too. We have but one record in the Gospel story of the use of either ass or room; but that one use was strategic, essential at the moment to God's whole plan. The element of prediction involved in the Lord's words here has already been discussed.[1]

The plain reading of the text of Mark suggests that this was the very day on the evening of which the Passover was killed and eaten, but the question is a vexed one, especially in view of the Johannine evidence.[2]

---

[1] See comment on xi. 2.
[2] The best recent summary of evidence is in Cranfield, pp. 420–422, but the question cannot be said to have been solved.

13. The Lord here shows a combination of supernatural knowledge and natural methods. In view of the fact that the upper room of verse 15 was ready laid for them, it suggests that the Lord had made some prior arrangements to keep Passover at the home of this resident of Jerusalem—a common practice of country pilgrims. But it was also divine foreknowledge, of the kind manifested by Samuel (1 Sa. x. 2–6), to tell His disciples of the signs that would lead them to the right house. Perhaps, even when Mark was writing, it was still unsafe or unwise to divulge the householder's name; it must have surely been known, not only to Peter himself, but to John Mark with his Jerusalem connections. It is probably over-exegesis to see in the sign of a man doing what was normally a woman's task (water-carrying) the mark of a disciple; in any case the man was but a servant, and the guide to the right home. It was with *the goodman of the house* that the disciples had business, and whether the servant was a disciple or no, the master certainly was.

14, 15. The very simplicity of the statement, *The Master saith* (Gk. *didaskalos*, 'teacher', i.e. Rabbi), shows both that the Lord was too well known to the man to need further identification, and that His disciples were known by sight. It is just possible that this was the home of John Mark in Jerusalem, for Luke at this point is almost as full as Mark; and, if Mark is in this respect a primary authority, Luke must certainly have had opportunity of contact with him. That would, then, by the usual rule, account for the anonymity of the householder in the Marcan account. (See Acts xii. 12 for later Christian use of this household as a place of meeting; but as the house is there named from Mary, we may assume that John Mark's father was dead by the date of Acts.)

16. As in the case of the tethered ass, one can almost hear the wonder of the disciples, in the wording of this verse; they found it just as the Lord had told them. But such divine provision did not absolve them from strictly practical duties such as preparing the lamb, the bitter herbs and the wine, that were needed for the meal. The Lord ever used common things (upper room, bread, wine, cup, plate) and invested them with spiritual significance, as He had done when He took a human body. Thus there is no contradiction between the first half and second half of this verse.

v. Prophecy of the betrayal (xiv. 17-21). All the Gospels make plain the Lord's knowledge that one of the Twelve would betray Him; the quotation here in verse 18 of Psalm xli. 9 makes plain some of the agony in the Lord's heart. As so often, if we note the Old Testament Scriptures either quoted or paraphrased by Him, we can see by what biblical types and analogies He understood His own experience, and thus we, in our turn, comprehend it more deeply. Even the Lord interpreted God's dealings with Him by Scripture—how much more therefore may we do the same.

20. Only John gives the exact detail of how Judas was pointed out by the Lord as the betrayer because, showing the consistency of the Johannine account, only John was close enough at table to hear the Lord's words (Jn. xiii. 26). Why did the Lord choose Judas initially? Scripture does not say; but it tells us that He had knowledge that one of the Twelve, whom He had chosen, was a *diabolos*, a very Satan, from the start (Jn. vi. 70). Was the choice of Judas a supreme token of love, like the dipping of the sop in the Johannine account? In a sense the cross of Christ, God's supreme manifestation of love, is just such another gesture. If men deliberately steel their hearts against this, then there is no hope, and they stand eternally self-condemned. Ultimately man is condemned by what he is, not by what he does; for the acts are but fruit and sign of character. Thus even the preaching of the gospel has a terrible aspect; man, by his reaction, is either saved or condemned (Jn. iii. 18).

21. Here again is a paradox of Scripture, seen again clearly in the apostolic preaching of Acts. The Son of man goes, betrayed by a friend, in fulfilment of prophetic Scripture; and yet His false follower is culpable for his act; he cannot escape individual responsibility for what he does. As always in the

New Testament, we are not called to an abstract condemnation of a 'third party', in Judas. Instead we are called to the solemn heart-searching of verse 19, 'Is it I?' When a great Christian said of a condemned criminal, 'There, but for the grace of God, go I', he was giving utterance to a deep biblical truth which should govern not only our attitude to the Bible, but also our whole attitude to life. The Sunday School teacher, who finished a stirring rendering of the parable of the Pharisee and publican (Lk. xviii) by invoking the children to thank God that they were not like the Pharisee, was typical of us all.

Peter (Acts ii. 23) shows his grasp of the 'divine paradox' outlined above when he stigmatizes the action of the Jews in betraying Christ to the Gentiles, and yet sees all as taking place by the plan and in the foreknowledge of God. Such an enigma cannot be resolved in human terms, but that does not mean that it is not capable of solution at a higher level.

vi. The Lord's Supper (xiv. 22–25). Whether or no the Lord's Supper was the actual Passover meal we cannot be sure; that depends on the exact day of the crucifixion. But even if the true Passover was taking place when the Lord hung upon the cross, and the Lord's Supper was but a *qiddūsh*, a lengthened 'grace' before the meal of a religious fraternity or *chᵃbhūrah*, the thought of Passover would have been prominent in the minds of the disciples, so that, in one sense, the question is almost irrelevant. It is arguable that the two meals bear almost the same relationship to each other as did the *Agapē*, or love-feast, to the Lord's Supper.[1]

22. What then would the meaning of the words of institution have been, for the disciples? Even if they failed to understand them, they certainly remembered them; and if they pondered them at all, they must have seen a reference to the eating of the *body* of the Passover lamb. John is clear, though admittedly writing long afterwards, as to the identification of the Lord's body with the slain lamb. He shows this beyond a shadow of a

---

[1] Cranfield (p. 422) denies the possibility of a *qiddūsh* in these circumstances, but his point does not seem proven.

doubt by his interpretation of the soldiers' reluctance to break Christ's legs (Jn. xix. 36, quoting Ex. xii. 46), and the offer of 'vinegar' (Jn. xix. 29, 30; Gk. *oxos*, Lat. *posca*, sour wine, the ordinary soldier's ration) at the cross, which could do duty for the 'bitter herbs' with which Passover was to be eaten (Ex. xii. 8). Had we not the Johannine Saying concerning Israel's feeding on manna in the wilderness (Jn. vi. 48ff.) this Marcan Saying alone would not be clear. To judge from John, the Lord at an early stage had introduced the disciples to the concept of eating His flesh and drinking His blood. It is noteworthy that, even at this early stage, many of His disciples found this Saying such a stumbling-block that they followed Him no more (Jn. vi. 60, 61, 66). This in itself is an argument for the genuineness of the Saying; had it been universally understood and accepted in early days, it would scarcely be misunderstood now.

In a sense, the taking, blessing and breaking of the bread is a deliberate way of recalling the Lord's usual action at the miracles of feeding (vi. 41, viii. 6); but it is also a picture of the Lord's taking common human flesh, blessing it and allowing it to be 'broken' for mankind.

23. The breaking of the unleavened biscuits (the *matzōth* of Ex. xii. 8) is an integral part of the Passover service, although the symbolism of the breaking is unexplained, in modern rites at least. Ceremonial washing is also a feature of the service; this reappears in John xiii, although not in the Synoptics. Four times during the service a cup of wine must be drunk, and three times bread must be broken, so it would be idle to try to equate the Lord's action with any one of these occasions. In view of the singing of the *Hallēl* immediately after (verse 26), it would seem to be an occasion toward the end of the meal, but we know too little of first-century Jewish liturgical practices to be dogmatic. The meaning of the action is unaffected in any position.

24. The wine stands for His shed *blood*, which is 'covenant blood', that is, inaugurating a solemn agreement between God and man, as that at Sinai did (Ex. xxiv. 8). Whether or no *new* should be read here, as an adjective qualifying *testament* (RV, 'covenant'), is a question of little moment, for while this disposition of affairs is parallel to that inaugurated by Moses, it is obviously not the same. Therefore, whether or no the word belongs here textually, it certainly belongs theologically. This 'new order' was a familiar prophetic concept in Old Testament times (Je. xxxi. 31; Ezk. xxxvii. 26). 'Covenant blood' is a slightly different concept from 'passover blood', so here again is a creative fusion of ideas.

The wording *for many* is a link with the interpretation of the Messiah's work and office in Isaiah liii. 12, again an example of the way in which many different lines of description converge in one at Christ. Christ's death is thus seen as a Passover; as the inauguration of a new covenant; and as a sacrifice (presumably a sin offering, even without the explicit statement of Mt. xxvi. 28). All three are distinct, though all three are sealed by bloodshed; but while it may be academically possible to isolate one concept from another for the purpose of study, yet to gain a clear picture of the work of Christ, we must combine all three into a stereoscopic picture.

25. This is the eschatological, the forward-looking, emphasis in the Lord's Supper. There is no Lord's Supper in heaven, for there it is 'fulfilled' in the marriage-feast of the Lamb (Rev. xix. 9) or the messianic banquet, as Jews loved to call it (cf. Mt. vi. 11). It is strange that, in modern Judaism, even the Passover has been set in an eschatological context, though it is a temporal and material eschatology. It will be interesting to observe in years to come whether the large-scale return to Israel affects this. Once Israel is keeping Passover in the land again, then eschatology, if kept, must become other-worldly; its goal must be beyond the grave.

b. The agony in Gethsemane (xiv. 26–42)

i. The road to Gethsemane (xiv. 26–31). At the end of the meal, the customary *hymn*, the *Hallēl*, or section of the Psalter, was sung, and the little band went out, this time not to

Bethany. This was presumably because of the lateness of the hour, and because they wanted to remain in Jerusalem itself over the actual festival season. Instead, they camped for the night among the trees of the Mount of Olives. Now the denial by Peter is prophesied, as the betrayal of Judas has already been foretold: this conversation may have taken place on the walk thither.

27, 28. The Lord used another quotation from Zechariah to illustrate the coming dispersal of His disciples, consequent on His death (Zc. xiii. 7). He saw this scattering, not as a result of persecution, but owing to a 'stumble' on their part. Their faith will be staggered by all the happenings that befall Him, despite all His previous warnings (e.g. Jn. xiv. 29). But this same chapter of Zechariah ends in a promise of mercy to the tested remnant; and so here, in verse 28, the Lord ends with yet another prediction of His resurrection, and a joyful reunion in Galilee—a rebirth, as it were, of the 'Galilaean springtime' after the dark winter of the Jerusalem days.

29. All the Gospels show the same picture of impetuous Peter, full of false pride in his own fancied strength, and scorn for the weakness of the others; he had no difficulty in believing the Lord's words to be true of his fellow disciples. But only Luke preserves the further Saying of the Lord as to Satan's desire to winnow Peter, and the Lord's prayer for strengthening his faith (Lk. xxii. 31, 32). Perhaps this was too personal a point to be included in the preaching of Peter, while the careful Luke may have culled it long after from any other of the surviving eyewitnesses (Lk. i. 1–3).

30. As Peter had signalized himself by boasting, so he was to signalize himself by failure, so that the others, as well as he, might learn distrust of all natural strength. As often, the Lord subjoined a prophetic 'sign', for the cock crowing is more than a note of time, although it may well include that. This was doubtless so that all might be reminded of His forewarning when the incident occurred (see verse 72). To those bred in the country, second cock-crow is a point of time, very distinct from the drowsy first cock-crow of midnight; but whether the Lord means this, or just two crows in quick succession from one particular cock, it is idle to speculate.

31. Peter's guilt is not concealed in the Petrine Gospel, but both Mark and Matthew make plain (cf. Mt. xxvi. 35) that it was a guilt shared by all the apostolic band, drily remarking, 'But that, after all, is exactly what every one of them said.' Peter was here, as always, just the representative disciple, the mouthpiece of the apostolic band, possibly because of his very impulsiveness and outspokenness. So it had been at Caesarea Philippi (Mt. xvi. 16), when that blinding discovery makes him the 'proto-Christian'; so assuredly it is as a 'representative Christian' that the Petrine promises are made to him (Mt. xvi. 18, 19) and thus, in him they are made to every one of us, who stand where he stood. So, too, the Petrine rebuke is ours, when we, too, fail to understand our Lord's ways (Mt. xvi. 23); we may not pick and choose, and have one without the other.

ii. The agony in the garden (xiv. 32–42). They move on into the Garden of Gethsemane, where the Lord, as it were, surrounds Himself with two rings of prayer-supporters, as a king in battle might be surrounded by his body-guard. At the periphery, near the garden entrance, were the eight; further in, the chosen three were closest to Him. To the three (for Andrew is as usual not included) the Lord revealed something of the inner struggle that was His; this is one of the points of His life at which we see how real were the temptations in the wilderness (cf. i. 12, 13), and why He rebuked Peter so sternly at the suggested avoidance of the cross (Mt. xvi. 22, 23).

34. The quotation from Psalm xlii. 5 or 11 is doubly suitable. This Psalm is not only expressive of the soul's deep longing for God, but also contains in the last clause of each of these two verses an affirmation of faith, and a promise of God's deliverance. Thus at the very moment when He seems most perplexed, He is most conscious of God's ultimate vindication. The same is true of the great cry of dereliction on the cross (Mk. xv. 34), for it is a quotation from Psalm xxii, which ends in a cry of triumph. This makes the cry one of faith, not of despair. The very verb used here, *grēgoreite, watch*, ought to have reminded His disciples of the parable of the door-keeper, told them just before (xiii. 34-37). The task of the door-keeper was to watch, and the Lord rounded off the parable by giving this as a general injunction to His disciples.

35. Standing was the usual posture for prayer in ancient times, with the hands lifted heavenwards (cf. Lk. xviii. 11; 1 Tim. ii. 8), but prostration was indicative of spiritual anguish (e.g. Nu. xvi. 22). Here again is a divine paradox, seen in the repetition of the adjective *dunaton, possible*. All things are by definition possible to omnipotence; but it was not possible for Jesus to be the Christ, and yet to avoid drinking the cup. That would have been only a verbal, not an actual, possibility, for it would have been a contradiction in terms. The early Church faced a similar ambiguity when they argued as to whether one should say of Christ *non posse peccare* (it was impossible for Him to sin), or *posse non peccare* (it was possible for Him to abstain from sin). In Him, both became one.

36. Only the Petrine preaching has preserved the tender *Abba, Father,*[1] from the original Aramaic prayer. Romans viii. 15 and Galatians iv. 6 show the quasi-liturgical use of this linguistic survival in the early Church. This was the more easy in that Paul, too, was a native speaker of Aramaic, familiar as he undoubtedly was with Greek (Phil. iii. 5; Acts xxii. 2). As in the Saying to James and John (Mk. x. 38), *cup* is a symbol of suffering, as well as of joy: and so the two meanings are blended in the words of institution at the Last Supper. But the thought may well go far deeper than a mere general symbolism of suffering, to the particular Old Testament concept of the cup of the wrath of God, designed for the foes of God, which Christ would drink at Calvary, in our room and stead (cf. Ps.

---

[1] It is a mistake, with some editors, to see this admittedly colloquial term as a 'nursery-word'; what other Aramaic word for 'Father' could the Lord have used? By this date, determinative forms were used very freely in Aramaic, with little appreciable difference in meaning. See also the comment on Mk. v. 41.

lxxv. 8). The last clause, *not what I will, but what thou wilt,* is a summary of the earthly life of obedience of the Christ; and such obedience was only perfected when it was 'unto death' (Phil. ii. 8).

Luke the doctor alone records, with medical interest, the extraordinary perspiration that accompanied the agony (Lk. xxii. 44). It is uncertain whether the reference is to the profuseness of the perspiration or to some other feature. But what caused the agony? To speak of the natural human shrinking from betrayal, mockery, scourging and death, all heightened by full foreknowledge, is too shallow an answer, while these no doubt were factors. All these the Lord had not only foreseen, but also foretold to His disciples (e.g. x. 32-34). During all of His earthly life He had been conscious of a steadily mounting pressure, which was not finally released until the cry of triumph from the cross 'It is finished' (Jn. xix. 30). The Lord used the parallel picture of baptism to describe this inner constraint (Lk. xii. 50), as in the conversation with James and John (Mk. x. 38).

37-39. The grave words of rebuke, though applicable to all, are addressed directly to Peter, using *Simon,* his 'natural' name, not Cephas (Peter) his name 'in grace' (see Mk. iii. 16). They are fittingly recorded in Peter's Gospel, as well as Matthew xxvi. 40. But they are not merely a rebuke for his recent boasting; they were to prepare him for the coming tests of the judgment hall. Yet Peter and his fellows were warned in vain, for they failed to take the only steps which could have saved them—earnest prayer in advance, and continual watchfulness at the time (verse 38). This is not arbitrary; such prayer is, at one and the same time, a confession of the weakness of our own *flesh* (38) and a showing forth of the readiness of our *spirit* by the very act of prayer, joined with a realization of the power of God to whom we pray. So prayer is one expression of Christian faith, as obedience is another; for faith is a simultaneous realization of our weakness and God's strength in any given set of circumstances. Peter's rebuke is that he had not the strength to watch. The Greek *ouk ischuō, couldest not,* is the same as that in ix. 18 of the powerlessness of the disciples to heal the boy at the foot of the mount of transfiguration.

40. The language is again reminiscent of that used to describe the drowsy three at the mount of transfiguration (ix. 8), where again even voluble Peter was finally lost for words. Here in the garden, the shame-faced disciples in all their pettiness are seen in the last clause; desirous though they were of justifying themselves, they were utterly abashed, and could find no words to say.

41, 42. The third visit of the Lord to the disciples, as the three temptations of the Lord (Mt. iv. 1–11), gives the idea of finality and completeness; so there is a fitting finality in the Lord's words to His disciples, *Sleep on now*. Their failure has been complete, and they may well sleep now; the crisis is over, and the betrayer near. In the Lord's words there is no hint of bitterness, but there is a world of sadness.

c. Christ taken captive (xiv. 43–52)

43. John xiii. 30 explains that Judas had slipped away from the Last Supper earlier that evening, immediately after receiving the final token of love. He left presumably as soon as he had found out what place in Jerusalem was to be the rendezvous for that night. He had then waited until the band might be safely assumed to be asleep; and the verses above show how right Judas was in his judgment. He was not lacking in worldly wisdom; it was indeed through worldly wisdom that Judas fell (see Lk. xvi. 8; 1 Cor. i. *passim*). So, too, he had brought a well-armed company of temple police and lusty young priests, with *swords and staves*, or cudgels, respectively, for a priest should not actually shed blood (thus Odo of Bayeux rode beside William the Conqueror, but with a mace, not a sword). Although Judas can scarcely have been present to hear the Saying about the two swords (Lk. xxii. 38), yet he knew his impetuous fellow disciples; and Peter's reaction showed how wise Judas had been here also.

44, 45. Judas had even made the identification of his destined victim sure amid the uncertainties and half-light of the garden with its olive trees. He was to be marked out by the *kiss* of peace and the salutation of *Master*, 'Rabbi', both natural signs between disciple and master. Here is the proof of utter moral blindness. Judas did not see the condemnation that would be eternally his for using the very signs of love as a means of betrayal. His sole concern was that the arrest should go smoothly; and again, his wisdom and efficiency were the snares that caught him. But such blindness was inevitable for one who had already used the sign of love (the sop at the Last Supper, Jn. xiii. 26) as a bolt to close the door, instead of a key to open it. Again, we must all ask, 'Is it I?' (xiv. 19). The miracle is that a man could live so close to Christ for three years, and yet could steel his heart against Him.

46. John xviii. 2–11 gives a much fuller account of what happened in the Garden, as is to be expected. See also Matthew xxvi. 50 and Luke xxii. 48, for the grieved words of the Lord in response to such treachery.

47. Who owned the two swords of Luke xxii. 38? Peter, James, John or Simon the Zealot, would seem to be the only likely candidates. Here Peter is wearing one of them; perhaps the Zealot wore the other. Only John, writing long after the event, finds it safe to mention Peter's name here,[1] writing as he does apparently after Peter's death (Jn. xxi. 19); he also is the only Evangelist to mention the name of the servant (Jn. xviii. 10). This last might not have been known to Peter, though it would certainly have been known to one who was personally acquainted with the high priest (Jn. xviii. 15). In any case in Peter's preaching such a circumstantial detail would have been dangerous. Only John and Luke mention the healing of the ear, though all Synoptists mention the blow; the precise 'General Practitioner', Luke, also mentions with medical accuracy that it was the right ear (Lk. xxii. 50). Like

---

[1] Lagrange, quoted by Cranfield, seems right in maintaining that Mark's *heis tis, one of them*, 'a certain man', implies that, although Mark knows well who struck the blow, yet, for reasons of his own, he will not give the name.

the blow of Moses to the Egyptian (Ex. ii. 12), this exhibition of 'the wrath of man' failed to work out God's purpose.

48, 49. This gentle rebuke must have stung the priests. They had not arrested Him by day for fear; not for fear of His disciples, but for fear of the crowds of simple men, unblinded by prejudice that theological learning can bring, who would have cried aloud against such an outrage (Mk. xii. 12). The Lord often thus appealed to the simple moral sense of the common man (cf. Mt. xii. 11, in sabbath controversy).

Such a violent arrest of the Messiah was a fulfilment of many prophetic *scriptures*. The one especially in mind here may be that quoted in Luke xxii. 37, immediately preceding the Saying about the two swords, 'and he was reckoned among the transgressors' (from Is. liii. 12). Those who have seen secret police at work in any part of the world will appreciate this. Arrests are usually made at night, for two reasons; the victims are liable to be confused and offer less resistance, and the neighbours are not likely to gather and protest. Life changes little over millennia in such matters.

50. So was fulfilled the Lord's prophecy about their 'stumbling' (xiv. 27); for, had they accepted God's way, they might have grieved, but would have stood quietly by their Lord as He was arrested. 'That is not natural', we exclaim; no, it is not; and that is why Christ's way ever makes natural man to stumble (1 Cor. ii. 14). Peter's puzzle was the greater, in that he had always striven for the natural way (Mt. xvi. 22). He must have thought that the Lord had encouraged man's path to the kingdom, in bidding them take swords (Lk. xxii. 38); and now the Lord had forbidden it (Mt. xxvi. 52; Lk. xxii. 51). To be 'offended in Christ', in biblical language, means to be utterly staggered by His ways, to lack the spiritual key that alone opens them, by that insight that God's Spirit alone can bring (1 Cor. ii. 15, 16).

51, 52. The Greek word *neaniskos, young man*, might denote one in late adolescence, in his teens. He is usually taken as being John Mark of Jerusalem, in whose father's home the

Last Supper may have taken place (cf. 'the goodman of the house', xiv. 14). Christians later met there for prayer and worship (Acts xii. 12), and Peter knew the place well. By then Mary, the mother of John Mark, is head of the house, so presumably his father had died. This in itself is a reminder to us of the strong physical link and continuity between the world of the Gospels and the world of Acts i–xii. It is after that date, with the vast Gentile expansion of the Church, that the break comes, a break which does not become final till the sack of Jerusalem. Mark would thus have been a lad, hurriedly aroused from sleep, with a sheet wrapped around him; presumably one of the frightened disciples had dashed back to John Mark's house with the news. Of course this may have been an irrelevant Petrine memory, a trifling incident stamped upon his mind, not by its own importance, but by the events surrounding it; but if Peter was already in flight, such detailed observation was unlikely. It might, it is true, be some other youth altogether; but if so, it is hard to see either the reason for the mention, or the failure to give his name. In any case he must have been a young disciple, or one known to the Christian Church. It seems unnecessary and unfair to spiritualize an incident like this; it is stated as a plain fact, and as such it must be accepted, whatever spiritual lessons we may then see fit to associate with the event.

d. The fall of Peter (xiv. 53-72)

53. In this account of Peter's denial, the exact chronology of the trial is in dispute; it is even uncertain how many separate court hearings there were. As this does not greatly affect the issue, however, we may leave it for lengthier works to consider.

On the face of it, this would seem to be late at night. This impression is heightened by the fire mentioned in verse 54. Fires are for light as much as for heat in any simple society even today. But Jerusalem lies nearly 3,000 feet above sea-level, and spring nights can be cold, so this in itself is no conclusive evidence; Peter was warming himself at the fire (verse 54), but he was recognized by the fire-light (verse 67).

54. Had Peter some obscure idea of rescuing the Christ by force? His lies need not have been altogether of cowardice; they might have been of some perverted strategy, though Scripture admittedly gives no hint of this. But even if this were so, he was still (as in Mt. xvi) thinking man's thoughts, and so came under condemnation (Mt. xvi. 23). Nevertheless this interpretation may be over-subtle, like that rejected above, which would impute good, though warped, motives to Judas. Probably Peter had no plan but was merely still thunderstruck. From whatever motive he did it, he stands condemned in Scripture as the man who denied his Lord after all his boast-fulness; and so he makes every Christian of every generation search his heart.

55. This appears to be a sort of preliminary fact-finding commission of the Sanhedrin. While they had long ago decided on His death for reasons good and sufficient to them, they had still to formulate a legal charge, adequate to justify the death penalty; they had no desire to assassinate Him, lest it provoke a bloody riot and consequent Roman action. Another proof of moral blindness was their failure to see that, in God's eyes, there was no difference between the quick knife of the dagger-men, who flourished at festival time (see Acts xxi. 38), and such judicial murder. But even if the high priests could find some single breach of the Torah, sufficient in Jewish eyes to warrant a death sentence, their task was still but half done. They also had to produce some political charge, sufficient in Roman eyes to warrant the carrying out of the death sentence. Both Pilate (Mt. xxvii. 23) and Gallio (Acts xviii. 14–16) show Roman reluctance to condemn a provincial on purely religious charges, especially when that religion was to them an offensive oriental cult, practised by an unpopular subject people. The Mishnah makes frequent bitter reference to the fact that the Romans had taken away the cherished power of capital punishment from the Jewish courts, even when dealing with their own people. As we read of the lynching of Stephen (Acts vii. 57–60), or of any of the mob attacks on Paul (e.g. Acts xxi. 27–30), we may wonder how effective such statute law was. Yet the rescue of Paul, with rough kindliness, by the soldiers of Castle Antonia, shows that no Roman Governor would tolerate even a lynching under his eyes, let alone a regularly-executed death sentence. Obviously, rough mob justice, of a quasi-legal character, was not unknown, any more than it is in many parts of the world today; but then as now it conflicted with the law of the land, and would be punished if detected (Acts xix. 40). Especially in explosive Jerusalem at Passover time, with the city tense and full of milling throngs of nationalistic Jews, the Romans were on their toes. Such judicial murder, especially if it provoked a riot (xiv. 2), would have dire consequences for the Jewish leaders, if not to the whole Jewish state (Jn. xi. 48).

56. For this whole section on the fabrication of the charges, see the author's *The New Temple*,[1] where the question is discussed at some length. The concept of false witness and judicial murder is found in the Old Testament (1 Ki. xxi. 10). The trouble was not lack of evidence, but too much; doubtless the same gold that bought Judas, bought these willing helpers, as could be done outside the law courts of many another city. But, as usual, it was harder to agree on a consistent lie than to tell the simple truth; and the very prolixity of these garrulous witnesses was their undoing. It is obvious that none of the early charges about sabbath-breaking would hold water, or they would have been produced at once, and all would have agreed on their truth. Common Jewish equity would not allow a man to be put to death for healing a sick man on the sabbath day, any more than for watering his stock on the sabbath; and the Pharisees, grumble as they might, knew this too well to proceed with the attempt.

57–59. Of all the Synoptists, Mark contains the fullest version of the content of this charge. That is not surprising, seeing that Peter, his source, was listening in the hall, as he warmed himself at the fire with the high priest's men. If Peter still had sword on hip, he might have passed the more unnoticed among the half-armed gathering. This accusation at

[1] *The New Temple*, Tyndale Press, 1951.

least was a true Jewish report of a Saying misunderstood by them, but preserved in John ii. 19. Indeed, without the preservation of this Saying by John, and its interpretation, we should be utterly at a loss to explain this charge except as pure fabrication.

In the Johannine way, the very quotation of the Saying in his Gospel probably means that he knew well of its use at the trial and that two of the Synoptists had referred to it, for Luke makes no mention of it at all. Indeed, as so often, the inclusion of the Saying by John is a tacit supplement to, and explanation of, the earlier Synoptic account. From John, we see that this Saying, only understood by the disciples after the resurrection, was a reference to the dissolution and raising up again, three days later, of the Lord's body; and from this springs the whole 'New Temple' concept. This metaphor was apparently freely used in Christian catechesis within the early Church, of which space will not allow a full discussion here. John was present at the trial, too, as an acquaintance of the high priest, and he must have heard this charge as well as Peter. But if this wild charge were taken literally, as apparently it was, it could only be construed as a claim to possess supernatural or quasi-magical powers; and no man could be condemned for that alone, for the source of His power might be good or evil. The Talmud is full of stories of miracle-working rabbis, and who is to say which magic is black and which is white? The bitter Pharisees might say that the Lord had a devil (Jn. viii. 48), or did cures of demon expulsion by Beelzebub (Mk. iii. 22), but the common man would scarcely believe that (Jn. x. 21). It is true that on the question of the profanation of the Temple (Acts xxi. 28), or destruction of the Temple (Acts vi. 14), the Jews were particularly sensitive, as subsequent Christian experience confirmed. But such charges could not justify a legal death sentence, the more so as the same Saying contained a prophecy of rebuilding. Also it is hard to see, even with the bitter Pharisaic reply in view (Jn. ii. 20), how any man could have taken such a Saying literally. Herod had performed this task already, demolishing Zerubbabel's mean Temple down to ground level, and rebuilding, with great blocks of Herodian masonry, the Temple which they saw now; could any Pharisee really believe that Christ intended to repeat this process?[1]

60. Even if the charges themselves could neither be defined nor substantiated, could He not perhaps be goaded by these charges into some utterance that would incriminate Him? But He remained silent; there was no need to deny such charges; even to the priestly court, they were worthless, save as make-weights. The silence of the Christ was in itself a prophetic sign (Is. liii. 7), as Peter saw (1 Pet. ii. 23).

61. The high priest must have known that the Lord at least accepted the title of *Christ* from those around Him (Jn. i. 49), but it may have been that He had avoided making such a claim unequivocally in presence of His enemies, until God's time had come. Matthew xxvi. 63 makes clear that this was no casual enquiry, but a question put 'under oath', as it were, in the solemn Name of God. Indeed the very word, *exorkizō*, 'I adjure', used by the high priest, may contain another reference to the priestly charge that He, upon whom the Holy Spirit rested (Jn. i. 33), was demon-possessed (Jn. vii. 20), and so must be solemnly exorcised. When under oath by the Name of God, even such a one must speak true (cf. Mk. v. 7).

But would He deftly extricate Himself from this ensnaring question, as He had from their well-planned dilemma about tribute to Caesar (xii. 14)? As with a modern Moslem, to claim to be Christ, the Anointed, God's Prophet, would be no blasphemy, although it might be hotly contradicted on point of fact, and a sign would be demanded. But to be *the Son of the Blessed* would seem intolerable blasphemy, and for such a blasphemy He might be condemned to death by the Sanhedrin. They must have known something of the stories of His birth, from the ugliness of John viii. 41; and the Lord's quiet question in John x. 34, based on Psalm lxxxii. 6, shows both that He consistently claimed to be the Son of God, and that He knew the reaction that it provoked. The bitterness of the taunt at the cross (Mt. xxvii. 43) again shows that this was a well-known

---

[1] See Cranfield, p. 442: but he goes too far in abandoning hope of discovering the original form of the Saying.

claim of Christ's, whether enunciated in these exact terms or not.

62. It may be significant that when 'exorcised', or put under oath by the Name of God, the Lord replied with the very Name of God, *I am* (Ex. iii. 14), thus putting Himself on an equality with God, which we know to have been a long-standing grievance on their part (Jn. x. 33). In the Johannine account, it has been pointed out that He used the Name of God in a similar reply in the Garden, and at the Name, the very men sent to arrest Him prostrated themselves on the ground (Jn. xviii. 6). But the present instance is reported only by Mark, and thus survives only in the Petrine tradition; even Matthew, with all his Jewish interests, knows nothing of it. The form of the Saying may therefore be more accidental than significant. In John's Gospel, it is true, it is sometimes hard to decide where plain narration of fact ends and interpretation by the Evangelist begins. But as fact plus interpretation is the definition of revelation, the point is of little moment, and in the Johannine context, the association with the divine Name seems sure, in view of the terrified reaction of the temple servants.

The Lord, while agreeing with the priestly definition of His nature, defines it further in terms of *Son of man*, His special self-chosen title. This is explained by another 'creative fusion' of Psalm cx. 1 with Daniel vii. 13. But, had the high priest only ears to hear, there was a solemn warning in this choice of Scriptures, for this was the Son of man vindicated and enthroned, and returning in judgment. So Stephen saw Him, before his death by stoning (Acts vii. 56), and thus prophesied judgment on his murderers, at the very moment when he prayed for their forgiveness. The priesthood stood on trial that day, although the execution of their sentence was yet to come, on that awful day in AD 70 when the priests were cut down at the altar as they steadily continued their sacrifices.

63, 64. This was the condemnation of the religious leaders of Israel: the high priest had asked not for information, but to trap the Lord. He must have known the Lord's claims long before he asked. Of course, had not such a claim been true, it would have been either madness (Jn. x. 20) or blasphemy (*aut Deus, aut homo non bonus* is an inescapable alternative). But the condemnation of the high priest is not simply that he did not believe it, but that he did not even ask himself whether it were true or false. Such a man was wilfully and culpably blind; he had closed his eyes in advance to the truth. But are we blind also? Who can cast the first stone?

The rending of garments, by now traditional on hearing blasphemy, was in origin a sign of grief, as is plain from the Old Testament (e.g. Lv. x. 6). Here it had become strangely warped into a sign of savage joy at a wicked purpose well-nigh accomplished. Joyfully, the worthless witnesses are dismissed: the high priest calls the *bêth dîn*, or court, to be themselves witnesses, and he formally asks for their opinion. Just as formally they give it: Jesus of Nazareth is liable to the death penalty for blasphemy. The agony is that, had His claim been false, it would have been a blasphemy of such magnitude; but what if He were right? None save Nicodemus seems to have dared to think of that (Jn. vii. 50–52) and he was scornfully dismissed.

65. With this condemnation, away went all restraint; no longer did the judges trouble to observe the outward forms of impartiality. Let them but act like this to the fiery Paul, and they would be told, as lawyer to lawyers, the injustice of what they did (Acts xxiii. 3). But Paul regretted his outburst at once (Acts xxiii. 5), and Peter never forgot the picture of the patient endurance of the Lord amid the taunts and blows (1 Pet. ii. 21–23). The derisive call, *Prophesy*, is given in Matthew xxvi. 68: 'Prophesy unto us, thou Christ, Who is he that smote thee?' This shows it to be a gibe at His claim to Messiahship, which would at the least involve prophethood, and had been shown above to involve Sonship of God. But the 'prophet from Galilee' was in any case a popular title for Him (cf. Mt. xxi. 11).

66–71. The whole story of Peter's fall leaves the reader helpless, powerless to intervene, as the tragedy unfolds inexorably, scene after scene, until Peter has passed the point of no return, and finally crashes. Rash self-confidence and scorn of others (xiv. 29); failure to discipline the flesh in the Garden (xiv. 37); the cowardice of the flight (xiv. 50); the following at a distance (xiv. 54); the close association with the enemies of Christ (xiv. 54)—all these in their turn made the actual denial logical and indeed well-nigh inevitable. No doubt Peter was sincere in his initial desires and protestations (xiv. 31), as a child is; and as a child's protestations, the Lord gravely received them, gently pointing out their utter inadequacy as He did so. But the battle against temptation in the high priest's palace had been lost long before; for the time for the Christian to fight temptation is before it is encountered.

This girl (66, 67) must have seen Peter before, in the company of Christ, and so recognized him as one of the Lord's disciples, just as the Jerusalem bystanders of verse 70 concluded that he must be one because of his Galilaean brogue. There were many Galilaeans in the capital at Passover time, true; but not among the servants of the high priest. The tragedy is that each step downward might have been a step upward; on each occasion, Peter was being forced to declare himself. At least he could no longer remain silent: now he must either admit or deny. God thus made the path of witness easier for him, and the issues more clear cut. But Peter chose, deliberately and thrice, to deny; and so these promptings of grace became occasions of condemnation, as they must always be if they are refused.

It is the fashion nowadays to make excuses for Peter, as some do for Judas, even if we do not go to the lengths of imputing good motives to either; and in so far as it means that we see our own weakness in him, that may be good. But unless we see the heinousness of his sin, we cannot understand the bitterness of his remorse, nor the depth of his repentance, nor the riches of grace in his restoration. The point is not to analyse by what easy steps the fall came, but to realize the terrible nature of the fall. Light thoughts on sin ultimately lead to light thoughts on redemption, and ultimately rob the cross of its glory.

72. It has been suggested above (on xiv. 30) that 'second cock-crow' is a definite point of time, not merely a prophetic sign. It denotes true dawn, as against the false dawn of first cock-crow; and xv. 1, 'straightway in the morning', supports this. But be that as it may, it was as a fulfilled sign that second cock-crow recalled to the mind of Peter the Lord's words; Luke xxii. 61 adds that at this moment the Lord wheeled round and looked full at Peter; and so his cup of remorse was full. The Greek *epibalōn, when he thought thereon*, is probably not 'on thinking it over', but 'he set to and thought', or simply 'he began to think'.[1]

e. The trial before Pilate (xv. 1–15)

i. The stage is set (xv. 1). This reads as if the night's proceedings had been but an attempt by a 'steering committee' to clarify the charge with the legal experts. Now a plenary session of the Sanhedrin formally bound Christ, and brought Him before the Governor. Thus begins, not the trial before Pilate, but the trial of Pilate, for he stands self-revealed as he attempts in vain, first to avoid the issue, and then to escape responsibility for the decision. But as in the case of Peter, Pilate is pushed inexorably to a verdict, and his verdict is condemned every time that we repeat in the Creed the clause 'Suffered under Pontius Pilate'. 'What is your opinion of the Messiah?' (see Mt. xxii. 42) is the question that everlastingly faces every man; and our eternal destiny depends upon our answer.

ii. Pilate condemns Christ to death (xv. 2–15). The trial proper begins (as can be seen from Lk. xxiii. 2) with a confused mass of general accusations, designed to paint the Lord in a black light as a revolutionary, a trouble maker, one who forbade the payment of Caesar's impost and who claimed to be an anointed ruler Himself. At this period the word *basileus, King*, was used equally of tetrarchs, subject kings, and the wearer of the Imperial purple at Rome, though the latter

[1] So Moulton, p. 131, quoting a Ptolemaic papyrus, also mentioned by Arndt and Gringrich.

might also be called *Sebastos*, corresponding in meaning to the Latin *Augustus*. The crime in this court would have to be one of sedition against Rome, and so any and every flimsy charge was added as a make-weight; for the charge about refusal of Caesar's impost was a palpable lie, as the high priests knew well. But at the mention of the claim to be another petty Jewish kinglet, Pilate jumped to action; that charge might well have some substance, and if so Imperial Rome would take cognizance of it. No 'client king' must rule save with Rome's consent. To Pilate's abrupt question the Lord gave a tranquil answer which was a full admission (Jn. xviii. 33–37) and yet showed conclusively that the legions had nothing to fear from such an other-worldly king.

3–5. Still the battery of charges continued, and still the Lord did not deign to answer them, to the marvel of Pilate. It is at this point that Luke inserts the story of the despatch of the prisoner to Herod, under whose immediate jurisdiction Galilee lay; Pilate had no desire at all to meddle with this case, the less so if it still further strained relations with Herod (Lk. xxiii. 12). But it was to no purpose; back came the weary procession, and the round began again (Lk. xxiii. 11, 13–16). This episode is omitted in Matthew and Mark, as not affecting the main movement of the trial. In Mark, the whole account is brief and 'telescoped'; were it not for the other Gospels, we might well miss something of the complexity of the sequence of events. But the Petrine source, for all its brevity, lays no false emphases; Pilate is still cynical, still knows that the Jews only accuse Christ out of envy (verse 10), yet desires to please them (verse 15). Turbulent Palestine was to be the grave of many an ambitious administrator's career; these Jews had influence at Rome. Finally, he knowingly frees a guilty man and condemns an innocent one (verse 15). All that John and Matthew add to this picture is to show us more in detail of Pilate's weakness and vacillations. It is interesting to speculate whether the reason for Mark's brevity here, where he is *kolobodaktulos* in style,[1] is that Peter, his source, was not personally present at

[1] See Introduction, p. 38.

the trial before Pilate, nor that before Herod, while earlier he had been present in the high priest's hall (xiv. 66).

6. There was still a possibility of escaping the responsibility of a decision by the time-honoured custom of releasing a prisoner amid a time of general rejoicing. Many of the new nations of Asia have celebrated their post-war independence by some kind of similar general amnesty of political prisoners.

7. There is not inconsiderable MS evidence for the possibility of this man's name being Jesus bar-Abba (or, more likely, bar-Rabba), just as the Lord's human name was Jesus bar-Joseph (Lk. iv. 22), although He was apparently more usually known as the carpenter's son, from His trade (Mt. xiii. 55). Jesus,[1] or Joshua, was a common first-century Jewish name. This would heighten the contrast between the two figures. Some exegetes have made play with the possible meaning of 'bar-Abba' as being 'Son of the Father'. But as the Gospel of the Hebrews (quoted by Jerome on Mt. xxvii. 16, the Synoptic parallel to this verse) had instead 'bar-Rabba', where the second element probably conceals a divine name, the point seems untenable linguistically, however helpful devotionally. As to the value of such 'Christian midrash', there have always been two violently opposed opinions in the Christian Church, and probably always will be; enough to say, with the early church of Antioch, that such handling, legitimate or not, is not true exegesis of the Scripture. At all events, the man seems to have been a Zealot, captured after some brush with the authorities in which there had been fatalities, and whose doom was thus sealed, but whose popularity with the nationalists was also assured. The outcome of such a choice was probable from the start; and the high priests made it certain, by their canvassing for Barabbas (xv. 11).

8. Attention is often drawn to the fickleness of a crowd, by comparison of the cheering throngs at the triumphal entry (xi. 9, 10) with this crowd, so soon to cry for His blood (verse

---

[1] Cranfield (p. 451) has an interesting explanation of Pilate's attitude, based on this coincidence of name: but it is too conjectural to be convincing.

13). But, although such mob fickleness is common (witness the quick change in the Lycaonian crowd in Acts xiv. 13, 19), yet, right up to the trial, the Lord's popularity with the crowd was undoubted (xii. 37). Indeed, it was precisely because of this popularity that the religious leaders dared not arrest Him openly (xiv. 2). The simplest answer is that these were two different crowds. The crowd of the triumphal entry was made up of pious pilgrims, no doubt many from Galilee, and an equally pious crowd from Jerusalem met them (Jn. xii. 12ff.). These last may equally well have been themselves earlier arrivals among the pilgrims. But, as Luther found, when he made his famous pilgrimage to Rome, piety is apt to flourish more away from a Holy City, than in it; and doubtless there were many residents of Jerusalem who were far from pious. We know from John x. 19-21 that even among the ordinary Jerusalem crowd there was strife concerning Him. This crowd at the trial must have been composed, in part at least, of the followers and servants of the high priests, seeing that all moved apparently *en bloc* from the high-priestly hall to Pilate's palace. Thus we are probably dealing with a mere section of the Jerusalem mob, a section specifically stated in verse 11 to have been deliberately inflamed by the high priests. Pious pilgrims had more to do at Passover time than to gape at Roman judges; indeed even the priests had scruples about Gentile defilement at such a time (Jn. xviii. 28).

9-12. The deep perverseness of human nature is clearly seen here. On the one hand Pilate genuinely wishes to escape from a difficult position by releasing Jesus, perhaps after a cautionary flogging (Lk. xxiii. 16). On the other hand, he cannot resist avenging himself on the Jewish leaders, who have placed him in a difficult situation. His way of petty vengeance is to taunt them with the claim to kingship made by the Lord. John xix. 15 makes clear how effective and galling this was to the Jews. Yet such vengeance by Pilate only made it the more certain that what he most desired could not take place, for it but exacerbated their bitterness against Christ. We cannot say that such perverseness is impossible; to him who looks within, it is a factor of daily experience; and the particle *for* in verse 10 makes nonsense unless we take some such common sense explanation. Pilate was no unnatural monster; he was a man of like passions to us; that is what makes his story such a warning.

13, 14. Even allowing for a natural preference for Barabbas, the 'patriotic' figure, it is hard to see why the crowd should thus shout, demanding a Roman death for Christ, unless the priests had deliberately inflamed them by stories of His supposed blasphemies (cf. verse 11). Beheading was the Roman death for a citizen, as traditionally for Paul; crucifixion for a slave or foreigner, as traditionally for Peter (Jn. xxi. 18); while stoning was the normal form of Jewish death-sentence, from the earliest days (Jos. vii. 25). After death by stoning, the bodies might be displayed upon a stake until the evening (Jos. x. 26; Dt. xxi. 22, 23). This last to the Jew was a public sign that the one who so died was under the wrath and curse of God (Dt. xxi. 23). So in the divine providence, the cross, besides its Roman associations of shame and a slave's death, had a deeper meaning to the Jews (Gal. iii. 13).

15. Nothing could be more cynical than the disregard for truth (Jn. xviii. 38) in this man who, knowing Him to be innocent (verse 14), yet flogged and crucified the Son of God, through a desire to ingratiate himself with the Jews (verse 15). It is true that Matthew and John give us extra sidelights which show more of Pilate's weakness and indecision; but this only shows us that he was perfectly conscious of the wrongfulness of what he did, and thus but increases his guilt.

f. The crucifixion (xv. 16–47)

i. The mockery (xv. 16–20). Now comes the mocking by the soldiers (see xiv. 65 for the mocking by the priests). Herod's 'men of war' (Lk. xxiii. 11) were probably either local Palestinian levies or some of his own hard-bitten Gaulish mercenaries, little more than hired assassins, of whom Josephus tells us. They, too, had mocked the Lord, but hardly with the venom of Pilate's men here, who may not have been full Roman citizens, but were certainly anti-Jewish in sentiment. If the 'Italian cohort' (see Acts x. 1) was stationed in Judaea in those days, there must have been some inhabitants of Italy among them, with the half-way gift of 'Latin rights'. None of these long-service regulars would have been locally raised in Palestine. Many were doubtless wild auxiliaries from other frontier provinces; but the one loyalty that bound them together was the rough soldier's loyalty to the Caesar and the Eagles.

The one charge that had penetrated their thick but honest skulls was that this prisoner claimed to be a king Himself, and was thus a potential rival to Caesar, despicable though He might seem to them. Hence the point of the rough mockery— the *purple*, or scarlet cloak of the Roman cavalryman, the crown, the sceptre, like the great commander-in-chief himself, to whom alone they bowed their knee as soldiers. There was a rough loyalty and patriotism in their very mockery; '*virtutes paganorum splendida vitia*', said the Latin father sadly—the very virtues of the pagans are only noble faults. The Roman exasperation against the 'cloak and dagger men' of first-century Judaism was growing, until it found terrible outlet in the massacres of AD 70, when easy-going Titus tried in vain to save the Jews from the wrath of the legionaries. Those who have lived with regular troops long, subject to such 'pinpoint' civilian terrorist activities, will know the exasperation it breeds in the rank and file. The bluff Roman soldier has an interesting concept of 'fair play' in war; even strategy he distrusted; Hannibal the strategist was *perfidus Poenus*, 'the treacherous Carthaginian', who always had something up his sleeve, and who would not come out into the open and fight man to man. Thus Jewish nationalism led to the arrest, and Roman nationalism to the mockery and the cross: so deep in all things natural is the 'old man'. Patriotism is not enough, as more than one patriot has found at the last.

ii. 'Take up thy cross' (xv. 21). Simon of Cyrene might be taken homiletically as a picture of every disciple, bearing the

Lord's cross for Him. His Greek name means literally 'snub-nosed', but as in the case of the apostle it doubtless conceals the good Hebrew name of Simeon (cf. Acts xv. 14 for the full form). He was doubtless a Cyrenian Jew; such had their own synagogue in Jerusalem (Acts vi. 9). He may have been a visitor to Jerusalem for the Passover, although his entry from *the country* at an early hour suggests that he was a resident of Jerusalem, as does the fact that his sons Alexander and Rufus were known personally to either Peter or Mark. They are mentioned as being of interest to the Christian community, and therefore presumably Christians themselves. If Mark ever visited Alexandria,[1] or even produced his Gospel there, one would expect to find more Cyrenians in the Church of Alexandria than in that of Jerusalem, and the point would become one of more relevance and interest. It is tempting, in view of the tradition that Mark's Gospel is the Petrine preaching as it took shape at Rome, to see a possible reference to the Rufus of the Roman Church mentioned in Romans xvi. 13. But the indefinite Greek particle *tina, one,* suggests that Simon himself was not known to the Christian Church; and in Romans xvi. 13 only a mother of Rufus is mentioned. Such an identification is too tenuous to press; and of Alexander we can say nothing, for none of the three New Testament candidates appear likely (Acts iv. 6, xix. 33 and 1 Tim. i. 20 with 2 Tim. iv. 14). In any case, Simon was 'impressed' (*they compel*) by the Roman Government for this piece of state service, designed to acerbate feelings further among the provincials.

iii. The crucifixion (xv. 22–32). Whatever the exact site of the crucifixion, the meaning of *Golgotha* is well translated by the Latin *Calvarium,* a smooth rounded hilltop devoid of vegetation, giving the appearance of a bald head, or skull. With deference to some topographers, who see plainly two staring eye-sockets in their chosen hill as proof of identification, in Hebrew and Greek the chief impression left by a skull was its roundness and smoothness, to judge by etymology. When the American troops nicknamed a bloodstained hillock in

[1] See Introduction, pp. 44 f.

Korea 'Old Baldy', they came closer to the sense of both languages. Modern English 'skull cap' preserves this old sense of the word.

23. The sour local wine was 'laced' with myrrh; this would give it a bitter taste, but a soporific effect. Thus is explained the reference to 'gall' (Mt. xxvii. 34), with its prophetic counterpart (Ps. lxix. 21). He would not take any anaesthetic; all His faculties must be unclouded for what lay before Him.[1] Such wine, tradition tells us, was provided by pious women of Jerusalem for condemned criminals.

24. Although Mark makes no specific reference to the fulfilment of prophecy in this verse, yet his choice of wording shows that both he and the other Evangelists see in this dicing by the soldiers for their perquisites, a clear fulfilment of Psalm xxii. 18. There was thus a divine appropriateness, not only in the Lord's death, but in its manner; and not alone in the manner of His death, but even in the incidents associated with it. This the disciples failed to see until after the resurrection; at the moment, as they watched from far away (xv. 40), sorrow and despair must have filled their hearts.

25. The exact time of the crucifixion is a problem; but normally *the third hour* would mean nine o'clock in the morning. The three hours of darkness would thus be from noon until three o'clock in the afternoon (verse 33).

26. As is distinctly brought out in John (Jn. xix. 21, 22), this identification-tag over the cross was Pilate's last revenge on the Jews who had forced him into such a difficult position. To the Christian, it is no irony, but God's very vindication of His Son, even in the hour of His death. The mediaeval hymn writers loved the concept of the King, crowned at last, reigning from the tree; and where there is an answering response of love from the human heart, picture becomes reality, and the King has come into His kingdom.

27. This suggests that an execution had been impending in

---

[1] Cranfield also suggests a second reason: it would break the Lord's vow at the Last Supper, recorded in xiv. 25.

any case, and that the Lord was but taking the place of Barabbas, a thought which must make every man ponder. The just dies for the unjust, the innocent for the guilty (1 Pet. iii. 18). That one at least of these two captured terrorists realized something of this is shown in Luke xxiii. 41; and the fruit of such a vicarious death may be seen in the Lord's reply to him (Lk. xxiii. 43). As in the case of the wise men, the Old Latin has preserved names for the thieves in both Matthew xxvii. 38 and here. *Zoathan* and *Chammatha* are one MS reading amid several variants, but more than this we cannot say. The Old Latin and the Old Syriac between them preserve several traditions undoubtedly early, but as to their truth, there is no independent test. Nevertheless there was no need to invent names, any more than there was for Caspar, Melchior, and Balthazar; so the survival of any name is strong presumption as to its genuineness, even if the exact spelling is uncertain.

28. This verse is missing in many MSS; it is easy to see how it could be added as an explanatory comment by the Evangelist, for, besides being an undoubted truth, it takes up the quotation of Isaiah liii. 12 by the Lord, in the upper room before the little party left for Gethsemane (Lk. xxii. 37). Whether or no it should be read in the text here is not of great moment, for it corresponds to a great theological truth, to which allusion is also made in xiv. 48. He was treated by the authorities as an evil-doer, it is true; but this was only an outward picture of the deeper truth that He was treated as an evil-doer by God upon the cross for our sakes (2 Cor. v. 21).

29, 30. The shaking of heads and the blasphemy, like the dicing for His clothing (verse 24), are all seen in terms of the Psalter. Again, it is the same Psalm to which reference is made (Ps. xxii. 7) and by which the significance of these events is interpreted. The climax comes with the great cry of dereliction (verse 34) which is again a direct quotation from Psalm xxii. 1. This frequent quotation means that not only did the disciples use this particular Psalm as a means of understanding the passion of their Lord; the Lord Himself so used it. The mockery of the crowds, and especially of the priests, at the

cross is the strongest possible psychological proof of the existence and nature of the Lord's claims; e.g., of the veracity of
the Saying about the destruction and rebuilding of the 'temple'
(verse 29); that He 'saved' others, i.e. He used this word in
connection with His own work on their behalf (verse 31); that
He indeed claimed to be the Messiah, and Israel's King (verse
32). These claims they undoubtedly disbelieved; but, had the
Lord never used them, then the taunt would have lost all its
sting.

31. There was prophetic truth in these bitter words of sinful
men, as there had been in the words of Caiaphas (Jn. xi. 50,
51). If the Christ desired to save others, then He might not
come down from the cross; that temptation He had repelled
first in the wilderness (Mt. iv. 6), then at Caesarea Philippi
(Mt. xvi. 23), and lastly in the Garden (Mk. xiv. 36). Hence,
to descend from the cross was not indeed a physical impossibility, but a moral and spiritual impossibility for the Messiah.
If He did so, He would cease to be God's Christ, treading God's
path of Messiahship; instead, He would become a mere
human Christ.

32. Their demand was impossible, for *see and believe* is not
God's order of working; that would be a denial of the rule of
faith which is 'if you believe, then you will see' (cf. Jn. xi. 40).
It was impossible, too, because as in the parable of the rich
man and Lazarus (Lk. xvi. 31), even if the supreme miracle of
all were to be vouchsafed to them, they still would not believe.
The resistance to God lies in man's stubborn will, not in his
intellect; and so, given a resurrection at last, these same men
made no question as to whether the sign was true or false, in
spite of the express testimony of the guards (Mt. xxviii. 11).
Their sole desire was to suppress news of the sign, for their
concern, like Pilate's, was not with truth. Against such men
God's judgment is clear (Rom. i. 18). Mark does not tell of
the terrorist who surrendered to God at the last, and thus
obtained an amnesty, and a King's pardon. Nor does
Matthew; it is Luke who has the full story (Lk. xxiii. 39-43).
Is this because Mark's informant, Peter, was far from the

cross, and would have missed such detail, while Luke, who certainly drew upon Mary for such information, had as source one of the little group of women who stood beside the very cross (Jn. xix. 25)?

iv. The death (xv. 33–41). As mentioned above (see verse 25), the usual interpretation of the time indicated would be that darkness—as in the plagues of Egypt, a sign of God's curse (Ex. x. 22)—fell on the land from noon till three o'clock in the afternoon. Luke xxiii. 45 explicitly says that this was a solar eclipse; it was no mere desert sandstorm, temporarily blocking out the sun. Darkness at noon, by its paradoxical nature, was a fitting sign for divine Omnipotence to give to those who had rejected the light.

34, 35. Linguistically, if *sabachthani* be read with most MSS, then it is not the Hebrew form found in the Old Testament, but the Aramaic of the Targum; while the *zaphthanei* of two MSS is the true Hebrew. Here we tread on holy ground, and so do well to tread reverently; but it seems likely that the Lord, in this hour, was staying Himself upon the Scriptures, not in the sacred Hebrew, but in the colloquial paraphrase in His own familiar mother-tongue.[1] This verse belongs to those where we have the very words of the Saviour preserved; for, while He may well have conversed freely in colloquial Greek, yet with His disciples He would have used the familiar Aramaic. There are similar linguistic variations on the form of the word used for *God* in the first part of the quotation, but unless the form *eli* be read, not *Eloi*, it is hard to see how the crude pun upon the name *Eliyahu* (Elijah, *Elias*, 35) could be sustained. For the connection in scribal tradition between Elijah and the Messiah, see ix. 11; the actual appearance of Elijah with Moses on the mount of transfiguration (ix. 4) shows that this was no misconception.[2]

But what was the meaning of this cry? Had God indeed

---

[1] See comment on Mk. v. 41.
[2] The crowds presumably had in mind the familiar late tradition of Elijah appearing to work miracles for pious Israelites—a commonplace of rabbinics.

deserted Him? No, assuredly, for this was God's path, and not what the Son would have chosen for Himself, were it not God's will; this is the whole meaning of the agony in the Garden (xiv. 36). More, it was God's path made plain to the Son from the commencement of His ministry, as the threefold prediction of the passion to His disciples makes plain (see viii. 31, ix. 31, x. 32). It has been well said that the opening words of the cry, *My God*, are an affirmation of faith. Since this same Psalm (xxii) ends in a cry of triumph, it is reasonable to suppose that the Lord chose it with this in view. Otherwise, there were many suitable passages (e.g. in Lamentations) which express suffering without any final consciousness of victory, and any of these the Lord might have used. So here we have the agony of One suffering the experience of abandonment by God, and yet certain of ultimate vindication and triumph. But in what sense was He abandoned? To betrayal, mockery, scourging, death—yes: but to limit the explanation to this would be superficial exegesis, for all this He had faced and foretold for years. There was a far deeper spiritual agony endured alone in the darkness, an agony which we can never plumb and which, thanks to the cross, no created man need ever experience. No explanation will satisfy other than the traditional view that, in that dark hour, God's wrath fell upon Him. Because wrath is no abstract principle, but a personal manifestation, that meant that the unclouded communion with the Father, enjoyed from all eternity, was broken. Some commentators have held that He suffered all the pangs of hell in that time; and if hell be at root an eternity of separation from God, then He assuredly did. But on such mysteries Scripture is wisely reticent, though it does tell us that He was bearing our sin, as a sacrificial lamb (Heb. ix. 28), that He bore the curse (Gal. iii. 13), that He was 'made sin' (or perhaps 'made a sin-offering', 2 Cor. v. 21) for us there. If there was a barrier between the Father and the Son at that moment, it could only be because of sin; and He knew no sin (2 Cor. v. 21); so it could only be our sin that cost Him such agony. Here is the heart of the cross; here is the mystery which no painting nor sculpture, with distorted face, can ever begin to show. We sometimes fail to understand the love at the heart of the atonement and thus use such crude non-biblical illustrations as grievously to offend the sensitive. This is because we fail to realize the true nature of the punishment for sin, in eternal separation from God, and thus the true nature and depth of the agony to be borne by Him. Both punishment and reward are ultimately to be seen in terms of God and our relationship to Him, be it utter severance or the closest communion; all else is consequent and corollary. Nor is saying this to minimize punishment and reward; it projects them on to an eternal screen, and gives a moral depth unthinkable otherwise.

36. The *vinegar* (Gk. *oxos*, Lat. *posca*) was the sour wine not only of the soldier's ration, but of everyday use;[1] those who travel tourist class on Italian or Greek ships about the waterways of the world will know it well. This is apparently quite a different occasion from the official offering of the drugged wine in verse 23. There may have been a touch of rough kindness in the deed, for all the coarse jest, especially if, as John xix. 28 suggests, it was brought in response to a word from the Saviour. Both the 'I thirst' (Jn. xix. 28) and the *vinegar* of this verse are taken from Psalm lxix. 21, another messianic Psalm which begins in sorrow and ends in triumph.

37. Why did the Lord ask for this moistening of His lips? Not solely through human suffering, nor through a mere desire to fulfil the wording of Scripture, but surely to gather His strength for the great cry of triumph that followed, and the prayer of committal before He died. Peter does not particularize the cry, other than noting how it rang out, even to the edges of the crowd where he doubtless stood; the softertoned commendation to God he missed altogether. But John, who stood by the cross along with the little group of women, heard every word (see Jn. xix. *passim*).

38. This tearing of the great woven *veil of the temple*, thus allowing any man to look at will into the holiest place of all (the 'Holy of holies'), is recorded in all three Synoptic Gospels.

---

[1] See comment on Mk. xiv. 22.

Luke, however, seems to put it at the beginning of the crucifixion and not at the end (Lk. xxiii. 45). The symbolism of this
rending is used later in the New Testament to denote the
breaking down of the barrier between Jew and Gentile, by the
rent flesh of Christ, in which all barriers between God and
man were abolished (Heb. x. 20; Eph. ii. 14). This also seems
to have been a favourite 'Catechetical Form' or Teaching
Simile, used by the early Church. Henceforth, man had free
access to the very presence of God (Heb. x. 19–22). Both
Jewish priesthood and Jewish Temple had ceased to have any
significance with the splitting of this curtain. Jerome (com-
menting on Mt. xxvii. 51, the parallel to this verse) reports
that the 'Gospel of the Hebrews' does not mention the curtain,
but says that the great lintel of the Temple cracked and fell.
An earthquake could produce both results, and an earthquake
is specifically mentioned in this context.

39. For the honest Roman *centurion*, or non-commissioned
officer, on duty with his squad at the cross, the evidence had
been overwhelming. He had watched and puzzled while his
men gambled, and now he was convinced. What he, a pagan,
meant by *the Son of God*[1] has been much disputed. It may not
have been by any means the peerless position that such a title
means to the Christian, especially as Luke has 'a just man'
instead of 'God's Son'. So, too, the Gentile jailor at Philippi
may not have initially intended, by his cry to Paul, all that we
now read into it; but even if not, the quick Christian oppor-
tunism of Paul soon found means of explaining to him the
deeper meaning of what he himself had said (Acts xvi. 30).
Nevertheless, at the least the Christian Church saw in this
word of the centurion an unconscious statement of truth, as
that of Caiaphas had been (Jn. xi. 50). The Lord demanded
little knowledge and much faith as initial steps, in those who
came to Him—witness His dealing with the dying thief (Lk.
xxiii. 43)—so that the centurion may have well become a true

[1] Moule (pp. 115, 116) discusses this passage, and seems right in following
Colwell, thus allowing us to translate '*the* Son of God' equally with '*a* Son
of God'.

believer ultimately. So Christian tradition assumed; for, true
or false, there are elaborate stories about this same centurion.
The account is not without suspicion, however, when we find
him travelling overseas in company with Joseph of Arimathaea,
who also appears in this context (verse 43). With all deference
to Glastonbury and early British Christianity, we may dismiss
both stories as pious and patriotic monkish fabrications. But
quite irrespective of the truth of this particular tradition, the
'non-commissioned officers' of the Gospels are a fine group,
numbering several examples of sturdy military piety among
them; and Cornelius (Acts x. 1) fully carries on the tradition.
There is no reason why several of them should not have been
true believers, the more so as we know of Christians in the
Roman army from a very early date, both from the recorded
martyrologies and from the military sites of early Christian
chapels (e.g. on the Roman wall in Britain). Further, it was
the Roman habit to move auxiliaries widely, from Eastern
frontier to Western, for it was only under the Late Empire that
the static frontier settlements grew up. We have actual evidence
for some detachments of troops being moved from Palestine to
Britain, and so it is just within the bounds of possibility that
this particular centurion was at some time later stationed in
Britain; but further we cannot go in fairness to the rules of
history.

40, 41. Here Mark mentions specifically the group of
women disciples, many of them wealthy, who followed Christ,
and doubtless supported the apostolic band from their worldly
goods (Lk. viii. 2, 3). John also speaks of them as standing by
the cross (Jn. xix. 25). The Church has always owed much to
devoted women, often to women of means, and it is the mark
of a fool to despise such. This same band was to share in the
burial (verse 47); to bring loving gifts of spices (xvi. 1); to hear
first tidings of the resurrection (xvi. 5, 6); to continue in
prayer until Pentecost (Acts i. 14); to open their homes for
Christian worship (Acts xii. 12). Finally, in the Pauline
Epistles, we find devoted women at the heart of many of the
New Testament churches, not least in the bands of the

'widows' and 'maidens' (apparently semi-officially organized as groups within the Church).

v. The burial (xv. 42–47). The agony of the garden is over and the suffering on the tree is now past. We are come to the hushed quiet of the garden tomb, where loving hands laid the weary body of the Lord to rest. True, the Easter story is not complete until that tomb is empty; but the great atoning sacrifice has been made, and the dividing curtain has been torn apart. That is the meaning of the final cry of triumph, 'Finished!' (Jn. xix. 30), perhaps better paraphrased as 'All has been completed' or 'The task has been fully done'. We do well not to hurry too soon to the resurrection morning; it is as though, after all the tenseness of the packed sequence from Gethsemane to Calvary, there is need for quiet meditation and rest before we are ready to come from the calm of the shady tomb to the joy of the early morning in the garden.

42. It was now evening of the day that we call Friday, as Mark (or Peter, his source) carefully explains for the benefit of his Gentile audience. Therefore, quite irrespective of the question as to which particular day of the week was kept as passover (14th Nisan, Ex. xii. 6) on that year, the Lord certainly died on the day before the Jewish sabbath. He thus dies before sundown on Friday when sabbath began for the Jew, since for him a day was from sunset to sunset, not sunrise to sunset, as we reckon it today. This accounts for the haste in removing the body from the cross, lest the sabbath be profaned, if the corpse be left hanging there after sundown on Friday, although we have seen that the pious Jew would remove the body at nightfall in any case (Dt. xxi. 23). John xix. 31 says that this sabbath had a peculiar importance for the Jews, presumably because of its association with the Passover; but the exact point of his reference is disputed, and closely hinges with the dating of the Passover in that year. Thus, if the body were hastily interred amid temporary arrangements, no proper burial would be possible until after sunset on the sabbath (Saturday night). In point of fact, no action was taken until early morning on Sunday, for the various funeral preparations would require both time to prepare and daylight to execute. After sunset on Saturday, the spices and linen could be bought, for it is unlikely that they were ready to hand in what was a poor home: but for the actual embalming, the women waited for the dawn of Sunday.

These, by Eastern reckoning, were the 'three days' in the tomb corresponding to the one sign which the Lord had promised would be vouchsafed to the unbelieving Jews (Mt. xii. 39, 40), the 'sign of the prophet Jonas'. This is an extraordinary example of the timing of God, for by no human calculation could the Lord have possibly guessed upon what exact day He would be put to death by the Romans. To talk of 'coincidence' in timing, if one is already prepared to accept the far greater manifestation of divine power expressed in resurrection, is ludicrous.

But besides being a prophetic 'necessity' (for Ho. vi. 2 was so taken by the Church), there were various other aspects making a third-day resurrection appropriate. The symbolism of the number three for completeness is clear. The Lord's reply to 'that fox', Herod (Lk. xiii. 32), 'Today and tomorrow I am healing men, and the third day my task is complete', perhaps again refers to Hosea vi. 2, and His own coming resurrection, as marking the completion of His task. There is also the common Semitic, and indeed early Greek, custom of contrasting an understood 'today' with an expressed 'yesterday and the day before'; this is often disguised in the colourless 'hitherto' of the Authorized Version. The 'third day' may thus be taken to denote perfection, culmination, almost 'prophetic inevitability'. Three temptations (Mt. iv. 1–11); three devils (xiv. 66–72); three questions (xii. 13–34), the list could be multiplied *ad infinitum*.

As to the reported Jewish belief that the soul lingered near the body for two days, but finally fled before the third day, it would but increase the evidential value of the resurrection as a miracle, by proving conclusively that this was no mere swoon, but very death. It was no mere re-uniting of a hovering soul with a waiting body, but an act of mighty power (Rom.

i. 4). Yet this seems but a makeweight, true perhaps, but too light to bear in itself much responsibility for the divine choice of the third day; for the rolling away of the vast stone (xvi. 4) or any of the accompanying miracles of John xx would have equally shown this aspect of God's power.

43. Joseph of Arimathaea, sketched in outline here, is often overshadowed in our eyes by his fellow-councillor Nicodemus, who appears with him here in the Johannine account (Jn. xix. 39). Nicodemus appears to be known only to John, while all the Synoptists know of Joseph. Both were Sanhedrin members, and their presence shows the truth of the reference (Jn. xii. 42) to the many secret believers in Christ among the ruling group. Both were rich (Mt. xxvii. 57, and the costly gift of Jn. xix. 39). Such wealth was to the Jew an evident token of God's blessing (Gn. xiii. 2, etc.), if only the man in question was not a tax-farmer, or some other 'sinner', who had gained his money by dubious means (Lk. xix. 2). Joseph was 'a good man, and a just' (Lk. xxiii. 50); and the text here with its *euschēmōn, honourable,* suggests a discreet, pious, sober, respected man. Many of the attributes remind us of Joseph, Mary's husband (Mt. i. 19). He was one yearning for, and looking for, the establishment of God's reign upon earth, doubtless through the earthly Jesus of Nazareth. Here was real courage, for a man of his position to risk an association with a leader already fallen and thus apparently incapable of benefiting him further. The very loving care for the body of the Lord showed that he had no belief in the resurrection. We can see how terrified the disciples had been by the trial and crucifixion, noting their failure to come forward even now, when all was over. The only exception is the group of women (verse 47); and they apparently did no more than watch from a distance. But Pilate would have almost certainly refused to grant the body to such humble disciples, for it was the property of the Roman Government, as that of any condemned and executed criminal was; but to a responsible man like Joseph, he was prepared to grant it. Like Esther (Est. iv. 14), Joseph had been prepared for a time like this.

44. Pilate's wonder was genuine; men might, and did, linger for days under the torture of the crucifixion, before dying of exposure and thirst under the pitiless sun. Hence the rough mercy of the limb breaking (Jn. xix. 31) from which the Lord was spared (Jn. xix. 33), a fact in which the disciples saw prophetic appropriateness (Jn. xix. 36). Hence, too, the *coup de grâce* of John xix. 34, although not required in the case of Christ. In the granting of the request, is there some stirring of Pilate's conscience? In the quick question as to whether the prisoner is already dead, is he trying to turn attention away from himself?

45. One wonders what testimony the centurion bore to Pilate; but although it is tempting to speculate and idealize, it was probably but the gruff military question and answer, certifying that death had actually taken place. A Roman sergeant had seen too many deaths to be in any uncertainty about such a fact. This, indeed, had been the very reason why a responsible officer had been posted with the squad on duty— to certify that the execution had been carried out as commanded. Common soldiers were not above temptation to bribes (Mt. xxviii. 12–15).

46, 47. This burial was but hurried and temporary; Joseph and Nicodemus wound the *linen*, or fine gauze (Gk. *sindōn*) around the body, loosely wrapping in the folds the aromatic spices of priceless value. They then laid Him in the new tomb, hewn out of the living rock near the site of the crucifixion, and rolled shut the great blocking stone that served as a door to secure it. After this, the two must have departed in haste, for it cannot have been far from the legal commencement of the sabbath. Matthew xxvii. 60, with its usual Jerusalem source of knowledge, explains that this tomb was one which Joseph had carved for himself. This was a royal burial, thus fulfilling the second half of the prophecy of Isaiah liii. 9, as the first part had already been fulfilled in His sharing in the death of the two criminals. So were the kings of Judah buried, in rock-cut garden tombs and with spices (e.g. 2 Ki. xxi. 26), although the modern attributions of the old rock-hewn tombs of Jerusalem are by no means certain. Nevertheless, sufficient examples remain from the turn of the Christian era to give a fair idea of the type of tomb meant, while exact identification of this particular tomb remains uncertain.

Peter doubtless heard of these things from the two Marys, who were watching (verse 47) and who returned home to prepare further spices themselves (Lk. xxiii. 56) ready to return after the sabbath and to complete the process of embalming the body; that was women's work, not men's. But they can have known nothing of the armed guard (Mt. xxvii. 62), which seems to have been an after-thought, even on the part of the Jewish authorities.

This can be seen from the fact that the women's sole anxiety, as they returned before daybreak on Sunday morning, was how to deal with the stone (xvi. 3). The possibility of the presence of an armed guard as obstacle apparently never entered their minds. If it be argued that they knew, but assumed that the guard would not impede them, the argument is nevertheless still valid. Had the Marys known that the group of men was in the garden, not ill disposed towards women who came on such a harmless and pious task, then the moving of the stone would have presented no difficulty to their minds. Since they had no knowledge of the posting of the guard, this was another Jerusalem tradition, and, as such, naturally known to Matthew's circle but not to Peter, and thus not mentioned in Mark's Gospel.

VII. AND THE THIRD DAY: THE MISSION OF THE RISEN LORD (xvi. 1–20)

a. The resurrection (xvi. 1–8)

1, 2. It was very early on Sunday morning, before full dawn (Lk. xxiv. 1). Sabbath was over, with its agonizing forced inactivity; now at least the women could do something, even if it was only embalming the dead. The men still gathered, talking aimlessly in the upper room of the events of the past week, behind shut doors (Jn. xx. 19). Here was love and deep devotion; but it was an adoration of a dead Christ, as in part of the Church today. The women looked for the familiar loved human body, so the first result of the resurrection was fear, almost resentment, at this new divine Christ (verse 8). A chapter in God's dealings had closed, and we are all such cowards that we would rather cling to the old familiar past than venture out continually into the new and unknown with God; yet this is the present and continual meaning of justification by faith, as Abraham found. Paul sees this transference of faith from the incarnate Lord to the risen Lord as necessary (2 Cor. v. 16); John expresses the same thought (Rev. i. 13–16), for the glorified Christ of Revelation is very unlike the lowly Christ of the Gospels. The disciples had always, even in His earthly life, shrunk from their beloved familiar Lord when He displayed supernatural powers (Mk. iv. 41). This only goes to show that, for all their closeness to Him, they had not yet understood Him, nor indeed could they until after His resurrection, as the Gospels reiterate. Only by the illumination of the Spirit can we see and understand the Person and work of Christ.

As God rested from His creative work on the sabbath (Gn. ii. 2), so had God's Son rested in the tomb. As man's fall was wrought in a garden (Gn. iii. 6), so was the triumph of the resurrection. As Joseph's bones had rested in hope (Gn. l. 25, 26), embalmed in an Egyptian tomb, so the Lord's body had been resting in hope (Acts ii. 26). As for Joseph, so now for the Lord there was a glad 'Exodus' morning, when God visited His people and led them from captivity (Ex. xiii. 19). The spices lavished on the Lord's body were thus like those lavished on Joseph (Gn. l. 26). They recalled the gifts of the wise men (Mt. ii. 11), which the Church has always linked with the Old Testament prophecy of Isaiah lx. 1–6. Such gifts recall, in particular, the lavishness of Mary (Mk. xiv. 3) and of the fallen woman (Lk. vii. 37). There is a closer link between the last few gifts, for, in the world's eyes afterwards, assuredly the hundred pounds' weight of spices used by Nicodemus and Joseph on the Lord's dead body (Jn. xix. 39) was just as much 'waste' as the ointment poured on the living Lord by the woman (Mk. xiv. 4). Did Joseph ever regret the cost, when the Lord's resurrection made his gift look useless? Assuredly no, although he may have regretted his own lack of faith; for the Lord had seen the love which prompted the gift (cf. xiv. 6).

3. The stone had been placed in position by Joseph (xv. 46), rolled down its sloping groove and slid into place, precisely to guard against any such unauthorized entry by individuals, so the anxiety of the women was well founded. The priests might be afraid of a theft of the body by the disciples (Mt. xxvii. 64), but Joseph equally feared common tomb-robbers, at whom so many tomb-imprecations of early centuries are directed. A hundred pounds of spices was worth a king's ransom, if stolen; and there were numerous cases of tombs being re-used by others for a second 'pirate' burial, after the expulsion of the first body or bones. But in confessing their own womanly helplessness, they had come the first necessary step; as in Genesis xxix. 8–10, there would be a champion that would roll aside the stone for these helpless women, One whose strength is made perfect in weakness[1] (2 Cor. xii. 9). A greater than Jacob and a greater than Moses (Ex. ii. 17) was here, to tend His flock.

4. The resurrection had made all their cares and anxieties unnecessary; that which they themselves could never do, God had already done. So the resurrection is a meet picture of God's work of grace in the heart of the individual (Rom. vi. 4). Henceforward, they must learn to live in the light of the resurrection (Rom. vi. 2). Matthew xxviii. 2 mentions the earthquake and the angelic visitation that moved the stone; but this only the guard witnessed (Mt. xxviii. 4), and so again we find it recorded in the Jerusalem source alone. This source repeatedly shows knowledge of events outside the immediate circle of the Christian Church. Obviously, in spite of the financial precautions taken by the priests (Mt. xxviii. 13), the true story had leaked out from some of the guard, and was known to some at least in Jerusalem.

---

[1] Cranfield (p. 464) seems undoubtedly correct in connecting with the thought of 1 Corinthians i. 26–29. See Singer (p. 6), where the Jewish man thanks God that he has not been created a woman, while the woman dolefully thanks God that she has been created according to God's will.

5. To dovetail the various resurrection appearances of Christ, or indeed the order of these early visits by disciples to the tomb, is not as easy as might appear at first sight, although the Gospel accounts are in rough general agreement and 1 Corinthians xv. 4–7 poses no insoluble problems. The discussion of this point, however, is more germane to a commentary on other New Testament books than Mark, for the text before us is quite straightforward, as far as it goes. It is obvious that much is omitted in Mark, either because irrelevant to the main 'run' of the story, and thus irrelevant to Peter's Western preaching, or else because Peter did not have the necessary close contact with Mary Magdalene, primary eyewitness of the resurrection events. Such eyewitness account by Mary is certainly presupposed in John xx. 11–18. What is harder to understand is Peter's omission of his own experience of the empty tomb recorded in John xx. 1–10, which apparently left a deep impression on his fellow-witness John. Perhaps this was felt by Peter to be too personal a matter to mention; or perhaps it was swallowed up in the joy of his later meeting with the risen Lord (Jn. xxi. 7). On this first occasion, Peter saw nothing to alleviate his gloom—no risen Lord, no angel; he saw nothing but an empty tomb. The empty grave-clothes meant nothing to him at that time, although they meant everything to John (Jn. xx. 8). Without the key of the resurrection (Jn. xx. 9), such evidence could only be interpreted as Mary Magdalene interpreted it (Jn. xx. 2); some other human, whether friend or foe, or mere tomb-robber, had removed the body. To tell of Peter's experience here would have been but to chronicle yet another failure on his part and a pointless chronicling at that, seeing that the supreme failure of the denial had already been sketched. This is then one of the Marcan omissions that exercised the early Church as greatly as they exercise us.[1]

But whatever the reason for this omission, it must be considered in the light of the larger omission of the restoration of Peter. This is recounted only in John xxi, but it would be ludicrous to assume that the memory of this lakeside interview

[1] See Introduction, p. 33.

had dimmed for Peter with the years. Certain of Peter's pastoral references in his Epistles seem to refer directly to the Lord's words to him on this occasion, and they appear to correspond very closely to the Sayings, preserved by John (cf. Jn. xxi. 15–17 with 1 Pet. ii. 25, v. 1–4). Thus we can only assume again a natural reticence on the part of Peter, an unwillingness to obtrude himself, especially in connection with an interview that must have stung him nearly as much as did the denial. There may be a further and even a nobler point; to the last, in his Western preaching, he is shown as Peter the Denier, Peter the Sinner, not Peter the Restored or Peter the Saint. There is only the one gentle reference in verse 7 to the fact that there was grace and forgiveness even for him. Like Paul, he was not preaching himself, but a crucified Messiah (2 Cor. iv. 5).

If the Longer Ending of Mark be correct (see section **b** below), then several viewpoints expressed in the above sentence must be reworded. Among other things, there is there a general reference to the restoration of all the apostolic band in verses 14–18. Thus Peter would be included. We have seen before how both Matthew and Mark set Peter in his apostolic context, so that he can stand in theological shorthand for the whole body. In his denial and restoration he is but the representative disciple, as surely as he had been in the Petrine promises (Mt. xvi. 18, 19); and thus there is no need to single him out here—all had fled, all had denied, all were restored, save only Judas.

Mark does not specify the *young man* as an angel, although his supernatural character is clear from the ensuing narrative. That realm of spiritual reality which we loosely call 'angels' reveals itself to seer and prophet in various guises. At times, it appears as living non-human creatures (Ezk. i. 5–14). At other times, as abstract mathematical forms (Ezk. i. 16). But the usual manner of revelation is as celestial beings who have assumed human form, at least temporarily. Youth and gleaming whiteness of garments may symbolize heavenly perfection and glory (cf. ix. 3, for the transformation in the very garments of Jesus at the mount of transfiguration). In spite of this accommodation to human terms of vision and understanding, mortal man quailed before these beings of pure spirit, as the shepherds had at Bethlehem (Lk. ii. 9), or Zacharias in the Temple (Lk. i. 12), or Mary at the annunciation (Lk. i. 29).

6. So here, too, as in each of the three other instances just mentioned, the first task of the angel is to reassure trembling man, by confirming to him that the purpose of this angelic coming is mercy, not judgment. Here was not only angelic announcement of the glad news, but also clear ocular evidence, in the empty tomb. We have already seen that this evidence alone, without the key of faith, was not enough to convince Peter (Jn. xx. 6–10). Even with the manifestation of the angel, invisible to Peter and John, it did not convince the women completely, to judge from their subsequent actions. That the ordinary word *neaniskos, young man,* is used, and not the specific *angelos*, 'heavenly messenger', probably implies that, apart from the sense of awe which he inspired, there was nothing else untoward or unusual about the appearance of the heavenly visitant. Thus we see that it is to the eye of faith that angels appear, for the unbelieving men did not see them; and further, that it is the eye of faith that thereafter interprets them for what they are. Whenever God acts, it must needs be with sufficient ambiguity for man to need the interpretation of faith that they may see the happening as an act of God. When God gave evidence on behalf of His Son, some said it was but thunder; others went further, but stopped short of the full truth, merely saying that some heavenly ministrant was speaking to Him (Jn. xii. 29). So the outward manifestations must have been superficially capable of any of these interpretations, as well as the truth. Christian faith is, in the last resort, an interpretation of all facts as the activity of a God who is at once all love, all holiness, and all power. So, without the key of faith, which is the system of interpretation, even the fact of the resurrection was as opaque to the disciples as it was unwelcome to the Jews (Mt. xxvii. 64). But faith is not subjective self-deception, for it does not create the fact which it interprets. Only God creates the event; faith is thus an intelligent appropriation for oneself of the act of God, a grasping hold of that which is real, even if at present unseen (Heb. xi. 1).

7, 8. If the women had believed, surely they would have witnessed as the disciples did in Acts iv. 33. But, in fairness, it must be said that such bold witness was after forty days of close association with the risen Lord Himself, and after the coming of the Holy Spirit. The women had merely had a momentary encounter with an angel, gracious provision of God although that was. Further, it is not clear from Mark that it was mere unbelief that closed the mouths of these potential witnesses to the resurrection. They were certainly afraid and *amazed* (verse 8), but *ekstasis* may contain a note of joy as well. This news was too great and wonderful to grasp at once, and it may be that only the abrupt ending of Mark at verse 8 stops us from hearing of at least a subsequent report to the eleven, as Matthew xxviii. 8 and Luke xxiv. 9 demand. Matthew xxviii. 8 has *chara*, 'joy', for the *ekstasis* of Mark, thus supporting the above view. Be that as it may, the commission was certainly given to the women, with the specific mention of *Peter* (verse 7). For the Lord's preceding of His disciples to Galilee, see xiv. 28, and the comment on that verse. Whether or no these women ultimately plucked up courage to witness to the resurrection, we cannot but contrast the behaviour of this group, who had just met the angel and seen the empty tomb, with the behaviour of those disciples who had met Christ Himself, like Mary Magdalene (verse 9, and Jn. xx. 11–18) or the two on the Emmaus Road (verse 12, and Lk. xxiv. 13–33). Those who have themselves met the risen Lord face to face cannot but testify to those things that they have heard and seen. So was the testimony of the disciples (Acts iv. 20); and so has been the experience of every true Christian since then.

b. The Longer Ending of Mark (xvi. 9–20)

This section is the so-called 'Longer Ending' of Mark, omitted in some mss, and stigmatized as spurious by some early authorities, such as Eusebius and Jerome. This poses a problem which may be put for convenience sake as follows. To end the Gospel with verse 8 is not only abrupt linguistically, but abrupt theologically.[1] Nevertheless, this particular Longer Ending is not found in some important witnesses, and is deliberately excluded by others. In addition, between verses 8 and 9 several early MSS and versions read 'But they told Peter and his group briefly all the things that had been commanded them. And after these things Jesus himself appeared to them, and sent out through them from east to west the holy and incorruptible proclamation of everlasting salvation', which reads like an early attempt to tidy loose ends; the last clause in particular does not sound very biblical in its expression. One MS actually ends with this summary, omitting verses 9–20 altogether, which is even more suspicious.

As regards the Longer Ending itself, it may be roughly described as showing knowledge of the subject-matter of John xx, the story of Mary Magdalene, along with that of Luke xxiv, the Emmaus Road, and Matthew xxviii, the great commission.

It is, in fact, a short harmony of resurrection appearances, a skeleton which can be easily filled in from the other Gospel narratives. But verse 9 here seems to have been introduced without reference to verse 1 above; and such an easy harmonization is suspicious in Mark, where we have grown used to unexplained problems, due to his brachylogy, and his strict use of his one source, as postulated in the Introduction.

Therefore it seems reasonable to see this as an early attempt, known at least as early as Irenaeus, to 'round off' a Gospel whose original ending had become in some way maimed or lost; that several such attempts were made is obvious from the different versions circulating. Further general textual uncertainty is shown in a long Saying added to verse 14 by one authority. Jerome knew of its existence in several MSS of his day, but as it is, from its content, obviously non-canonical, it will not be further mentioned except as evidence for a general textual dislocation at this point in Mark's Gospel.

What, then, is the theological value of this Longer Ending?

---

[1] *Pace* Lightfoot and other modern scholars: they have only proved the *possibility* of such an ending, but certainly not its *likelihood*.

It may be compared with the story of the woman taken in adultery, in John viii, as an example of an early tradition which may very well be genuine and is undoubtedly primitive, but does not belong to the actual Gospel text as it stands. In the case of the Marcan ending, we can go further; the contents are in any case evangelical, even if perhaps derived from other Evangels, and there is always the strong likelihood that this is an 'official ending', subjoined to a sort of 'second edition' of Mark. We know so very little about the actual circumstances of the primary composition and first written forms of the Gospel that it is unwise to be dogmatic. We shall therefore comment briefly upon it, for even if it be only a patchwork of pieces from the other Gospels, yet it does no more than represent on a large scale what is undoubtedly true on a small scale, probably much more frequently than we suspect—the mutual assimilation of originally independent Gospel texts. However, it would be unwise to build any theological position upon these verses alone; and this no responsible Christian group has done.

9. This is clearly the appearance to Mary, alone in the garden, as mentioned in verse 1 above, unless verse 1 refers to John xx. 1, 2, Mary's first visit to the tomb, before she met the Lord. She, to whom much had been forgiven, loved much (Lk. vii. 47). It may well have been Mary Magdalene, who anointed the Lord's feet in the house of Simon the Pharisee (Lk. vii. 38); for she was not only from a different place, Magdala, but also a very different character to the gentle Mary of Bethany, who anointed the Lord's head (xiv. 3).

10, 11. As in John xx. 18, love's feet were swift to bear the news; but as Luke xxiv. 11 and 22–24 makes plain, the disciples regarded all such women's talk as *lēros*, 'rubbish'. There is nothing more tragic than the refusal of natural man to receive such Christian witness (1 Jn. v. 9, 10).

12, 13. So it was not surprising that two of these same disciples failed to see, in the Stranger of the Emmaus Road, the risen Christ; but it was true irony that they should actually pour out to Him Himself their contempt for such women's tales (Lk. xxiv. 22, 23). Again, it was poetic justice that those who had disbelieved the women's witness should now find themselves disbelieved by the other disciples, when they returned by foot to Jerusalem, careless of the late hour.

14. This is the appearance to the whole body of the disciples, chronicled in John xx. 19ff. It almost seems as if the disciples, in the stubbornness of their sorrow, actually preferred unbelief and despondency to God's joyous truth of resurrection. Indeed, this attitude of dogged unbelief is portrayed for ever in the Thomas of John xx. 25. Unbelief and hardness of heart had long been the besetting sins of the disciples (e.g. Mk. ix. 19), and nowhere were they more apparent than in this reluctance to believe in the resurrection. Yet, by God's law, these two very things would be the greatest obstacles in the apostolic preaching of the gospel to others. If we want to understand the blindness and perversity of the man outside Christ, we need only look at our own hearts to understand and be humbled.

15, 16. This is the great commission which, Matthew xxviii. 16–20 tells us, was delivered in the hills of Galilee, where so much of His earlier teaching had been given. This explains His expressed intention to precede His disciples to Galilee (verse 7). Until the disciples had met the risen Lord, and were thus convinced of the resurrection, they had no gospel to preach, and so it was fittingly not until then that they received the great commission. Indeed, so far from generalizing their mission, during the days of Christ's earthly ministry, the scope of the healing and teaching work of the disciples had been deliberately restricted to the 'house of Israel', and preaching to Gentiles was excluded (Mt. x. 5, 6). Even Christ Himself made no attempt to reach wider Gentile circles, though He was fully conscious that they would have been more responsive than hard-hearted Jews (Mt. xi. 21); He, too, saw His earthly mission as restricted to 'the lost sheep of the house of Israel' (Mt. xv. 24), although He did not turn away from the needy Gentile (Mt. xv. 28). This earlier restriction, combined with the expressly general terms of the commission now, and the symbolic use made of the coming of the Greeks to Christ as a sign of His approaching death (Jn. xii. 20-23), seems to show that Paul (Eph. ii. 14) is justified in interpreting the tearing of the temple curtain as not only a union of God with man, but a union of Jew and Gentile in Christ. Henceforth, the Jewish race had ceased to have its old significance as the chosen people, a term now to become synonymous with the Christian Church; thus a restriction of preaching to Jews would have been meaningless. In other words, the earthly ministry of Christ was to the Jew first (Rom. xv. 8); the ministry of the risen Christ is to all mankind without distinction. This, to the Jew, was a great stumbling-block (Acts xx. 21), when they first heard it in early Christian preaching. In fact, so great a stumbling-block was it, even to the disciples themselves, that it took persecution and flight to drive them to preach to the Gentiles, almost by accident at first (Acts xi. 19-21).

16. As always in God's dealings with man, it is faith that justifies and unbelief that condemns. We have no record of Christian baptism earlier than this, except a cursory reference (Jn. iv. 1, 2) to the fact that the Lord's disciples baptized, although He Himself did not. As several at least of the apostles had been disciples of John the Baptist (Jn. i. 35-40), the practice would have been a natural legacy; but until now, it can only have been like John's 'baptism of repentance' (Mt. iii. 11). Matthew xxviii. 19 gives the full Trinitarian formula, but it seems that early converts, being in any case all Jews, and thus believers in the one God, were sometimes at least baptized simply in the Name of Jesus, with a view to the reception of the Holy Spirit. It is striking that in some at least of these early cases, we have no evidence of the Spirit's coming as accompanying baptism (Acts viii. 16). This is not of course to say that a mechanical repetition of a Trinitarian formula in baptism can produce a desired spiritual result, but simply that, in the Bible, to baptize 'into a name' means to baptize into a nature. Naturally if there is no clear teaching about the Person and work of the Spirit, then baptism can be as hollow as that of John's proved to be in some cases (Acts xix. 1-6) despite its preparatory significance. To baptize into the threefold Name of God, then, is not a theological quirk or quibble; it corresponds to a baptism into the fully revealed nature of God, and thus into the fullness of Christian experience. In early unsophisticated days, however, the name 'Jesus' could conceivably stand for all this, especially if the candidates were already Jewish monotheists.

17, 18. Here again is the great rule of the spiritual life; signs are given to those that believe, not primarily in order that they may believe. This was the ceaseless battle between the Pharisees and the Lord, the Pharisees reiterating demands for a sign, and the Lord gently adamant that no sign would be given to unbelief, save that of 'the prophet Jonas' (Mt. xii. 39) —in other words the sign of the resurrection, which had at last been vouchsafed to them. This promise, then, is a word for the Church; it is for those within, not those outside. Every one of these evidential 'signs', except possibly the drinking of lethal draughts, was fulfilled in detail in the history of the early Church. The phenomenon of tongues, for instance, is particularly prominent from Pentecost onwards (Acts ii. 4, etc.). For the rest, in Acts xvi. 18 Paul expels a demon; in Acts xxviii. 5 he shakes off a snake into the fire; in Acts xxviii. 7, 8 he lays his hand on many sick and heals them. Whether or no such evidential manifestations were intended to be continuous in the life of the Church, or restricted to this period, or sporadic, must be considered in the light of the rest of the New Testament; in view of the uncertain textual evidence for this longer Conclusion, no dogmatic assumptions should be made from it alone. Paul's cautious words (1 Cor. xii and xiii) are a wise guide to follow. If, as suggested, these verses are a subapostolic attempt to restore a lost ending to Mark, then we must assume that known cases of drinking lethal draughts survived, otherwise there would have been no point in including the phenomenon here amid a list of other known miracles.[1]

[1] Eusebius III. 39 does mention this as happening to Justus Barsabas (cf. Acts i. 23) but only on the authority of Papias, for whom he has very little respect. Still, this may well represent an early tradition.

19. With this verse, compare Luke xxiv. 50, 51; the phraseology is borrowed from the Old Testament, although it is difficult to speak of specific quotation. The clause seems a combination of 2 Kings ii. 11, the ascent of Elijah, with the messianic Psalm cx. 1. Thus the early Christian interpretation of the Lord's ascension is clear; it is a triumphal ascent, to be followed by a 'heavenly session' awaiting God's ultimate vindication. Psalm cx is the great messianic Psalm, where Melchizedek's priesthood is promised to the Lord; it is also the very Psalm quoted to the scribes by the Lord when He asked them His hard question about the identity of David's Son, who was also David's Lord (Mk. xii. 37).

20. This is the peaceful closing verse, like Luke xxiv. 53; but Luke leaves the disciples at worship in the Temple, while the Longer Ending of Mark shows the Church expanding on all fronts. The reason for this may be that Luke's Gospel is but Volume One of his Church History; there is a sequel to come. Not so Mark; the whole of the Acts of the Apostles is covered here in this single twentieth verse; and it may be more than an accident that the style of this last verse is much more the style of Acts than that of Mark. There can be no going back to the old; the Church must move forwards, with her Lord—we as well as they.